Praise for *The Unquiet Daughter*:

"I loved it."

- Sara Nelson, former books editor of *O, The Oprah Magazine.*

"Passionate and unflinchingly honest, this is a fascinating memoir that explores the tangled connections between Graham Greene's fictional version of wartime Indochina, and the real people there whose actions have haunted the author for most of her life. Danielle Flood is the child of an affair so much like the one described in the love triangle of Greene's novel that she is perfectly right to make her startling claim, 'I am a sequel he never wrote.'"

- Michael Shelden, author of *Graham Greene*: *The Enemy Within.*

"Holy Moly, Mother of God. Ferociously honest and gorgeously written, Flood's memoir is the fiercely tragic story of her search for her real father, her knotted relationship with her complicated mother, and her hard-won understanding of herself. About memory, love, loss, and time, Flood's engrossing debut shines like mica and is as polished as platinum."

- Caroline Leavitt, author of *Cruel Beautiful World* and the New York Times best sellers, *Is This Tomorrow* and *Pictures of You.*

"Every once in a while a memoir will appear that has the power to stop us dead, to shake up our mundane, everyday lives...This book relates to the triumph of the indomitable human spirit in the most trying of life's circumstances..."

– Jo Manning, author, *My Lady Scandalous*, the biography of 18th century British courtesan Grace Dalrymple Elliott

"*The Unquiet Daughter* by Danielle Flood is the true story of an exceptional woman. It takes the reader on an amazing journey. Exotic, mysterious, exciting, and romantic. Bravo Danielle Flood. It's a classic."
- Elliott Gould, Oscar-nominated actor.

"In Danielle Flood's clear eyed memoir of her early life with her exquisitely beautiful and deeply troubled mother, this truth echoes: the fact that a child could survive such emotional devastation and cruelty is a testament to her resilience and her valiant spirit."
– Leslie Daniels, author of *Cleaning Nabokov's House.*

"Extraordinary and spectacular…a story that can connect powerfully and poignantly with most of us."
- David Lawrence, Jr., international child advocate and former publisher of *The Miami Herald.*

"...a work that will outlive us all: compelling, acutely honest and profoundly moving, without being whiny or cruel. That's rare."
- Joe McGinniss, author, *The Selling of the President 1968.*

THE UNQUIET DAUGHTER

A Memoir of Betrayal and Love

Danielle Flood

Piscataqua Press
Portsmouth, NH

The Unquiet Daughter

Published by Piscataqua Press
142 Fleet Street | Portsmouth, NH 03801 | USA
603.431.2100 | www.riverrunbookstore.com

Printed in the United States of America
ISBN: 978-1-944393-18-2

Library of Congress Control Number: 2016940390

Grateful acknowledgment is made to the following for permission to reprint copyrighted material:

Excerpt from "Like Wings" from THE GOD OF LONELINESS by Philip Schultz. Copyright © by Philip Schultz. Reprinted by permission of Houghton Mifflin Harcourt Publishing Company. All rights reserved.

Excerpt from THE LIFE OF GRAHAM GREENE, VOL. II by Norman Sherry, copyright © 1989, 1994 by Norman Sherry. Used by permission of Viking Books, an imprint of Penguin Publishing Group, a division of Penguin Random House LLC.

Cover: (left) The author's mother in a promotional photo as an exotic dancer.
(right) The author and her mother in a Saigon public park, January 12, 1952, around the time of the biggest bomb disaster to date in the city's history.

Visit Danielle Flood on the World Wide Web:
www.danielleflood.com

For Jim Morin,
who stood by me,
and my children,
all children.

Saigon, French Indochina. Circa 1952.
The author with her amah in the Luyen Photo studio, Place Dakao.
From the collection of Danielle Flood.

I have read of ancient people
who held razors to their doctor's throat
as he operated – as if love could have such balance,
like wings.

Philip Schultz
from "Like Wings"

Prologue

I have been looking for home in my house again through these windows that are my eyes. Home comes and goes, like thoughts, like the clouds drifting over our slightly wild blue garden. It doesn't make sense, for I am loved by my husband and our children who scamper in and out during the day. I am loved by the dog even, who likes to listen with me to opera in the evening. Still, the feeling that home is somewhere in general and nowhere in particular returns, quite predictably, when I remember my mother.

She was beyond liberated in the feminist sense; a maverick. She did what she wanted to do, discarding convention – and, often, motherliness – like a dancer peeling off clothes. Her ex-husband called her the Dragon Lady, for she was dangerous, especially when she was bored, and she was easily bored. She could inflict pain and, just as readily, radiate charm. In a thick French accent she would say, Who cares what *zay sink*, Dani? And then she would laugh, throwing her head back. It was a laugh that drew close those who loved her, or sent them scattering, me amongst them. Even now, as the ashes of her remains play in the wind in France, the thought of her threatens to shake the center of me. Yet I prevail.

I lived for decades in mystery. What she did and did not do and what she did and did not tell me – about who she was, who I am, our past – made me a writer. Even as a small child, I could sense that something was missing; what was evident didn't quite fit together. This formed me. Made me spend my life learning to find the words and arrange them, to be ready, poised for the answers. Made me curious, driven, to find out what I needed to know. Made me haunt, when pieces of truth emerged, my dear England, that I had inexplicably always loved.

And then, after I found out as much as I could, I floated for a while, like a ghost, if there are ghosts. Resting, reflecting, recuperating. I wrote about anything but what I knew I was born to write, avoiding the subject, hiding, for years. Then I had children. Aha. Then came some perspective. As they passed from stage to stage, developed, I became struck by the contrast between their experiences and mine when I was their age. The realization, like a vague picture coming into focus, became stark, and I knew it was time to tell. It has taken me more than half a century to get here, tapping at the keys of my life, for I have been embarrassed, ashamed and afraid, afraid that I might die once I tell the story, as if it is all there is of me. But that is not so.

Finally, I asked them. The children – well, teenagers. What will your friends think? I asked my daughter on the back porch and later, my son while driving in the car. I was startled by their separate answers. They said: Who cares what they think, Mommy?

Something happened in Saigon. For most of my years I knew only that I was born there. Later I learned that the English author, Graham Greene, was there many times when my parents were living there, gathering material for his classic novel, *The Quiet American*, which became two movies; the second one, released in 2002, starred Michael Caine. It's about a love triangle in Saigon between an older British man, his young Vietnamese mistress, and a young American Foreign Service Officer who falls in love with her and asks her to marry him. I came from a love triangle much like the one Greene describes in this novel. I am a sequel he never wrote.

From what his authorized biographer says, Greene knew much more about my beginning than I did – he knew about my three parents.

Greene first arrived in Saigon in January, 1951, during the war between the French and the Vietnamese communist revolutionists – the Vietminh. Since long before the American war there, what we now know to be Vietnam had been part of French Indochina, which was part of the French empire, later called the French Union. Since the late 1800s, for the most part, France had ruled *Indochine* and infused it with its culture, so much so that French was not only the spoken language, it was taught as the primary language in the schools.

It's a war story. Vietnamese communist-instigated bicycle bombings, grenades exploding in restaurants and sidewalk cafes and assassinations were common in Saigon at the time. When I was almost three months old, the 100th U.S. shipload of military aid to France arrived at the downtown dock there. When I was in utero, there was a spectacular suicide-bomber double assassination outside Saigon. Greene wasn't there for that. The bomber mortally wounded, amongst others, a French brigadier general and a South Vietnamese governor, which at the time was more significant to some than murdering a French editor or publisher, which was also not unusual in those days.

Greene left, then came back to Saigon just before I was born and then again and again. He was very interested in my parents. This is evident because his authorized biographer says Greene heard about them when he first arrived. But also Greene knew details about them that only someone who had followed their story for the better part of two years could know.

Because there are so many similarities between what happens in the novel and what happened in their lives, I have long engaged in the unique pastime of comparing my parents to characters in *The Quiet American*, characters who Greene insisted came from his "unconscious." The first comparison I made is: Dad was too smart to get murdered. So were his friends at work, some there undercover for the Central Intelligence Agency.

Chapter One

In the beginning of what I remember, we seemed to be a typical American family – Mom and Dad, Evalyn, Patricia and me – as much as any family can be typical. I mean we had a lot in common with other American families. But even during the most normal part of our years together, I knew something was different.

It is 1957 and we live in Silver Spring, Maryland, in a red brick house with yellow and white trim and a front lawn like a green apron. Jello glistens as it is shaken out of copper molds. The stink of canned spinach is proof that Popeye The Sailor Man is a traitor to us all. The sounds are of Wonder Bread popping out of the toaster mixed with me, age six, and Evalyn, age five, and Patricia, age three, shouting *me first* or crying in harmony *oh noooooo, whoaaa, nooooo* as we stand three abreast waiting for our spankings in the laundry room. Serious business is: How high we can swing in the back yard; getting a nickel from Mom for a popsicle before the jingling ice cream man's truck leaves the block; getting to watch *The Wizard of Oz* on TV with a piece of red licorice; making the biggest snowman; and fighting sleep on Christmas Eve, for we believe with all our might that before long reindeer will be clomping on the roof.

We are bored when Dad gives his slide show of Hong Kong harbor at night with its colored lights mirrored on the water and of Marilyn Monroe carrying me around on her hip in Fukuoka. We like to poke our fingers through the rice paper in the shoji screen in the living room; we do not like having to cut up pieces of it and glue it back on. The many Buddhas make lousy dolls; they're all boys, you can't move their limbs or dress them up because they're made of iron, jade or ceramic – stuck in one position – like the geisha doll in the glass and lacquer box that Mom says a Japanese city gave to me; her hair is fixed into a bunch of chignons and you can't comb it. Once in a while Mom lights incense in a porcelain boat and it smells nasty. The teakwood trunks, some carved, are fun because every once in a while Mom opens them and takes out beautiful embroidered Thai silk shawls and drawstring purses and silk brocade Vietnamese and Chinese dresses that were made for her, woven with crane, dragon and chrysanthemum images in them. There are bolts of silk brocade and beautiful scrolls – two of an emperor and empress of China.

The trunks also hold boxes of photographs. There's me with my Chinese amah in a studio portrait made in Saigon. My amah has scary very long thumb and pinkie fingernails, indicating, Mom says, that she doesn't wash dishes or cook or do anything else but be a nanny to one child. Another amah, wearing a kimono and holding me and Ev, also looks scary, with gray, slicked back hair and a wrinkled face. My earliest memory is of calling to Boy, the cook's son, to play with me but he ran off into the tall grass behind the house in Bangkok, where Pat was born. I couldn't understand why he wouldn't play with me; maybe it was because I spoke Chinese, Mom says, like my amah, even for a short while after we came to the States.

I still do not speak great English when I first go to Parkside Elementary School in Maryland because I really need the pictures in the books to understand what See Spot and See Spot Run mean. We have no idea what Mom and Dad are saying to each other because we don't speak French and they do. Mom knows how to say many things in English, like eat, wee-wee, ca-ca, clean up, go play outside, toys, and I love you. But it takes her a while to speak at length in whole sentences. I know what *viens ici* and *non* mean. We get most of our English from Dad, who corrects us. He tells us not to say ain't when we bring it home from school. Eventually he uses phrases like: was to have been. We copy the way he speaks with no accent. For the most part, Dad is the apex of the family because he is fluent in both languages. He also speaks several others. When we go to Chinese restaurants the waiters are always surprised: he is a tall, very fair-skinned, blue-eyed, dark-haired man of Irish and English descent from Pennsylvania; he bears a resemblance, probably because of his large horn-rimmed glasses, to Clark Kent; but he orders, casually, in Chinese – I don't know which dialect.

He is, at the moment, a United States Information Service Foreign Affairs Officer stationed in Washington but to us he is the handsome prince who takes Mom out all the time. He wears tuxedos with a fuchsia Thai silk cummerbund. She wears evening gowns – gold or purple or black – with twinkling necklaces, dangling earrings and beautiful gloves so long they go over her elbows.

When they don't go out, the three Asian women wearing pale blue Mao jackets and loose black pants come and spend the day and evening in the kitchen chopping pork and ginger with a meat cleaver, making dough and steaming *dim sum*. The men with trucks come and deliver cases labeled Vat 69, Beefeater, Smirnoff and Piper Heidsieck. The cigarette boxes are filled and we are sent to bed, but later, after we see through the window the cars and limousines arrive, we creep down and peep from the staircase at the men in suits or tuxedos, the women in evening gowns or cocktail dresses. The living room and the downstairs recreation room with the big bamboo bar are packed with embassy and government people from France, Vietnam, Cambodia, Laos, Thailand and Washington. How can they see the tiny roulette ball through the cloud of smoke? It clicks and clatters all night in the black wheel on the round red lacquer coffee table. You hear ahhhhs when it stops, laughter and excited chatter in English, French and Southeast Asian languages until at four in the morning Mom and Dad go to bed, leaving the brass ash trays full beside *Foreign Affairs* and *Time* magazines. It seems they have parties or go out many nights in the week. We think this is what marriage will be like when we grow up: evenings in Cinderella dresses with a husband as handsome as Dad.

We make up games. We flip through Mommy's *Vogue* or *Harper's Bazaar* and as soon as we turn the page, we each point to a model and say: that's me. The winner points at the prettiest one the fastest. We make evening gowns for our dolls out of toilet paper. We make tents with sheets between our beds and go to *The Arabian Nights*.

I take Ev to Sunday school and afterwards I vacuum the whole house. I have to do a lot of things my sisters don't have to do because I am the oldest. I have to take care of them. One day Ev and I are late for Sunday school. We are too scared to go into the classroom because Sister will be mad. I decide we should go to Mass in the big church because we have been learning in catechism that if we don't go to Mass on Sunday we will have a black mark on our souls and if we get hit by a car and die, we will go to hell. The ushers in the back of the church say, come in, come in. But when we get home we get in a lot of trouble because Sister called and said, Where were they? How come they didn't come to Sunday school? Mommy is mad and when she's mad I get so that I can't talk. Then she gets madder because I can't answer her and I put my arms up to fend off a slap.

I figure slapping is very French because Dad never does that. He makes a speech first, saying, Now I want you to know why you're getting a spanking. Though we moan in fear, again in harmony, he then makes us march down to the laundry room, turns us over his knee and spanks us, in an orderly manner. Then, just as predictably, we cover our behinds with our palms crossed and facing outwards, fearful that it might happen again, and continue to moan as we go up to our rooms with his words following us: This hurts me more than it hurts you.

Except for spankings, I love everything about Dad. The way he taps his unfiltered Camel against his wrist to pack the tobacco. His corn cob pipe. His face that feels like sandpaper when you kiss him. His relaxed demeanor. His reserve. His stance that says all is under control. In the morning he sits in the living room in a brown jungle flower print sarong, as if this is the most natural thing for an American man to wear in a suburban Maryland house in 1957, as he reads *The Washington Post*. I climb onto his lap and put my arms around his lean torso and rest my head against the dark hairs on his chest and he says, What's this?, and I say, I love you Daddy, and he says, You do? And then he gives me a squeeze or pats my shoulder and I feel safe.

And then one day he does not come home to watch the news and eat dinner or to take Mommy out to a ball.

We ask where Daddy is and Mom says, overseas. This is strange. He has not said goodbye. We have not seen suitcases or trunks. I ask where overseas is. Formosa, she says. Where's that? I ask. Taiwan, she says. Where's that? I ask. Overseas, she says.

Every time we see an airplane we say, It's Daddy! Dad's coming back. But he doesn't.

I take to walking in my sleep. The thing about walking in your sleep is that you don't remember it, so I can't tell you how many times I did it, or what happened until I woke up somewhere I wasn't supposed to be and Mom would be trying to explain it to someone.

We move to a basement apartment in a modern five-story building in D.C. and I walk in my sleep out the door. The door locks behind me. It is the middle of the night. The cold in the hallway wakes me up and I am bewildered, sitting on the floor outside our door. I imagine Mom will be mad at me for this because she seems to get mad at us for everything now. So I try to wake up Ev by whispering through the keyhole. Ev, open the door. Ev, open the door, damn it; open the door or I'll kill you. This goes on for a while. Finally the man who lives next door opens his door and sees me on the floor in my pajamas with feet and says: What's going on here? He reaches to ring our doorbell and I say, Oh, mister, please don't do that. An incredulous look crosses his face and he, determinedly, rings the doorbell. I cringe. Mom opens the door and looks aghast, then starts apologizing to the man and says, She does not know what she's does; she walks in the sleep. Finally, we all go to bed.

We move to a big red brick house. Mom sleeps until noon. There is no heat. So I'm glad to get up at six o'clock in the morning when Fat Doris, the maid, arrives to warm up the kitchen by cooking herself pork chops and fried apples. She watches us get ourselves cereal and off we go.

This house is in a good starting place for three little girls on foot because it is a little more than half an hour between frequent destinations: The White House is to the east, and to the west, our public school in Georgetown, an old neighborhood with lots of trees and pretty old townhouses, often fronted with tiny gardens. Both places make us feel good and the walking makes us feel free, grown up, on our own.

We walk all over town, holding hands – I insist on that. On Saturdays we walk all the way past the White House to the movie theatre around the corner and down the street where we each buy a caramel candy for a penny.

The movies cost 25 cents. One day we get there and the lady in the booth says it costs 50 cents. We look like we've just witnessed a murder. I say, But we just walked from 26th and K (about forty-five minutes away). She lifts her bag to the counter and lays out three quarters for us and says, Go ahead in, but now you know for next time. We skip into the theatre. I do not remember the movie, but movies then always seemed to be happy, like that blonde actress, Doris Day.

Mom becomes a beatnik. We know this because she brings home bongo drums. She's been out with some other students from the Corcoran Gallery of Art school and says beatniks go together with bongo drums. She wears tight black toreador pants and black sweaters with a straight neckline and sleeves pushed up. She starts painting pictures of me and not Ev and Pat and I wonder why I have to be the one to sit still for hours. Even in my striped Dennis-the-Menace tee shirt, she paints me. A long word, and smell, comes into our lives: Turpentine.

She paints a guy named Tony smoking a cigarette. Who's that? I say. Another student in the class, she says. She draws naked ladies and guys. But, Mom, I say, why aren't they wearing any clothes? She says the models at school pose like that. Why? I ask. Because, she says, *Zee body eeze beaut-ee-ful.*

We, too, do some painting. She gives us gray enamel paint and tells us to paint the kitchen. It's boring so after a while we decide to paint each other gray enamel. She gets mad and sounds like an ambulance. I assure her that we won't do this again – it's hard to get it off with Turpentine. After she calms down, she shows me how to strip varnish off the buffet in the kitchen. I brush it on, and when it rises a little, it's time to scrape. It burns my hands, so she gives me rubber gloves, but the stuff eats through the rubber gloves and burns again. This is the job I like least and I don't care if it's an honor to do because I'm the biggest. The stuff makes me dizzy, like the oven cleaner does. And so I'm pleased when she says to paint Evalyn and Pat's room powder blue.

I want my room to be blue too, but she says there's not enough paint. Then she gets some white paint and paints gigantic angels on the wall over Ev's and Pat's beds. I say I want a big angel over my bed too but she doesn't answer me. It is as if she doesn't hear me.

I am reading upstairs when I hear the outside front door slam. It is a sunny afternoon. A Saturday, no school. I am eight, Ev is seven and Pat is five. It is a big slam, and Mom is not yelling at Ev and Pat for it, so I am curious, about the silence that follows. I go downstairs and find Mom sitting at the dining room table in front of the big silver samovar. She's staring straight ahead of her. I run to the front window. Ev and Pat are climbing into a big yellow taxi and Dad is standing there. He begins to fold himself into the back seat beside them as I run to the front doors. But by the time I get through the first one with its glass window and the second big wooden one and down the front stoop, the taxi has pulled away. Hey, I yell. I run down the walkway and out to the sidewalk. Dad, I yell. I wave my arms, hoping Dad or Ev or Pat will look out the back window, but they don't. The taxi is a block away. They can't hear me. I stand on K Street for a long time, watching the taxi get smaller. Then, I go inside.

Mom is crying. I get scared and start crying too because I've never seen her cry before.

I stop to catch my breath and ask, Why didn't he take me too?

She shakes her head and cries some more.

But I want to see him. What about me? I want to go with them, too.

You can't, she says.

But why?

Because they are going overseas.

But what about me? Why can't I go?

Then who will take care of me? she says.

I feel the pulling inside, the tearing of allegiance. How can I leave her all alone? And so I say, I'll take care of you, Mommy.

You were so much work, all of you, she says.

I decide I am not going to be any work. I go upstairs. My sisters' room is a mess of doll heads and legs, broken crayons and paper with Pat's triumphant scribbling on it. I get a broom and sweep. I make the beds. Miraculously, it seems, the room stays neat for the rest of the day and night and for the next day and the next. Life, I think, may become less hectic and perhaps, finally, I will have Mom all to myself.

Not exactly.

We never lived together again, Mom and Dad and Pat and Ev and me. After what was to come, at least we knew what it had been like to share, for the most part, peace and predictability; thereafter that life would forever seem like a distant fantasy.

Chapter Two

My mother lied to me more than once about my real father's identity. I'm not sure which tale affected me the most.

The first lie was perpetrated for my first dozen years. I believed Jim Flood was my father from the time I could remember. Because I loved him so much, it was for the rest of my life impossible to not think of Dad, Jim Flood, as my Dad even though my mother told me on a particular afternoon that someone else was my real father. She did this in timeless minutes that still feel surreal.

She said my real father was a British intelligence officer in Saigon and so I thought he must be really intelligent. I felt proud and hoped I had some of his intelligence. She said it didn't matter that they weren't married – which I didn't like. By then the idea, *married and lived happily ever after*, had become part of my sinew. She said he was very nice but she didn't know where he was. She said she couldn't look for him because she married Dad and had come to America.

Being twelve in 1964, I was ignorant, naïve and gullible, far more so than someone that age normally would be these days. Then, more than fifty years ago, romantic relationships were generally not put before children in complicated ways on TV, in movies or in books that we saw. Children were children and grownups were grownups and as far as I knew, whatever grownups said was true.

I absorbed all this and thought: what a romantic, sad story. I sort of felt sorry for her; sort of, because I was aware that I had also lost out on this situation. Then she gave me a photograph of a handsome man who did not look like me, but who did not look very unlike me. I accepted this as proof that what she was saying was true. I kept this black and white photo in my jewelry box for almost twenty years. Though it was an insufficient replacement for Dad, it was the most precious thing I owned.

For years after that, in Manhattan, in London, even in Paris, when I stood waiting for the light to change to cross a street, I studied men's faces. Looking at them, I would wonder: Is it you?

I was especially nervous when we traveled, for a year was a long time for my mother to stay anywhere. How could my father find me, I wondered, if I kept being moved around from this school here, to that summer camp there? I thought: He must be trying to find me. I decided that one day when I could, I would stay in one place for a long long time, so he could find me. Meanwhile for nineteen years when I traveled, in every city I was in, in every new phone book, I looked for this man. Nothing.

I discovered in the early 1970's that phone books were for free, at least in Manhattan. I ordered, gradually, so as not to cause alarm at the phone company, the phone books of dozens of cities in the world. At the most, at one time, I had 73 phone books. I kept them in my brownstone apartment on West 74th Street in the kitchen cabinets, under the bed, in the book cases, in a big wide basket. They were comforting somehow. I especially liked the Paris phone book. Though John Orr was not listed, I liked to think he might be living there, wearing a beret, saving lives under cover, like James Bond.

During these 19 years I coveted other people's fathers, though not in a personal way or with ill will. I never wished someone else's father was my father. But in school, when I saw a friend's father come to a function, I wished I had my own coming to a school play or picnic. Even today, in social situations, when I meet someone's father, I am often silently emotional. I want to say, What a great guy you are for staying by your son or daughter as long as you have. Later, when I hear of sperm bank conceptions or of mothers making the single parent decision and sometimes not telling the father he is a father, I wonder: Why is it that how the child might feel about such conception appears to be of little or no consideration? As if the child were a pet.

There was one slight moment, 18 years after my mother told me about my secret agent father, when I felt that she knew more about him than she had let on. I had shown her a story I was proud of – a magazine cover story. In it, I wrote that I am middle class, when I meant to say, that I was an average citizen. My mother objected to this. She said: You are not middle class; You are high class. I said, How do you know this?

I stared at her. Did she know something more? Where he was? More than what she had told me? It felt like the answer was circumnavigating my head, invisible, intangible – and I couldn't capture it. She said: I just know. Then I thought about men she had dated – they were all somewhat genteel. I guessed that was it. That he had been a genteel intelligence officer. After all, I thought, gazing at her middle-aged but still beautiful face – she wouldn't dare withhold information about my father from me. Who would do that?

I was almost 32 the third time my mother lied to me about who my father was. This time she said she had lied about the secret agent and that my father was a Swedish businessman in Saigon. She was not sure about the spelling of his name. She said she didn't remember his first name.

By then, almost two decades after the your-real-father-is conversation, she had done so many things that made me feel excavated I was wary when she phoned. I knew her much better at this point in my life. I knew she was lying again.

My mother didn't sleep with just anybody. After the Mexican divorce from Dad, she'd had a heavy affair with one man and a relationship with another; they had lasted years. I am sure that she never slept with a man without knowing his name, rank, serial number, bank account numbers, education, real estate holdings, parents' names, parents' education and real estate holdings, siblings and blueblood ties. Ex-wives? Ex-wives were too expensive. My mother would not blink at someone with an ex-wife.

I felt like part of a TV game show called: Your Real Father Is. Years later, I found a photo of this businessman. He was wearing a kilt. On the back of the photo she'd written that he was from Hong Kong and that he was "Norwaygian."

Your Real Father Is: Swedish or Norwegian, in a kilt, in Saigon, during wartime in French Indochina.

My mother's birth certificate was handwritten in elaborate script in French. It says a chevalier of the Legion of Honor, decorated with the *Croix de Guerre*, and chief of medicine in the hospital in Vinh, Annam, in the French colony of *Indochine* witnessed the birth of Suzanne Marie Eugenie Clara Jullien, the daughter of Aymond Damien Henri Charles Jullien, entrepreneur, and his wife, Marie-Jeanne Jarno, without profession. My grandfather left France in 1896 to serve in the military in the Boxer Rebellion in China and made his life for more than fifty years in north French Indochina as a civil servant and sometime entrepreneur. My grandmother, who was half-French and half-Vietnamese, had been the tutor to the children of a wealthy French family in Annam when she met her employer's friend and married him. They had five children and lived in Tonkin with, usually, five dogs, some pet monkeys and birds, and employed a chauffeur, a cook, two gardeners, an amah or several amahs, a laundress, a seamstress and a young servant called Boy; my mother said you had to have many servants because the laundress wouldn't cook and the cook wouldn't clean; she said the test for the cook to work for her mother was a perfectly-made Baked Alaska. When I was a little girl, my mother told me that when she wanted her shoelaces tied, she called for Boy to do it. Her father hunted with three German shorthaired pointers; she said the wastebaskets in the house were elephant feet and the paperweights were rhinoceros tusks. He shot three panthers on different occasions who were sometimes drawn to the back of the house by the dogs. My mother helped her older sister, Nicole, cut up the skin of one of the panthers to make a bikini, which their father didn't appreciate. Her brothers said my mother was born headstrong which didn't mesh with a strict French Catholic household. She and her older sister Nicole were sent to boarding school in Hanoi for their teen years – to the *Couvent des Oiseaux*, modeled after the one in Paris. Their mother, Marie-Jeanne, had lived in a convent from the time she was three until she was 19. Once, my uncles confirmed, my grandmother went to retrieve the pierced earrings from my mother and her sister after a nun in their school ripped an earring out through another student's earlobe. I knew many nuns of yesteryear and I doubt they liked the way my mother looked.

Barefoot, she was five-foot-eight, and beautiful to the point of inconvenience. Years later when we lived in New York, it was difficult to walk down the street without some gentleman passing by, stopping, then running back to catch up with her and asking if she would have dinner with him, or if she was a movie star, or if he could have her phone number, or autograph, or once in a great while, if she would marry him. She would laugh, if she was in a good mood, or continue walking as if she'd heard nothing. It was best, when going out with her in a heavily populated urban area to quickly shove her into a taxi, and then into a building or vice versa, otherwise it would take forever to get anywhere. It was easier in southeast Asia, where we had an entourage of servants, or when traveling, a slew of airline stewardesses to carry us children. And it was easier when we had Dad, who was taller than our mother was in four-inch heels and Clark Gable handsome.

I tried to comprehend the meaning of these lies. I guessed that they meant she had no idea who I was, or am – or how understanding I could be. That she had no respect for me as a person. It was a pity – this penchant she had for doing whatever she wanted. She was sometimes talentless when it came to second-guessing how people might react to what she did or said. In my reactions to this third lie, it crossed my mind, ridiculous as it might seem, that there ought to be a law. Knowing who your father is should be a right. She knew who she was, who her mother and father were; I knew instinctually that this gave her at least a part of her sense of self. How could she not understand that I needed that too? That knowing my father and who he was would help me to know and understand me.

I realized I would have to question the first of my not-fathers – Jim Flood, which meant that I would have to take a big emotional risk.

For two decades, I hadn't asked Dad, Jim Flood, who my real father was because I thought he was the British secret agent. It never occurred to me that Dad knew about any other father I might have had. Dad never brought it up and I figured if we never talked about anyone else being my real father, then Dad would stay my Dad. Having a stepfather you loved even though he was overseas most of the time was better than having an unknown father, I thought, until I learned of the third lie, about the Scandinavian businessman, which was so preposterous I had to know, finally, why she was creating these not-fathers.

If I asked Dad to tell me what he knew, would I lose him, his love, his role-playing as my real father for all these years? Would I lose the safe feeling that I was part of him and his family in so many ways? And if I did that and found my real father was dead or didn't want me, would I be left without any type of father?

I could not phone Dad I because in retirement he lived in a villa in the Algarve in southern Portugal and chose to have no phone. His last post was U.S. consul in Madras. By now Ev and I suspect he worked for the Central Intelligence Agency some of the time that he was supposedly working for the State Department or the United States Information Agency (USIA), but don't tell anybody I said this because some people retired from the CIA, the State Department and USIS balk and/or get annoyed when you breathe the thought that anyone in State or USIS might ever have worked under cover for the CIA. It's just that Dad was always someplace where a war, usually with Communists, was brewing or had been brewed, like south China, in 1949 before Mao Tse Tung took over, or French Indochina in 1951 to 1953, Taiwan in 1958, Korea for the first half of the 1960s, and Laos in 1966 and 1967. After he "retired," he went on "holiday" in Afghanistan in 1976 or was it 1977? In French Indochina, two friends with whom he worked were career undercover CIA officers. Also, he wrote, under a nom de plume, a novel called *The Jing Affair*, with characters who are CIA officers or recruits. In keeping with a family bent toward mental over manual work, Dad's father, Edward Houston Flood, a gentleman lawyer, was an intelligence officer for the U.S. Army during World War I. His mother, Evelyn, from Wisconsin, was often immersed in *Foreign Affairs* magazine and discussed politics with Dad, though she was offended by certain phrases in Dad's novel: God-damned, bastard, and son-of-a-bitch. She was concerned with being proper. Properly, her family tree, on the Spencer side, published in a hardback book, goes back some fourteen generations to the Spencers in England, whose descendants came to Cambridge, Massachusetts in 1630. But Dad didn't care about stuff like that.

He cared about truth. It was a big deal when we were small children. He had been a reporter for the Associated Press in Singapore before he began working for the State Department in Saigon. Inaccuracy was his special peeve. I knew him to have told the truth to the best of his knowledge, except for one time, which I would learn of – which had to do with the recording of my birth.

Dad wrote me a letter about Mom being involved with a married British air attaché in Saigon. He said Mom told him the attaché took her on holiday to Hong Kong where she met a British intelligence officer who had been in a bad motorcycle accident and had burned both legs. Dad said Mom said that was the man who was my father.

Your-Real-Father-Is...a British intelligence agent in Hong Kong with burned legs from a motorcycle accident.

After I read this letter I had a great desire to be anyone but me. Someone in *Leave It To Beaver* land would have been fine. I wanted to crawl into the television set. I saw myself tapping someone's shoulder in an elevator and saying, Excuse me, could I borrow your body? Or saying, On second thought, could I borrow your mind?

It occurred to me, considering the ways to tell this story, that it might be easier to write it in the third person because I kept feeling like all this was happening to someone else.

My mother was 24 when I was born. Jim Flood was 27. I can see him, amused, watching her intently as she created this fantastic story in the fast French that flew between them about the man with the burned legs. My mother was allergic to maimed people. Physical beauty was so important to her that in her late forties she had her toes shortened so that her feet would be smaller. Why would a woman, who so cared about appearance that she spent hours preparing to go out, have sex with a man with burned legs? She probably felt sorry for him, the way Americans feel sorry for Osama Bin Laden. And, in this story she's with one gentleman while visiting Hong Kong and then she betrays him with a stranger there? That's a very funny idea. Really. She would never do that. She didn't hop from man to man. And she would never risk being stranded in a foreign place by deceiving her host. She watched out for her well-being first and foremost.

I remember asking Dad once, a quarter of a century after their divorce: You loved her even though she was a liar? And he said: Yes. To complicate matters, she didn't always lie, so thinking about why she would lie in any given situation was helpful when searching for the truth. But sometimes figuring out whether or not she was lying was futile.

My real father. Dad's letter gave me hope. Sometimes you don't really know how much you miss someone until you know that the idea of him could be a reality.

The past was still alive in me – bewildering me. For years Dad as my father was an overseas dream. My real father was a figment full of whys. The decades without him became a whisper and a roar. I needed him – perhaps because life with my mother was so unusual, sometimes bizarre.

Chapter Three

It is 1960 and I still think Dad, Jim Flood, is my father. Mom and I are still living in Washington, D.C. I do not appreciate the recent Big Yellow Taxi incident, so I tuck it away since I can't do anything about it. There is a heaviness inside me. Every airplane reminds me of Dad. Every issue of *Vogue* and *Harper's Bazaar* reminds me of Ev and Pat and the game we used to play, pointing at the beautiful models as soon as we turned the pages. But one person can't play that game.

Mom and I move around the corner to a small apartment in a new building where children are not allowed, a fitting beginning for my new role as a hybrid child-adult, adult-child at the age of nine.

Of course, there, most of the time I do not exist, since children are not allowed and so I voyage through the stairwell and the basement back door of the building, instead of in the elevator, where people might point at me, whip out a big magnifying glass, look through it and say, Hey, you're not a grownup, You are going to be *dans la rue*. Stairwells with their echos are great places to sing, but in this building I have to be quiet. This rule against children also means I can't have any friends over from school and that there will be no one else to play with in the building. This is convenient for my mother who has an attitude about children in general; she once told Dad's sister: Children should be kept in cages, like animals.

I think this attitude doesn't apply to me because now she generally tells people I'm her younger sister, which makes me not her child, and therefore not a child, maybe, and so I sometimes don't think like a child; I have special privileges, like saying non-child-like things and getting away with it, as long as I'm not intentionally rude. To wit:

Mom: (exasperated and annoyed) You're sad! You're sad all the time.

Me: (exasperated and annoyed) I wish I was never born.

Such a startled expression on her face. I have never seen her look that surprised. This is a major accomplishment for me. Then she looks sad. I have not meant to hurt her, or anyone. It's just come out and I see the power of truth put into words. This is the moment I become a writer. I cannot write much now, because she would read it. Except for what is in my mind, I have no privacy. My world is under her control, but I see that one day I could have freedom, in a sentence, or a paragraph, in many paragraphs, to tell the truth without her changing it. I feel better. Until I can write everything down, I memorize everything I have to say.

Sometimes she asks me what I think, which makes me feel important. I know it's just one of her ploys to make people think she cares about their opinion when in fact she's going to do what she wants to do anyway. The reason she does this is that she wants people to think they're smarter than she is and that makes them feel good, so they're nicer to her than they might otherwise be. She also wants them to think she's helpless – with her French accent that is so heavy that even after she learns to speak English it sounds like she's still speaking French – so they have to help her do whatever she's trying to get them to do for her. Also, her accent causes some people to underestimate her; danger.

I often forget she's not helpless. Her indications that something needs to be done can seem to fill all space and time, so I do many things for her because I want her to be happy and because I want her to leave me alone so I can read, because there's nothing else to do since we have no TV and because I'm not allowed to go to other kids' houses or to play with them on the street – that's very low class. But I often remember that she said the three of us were so much work.

So I make the food list and go to the store and save the green stamps and put them into books. I cut out the coupons and use them while food shopping. I make the rice and wash lettuce and cut the onions and garlic. I wash all the dishes. I vacuum the apartment and make the beds. I dust and put Old English lemon oil on all the trunks – the carved one takes forever – and on the red lacquered Japanese table. Stealthily, like a thief, late at night or early in the morning, looking both ways in the hallway, I make a dash to put the garbage in the incinerator, then hurry back into the apartment. It's too dangerous for me to go back and forth to the laundry room but I fold the laundry and iron it and put it away. I make the coffee and seemingly endless cups of tea for her. I run her bath. I wash the bathtub and the toilet with BonAmi and the floor and kitchen with ammonia. But this is not enough.

I also have to walk around with a book on my head, shoulders back, back straight. I read Emily Post's *Etiquette* because my mother says I have to know how to be polite. A problem develops.

I am supposed to put only small portions of food in my mouth. Sometimes the lettuce in the salad is not small enough. So I cut the lettuce with a knife. She starts sounding like an ambulance again. Oh, man, faux pas. I feel this is unreasonable. But she goes on and on. *Jamais* cut the salad with a knife.

There are other rules. They are not in Emily Post and may have come from Indochina, but, if broken, can elicit her displeasure: Do not put new shoes on a table, never bring a peacock feather into the house, never give anything sharp as a gift – no pins or letter openers – and never walk under a ladder or let anything come between you and the person you are walking with or else you have to say, bread and butter, and that might not fix it. Once, I broke a mirror and she acted as if I might give her a disease. Speaking of which, do not kiss her on the face, do not touch her face or head because the head is sacred, and also you might give her a cold or the flu. In order to kiss her you are supposed to kiss the air in the vicinity of her ear. If you break these rules the consequences are: her siren-like chastisement, a slap or doing *sumi ma sen.*

Sumi ma sen means you have to get down on your knees and kowtow to her and say, *sumi ma sen*, which means I'm so sorry, in Japanese, over and over for about four minutes, which is a long time in that position; even then, she might not speak to you for a couple of days or more.

I am beginning to think that the only way to get out from beneath her microscopic eye is to provide her with a distraction and the best one I can think of is Dad, Ev and Pat.

There is a crucifix in the living room over the phony couch, which is a bed with a brown corduroy slip cover and throw pillows. One day when I am alone in the apartment I get down on my knees. Hi, Jesus, I say. I know you have a lot to do. But I have one thing, well, maybe two that I need to ask for. Considering all the important things you have to do, like saving lives and making cripples walk, you might not think this is important but then it might not take up as much energy as other miracles. So, do you think you could send my sisters back? And Dad? Please. In the name of the Father and the Holy Spirit and you? Also, could you give me a sign that you heard this and it's going to happen? How about the Virgin Mary appearing? How about no sign and my sisters and Dad just come back?

Nothing happens. I start to see that maybe, if I think of something, that Jesus will be answering me that way. And so I wash the dishes and the kitchen floor. Then the answer comes to me.

It's a hair dryer. It won't bring Dad back, but at least it will help her stay ready for when he returns, if he returns.

Mom said I could have the green stamps that come with the supermarket food. At the redemption center, I figure out that I will have enough stamps for a hair dryer by Christmas. It's going to save her money at the hair dresser and also make her feel loved and make her look even nicer so she can get a job as a model or as a movie star; then Dad will see her and be reminded of how beautiful she is and come back. She has to do something. I know her efforts to become a secretary are not going to work out because her typing sounds like this:

Tap. Silence. Tap. Silence. Tap, tap. Silence. Tap. Silence. (The problem, I learn years later, is the French keyboard in her head is different from the American one.)

Just before Christmas I get the hair dryer. It has a hood that comes off and hooks up so you can sit under it like at the hair salons.

I bring some food coupons to the man in the corner grocery and say he needs to give me the money for them because I need to buy some Christmas wrapping paper. He says you need to buy the food that goes with the coupons. I say, I can't, but he can give me the cash for the coupons that someone else doesn't use when they buy the food. He says no. I say, yes. I stare at him so he will get the idea that I won't leave until he gives me the cash. He presses a key on his register and gives me the two dollars and change I need. He does this with a grudging attitude, pressing the change on top of the bills into the palm of my hand.

Christmas is a quiet affair. Not like it used to be with Ev, Pat and I exclaiming as we tore open our gifts and the box from Grandma, Dad's Mom, that was bigger than the three of us put together. There is nothing from Grandma this Christmas. Or Dad or Ev or Pat. I get a foot-high stack of comic, coloring and crossword puzzle books from a nice lady down the hall who keeps the secret that I exist in the building and a very nice yellow quilted bathrobe.

Then, *voila*, the hair dryer. Mom says wow and *oo-la-la* and *formidable.* Am so pleased. Now, when she's a movie star, Dad will see her, even Overseas. But this doesn't quite work out the way I had planned.

I end up washing and setting her hair, teasing it, combing it out and spraying it, so she can save money instead of going to the hairdresser. Then I see she's up to something. She starts getting dressed up and going off someplace after hours of preparation – the nails, the make-up, the hair, the suit, the stockings, the high heels – which is normal for her, if she's leaving the apartment.

She drops me off at art museums for three hours at a time. Where are you going? I ask. To get a job, she says. What kind of job? I don't know yet.

Meanwhile, I am required to describe, upon her return, which Impressionist or Old Master painted what painting by the style alone and not by the name on the plaque beside it. In the beginning this is difficult.

One day I get a break from the museums because Mom says some friends we used to know from Dad's work in the government want to take me to the zoo. This sounds odd, since the general message in life at the time is that grown-ups can't stand children. But I'm definitely interested. A trip to the zoo instead of a museum? I would have gone to the zoo with Jack the Ripper to get out of that routine. I get dressed up, braid my hair down to my waist and proceed to go to the zoo with the pretty blonde lady in a shirtwaist dress with the matching fabric belt with her husband who wears a V-neck sweater with the shirt collar neatly framing his neck, like in a magazine. Very well thank you… Would I like some ice cream? The last time I had had something sweet was some red licorice while watching *The Wizard of Oz* on TV with my sisters when we lived with Dad. Would love ice cream, thank you. Vanilla, please, and thank you.

And so, I say, where are your children; can I play with them? Oh.

No children. The lady acts like her feet are made of cement as she says this. She looks sad, which seems quizzical again, since without children, she's supposed to have it made. But she is definitely not happy about the situation. I am thinking I could offer myself as their child, temporarily, from time to time, but then swirls of feelings start churning inside me. What about Mom? What about Dad and Ev and Pat? I think: I could say we could be friends, but that would be a really forward thing to say to a grownup, like we're equal, which as you know children and grownups are not. We're supposed to be seen and not heard. So I say nothing. I take the lady's hand and her husband's hand. We walk around, talking about the animals and Impressionists. It does feel good to hold their hands. I can see a kid like me could be the center of their lives. They want to know if I want to do this again.

Love to, thank you very much.

In two weeks?

Love to.

But in two weeks they do not call. I am going to miss an ice cream cone and being the center of their attention for two hours, so I say to Mom that I want to call them and invite them to the zoo. She is hesitant. She is sad. What is this? She doesn't want me to. What is this, jealousy? I don't have time for this. I want the truth. I want to know if they want to or they don't, so I can get on with my life. Finally, Mom gives me the number. I call the lady. She says their uncle is very sick and they can't go to the zoo.

Maybe later on.

Sure.

The weekends go by and when the phone rings, there's a pause, and Mom starts speaking French, so I know it's not for me. The blonde lady and her husband are the only people who might phone me. I know better than to bother giving our number out to someone from school. So it's back to the museums I go.

There I decide I do not care for the work of some artists like Picasso. I like the Dreamies – Monet, Manet, Van Gogh. I pretend to float in the paintings, like Chagall's brides. I like to disappear into them, watching people watch me in silence. You're not allowed to touch paintings. It's safe in there.

One day the doorbell rings and Mom says I should go stay in the bedroom until she calls me. This is our only visitor during this phase of our lives. Picasso had a Blue Period. This is the beginning of my mother's Demure Period.

It's a woman's voice. I don't dare open the bedroom door enough to see her. I just want to hear what's going on. I hear phrases: the more you take off, the more you make... There is a silence, then sounds of departure – a murmuring, the dining chair legs grazing the floor, the click-clack of heels, the close of the door, the resonance of the doorbell chime after it shuts.

Take off? Take off for where? I come out of the bedroom.

She is sitting on the dining chair, her legs crossed, one wrist crossing the other, resting on a slender knee, the polished nails falsely cheerful at the tip of her limp fingers.

What? What's going on?

The lady is an agent, someone who gets you jobs and you pay her ten per cent of what you make. Mom says she is thinking of becoming a dancer. Not like the Rockettes that we saw in New York with Dad. She might become an exotic dancer. Exotic dancers take their clothes off at the end of a show. Not all their clothes. Down to something like a bikini. Bikinis are O.K. to wear because we're French. It's normal for French people to go topless on the beach on the Cote D'Azur. But of course, she's not going to be doing *that* on stage. Miss America contestants wear bathing suits. So she would be simply going down to a French-style bathing suit. She is solemn as she explains this. She also seems unsure.

She proceeds, on the cusp of her new career, as if she has no one else in the world – though this is not true, but I do not know this – and I, thinking she is so alone, feel sorry for her. I still have Dad, even though he is Overseas, but generally I feel that except for her, I, too, am alone in the world, though I seem to be getting used to it. One day she says she is divorcing him. Am sad, though I dismiss this as a mere technicality; she can divorce him as her husband, but she can't divorce him as my father. He will always be mine, Ev and Pat will be my special angels. I still hope that everything will settle down and that we will be a family again.

We move to Baltimore, to a third floor walkup over an art gallery on a street lined with ginkgo trees. There is work, Mom says, in Baltimore. There aren't as many museums as there are in Washington, so when she looks for work, she drops me off at the library.

The librarian spots me and asks what help I need. I am too proud to tell the truth, which is that she is my new free baby-sitter for the next three hours. So I say, I'm interested in the War of 1812. This is not a lie because I am actually interested in most everything. The librarian asks if this is for school. No, I say, seeing that I could possibly be considered a child prodigy; I just want to know everything about the War of 1812.

What a boring war. I sit and stare at the pages of the encyclopedia, pretending to read. To this day I still cannot tell you what the War of 1812 was about, who fought in it, or where it was fought.

Thank God for *Superman, Archie, Betty and Veronica* comic books. Since I am not allowed to play with other children after school or on weekends, I am frequently alone over the next few years, for much more than three hours, so leaving me in a library doesn't always work out.

You can't stay in the public library until 4 a.m. though I think it might be one spooky fun time. We get a beat-up television which works sometimes, when I renew the electrical connection, by shaving off the covering of the wire with a knife and twisting the fresh copper around the screws in the back of the set. I love war movies, especially with bomber pilots in cockpits referring to the Germans as Jerries. My favorites are Veddy-Veddy movies, where people are mostly cheerful, polite and act like it's normal to dress up in evening gowns and tuxedos for dinner every night;

they speak with an English accent, or what sounds like an English accent sometimes even when the movie has American characters. They say, veddy, instead of: very. But I learn there is no more handy company than an author's silent voice in a book. Comic books are too short, televisions are too heavy to carry.

My most frequent companions include Nancy Drew and the characters in many poetry and fairy tale books and the real people in the *Encyclopedia Americana*; also Johnny Carson. In the middle of the night, Mom comes home to the speckled grey screen on the television making a shushing sound. I get mad when she leaves me alone until the sun comes up or beyond; then she's penitent. When she's going to be gone longer than that, she leaves me with babysitters. The most unforgettable one is a legendary strip tease dancer named Blaze Starr.

Chapter Four

Blaze Starr, the burlesque queen, was probably the most stable of my live babysitters, though our relationship was short. There was a nanny whose name I forget who got fired for smoking when we were on the road in Louisville. There was a German governess, Marta Uckert; more about her later. And then there were the dozens of nuns.

From the time I was almost ten – when Mom began her new career, Blaze babysat for me and I began going to school and camp with nuns – sex became the root of certain tension in my life. The nuns were obsessed constantly with being opposed to it without mentioning it specifically. My mother was so volatile about any possibility of my personal involvement with the opposite sex that, long before my body took on any appearance of womanhood, the subject of having anything to do with boys or men mortified or embarrassed me and did so for many years.

This, I now understand, was part of her deliberate and successful crusade to keep the details of sex from me that resulted in my being as a child somewhat a prisoner. I was never allowed to go to another child's house to play. When I was nine, I disobeyed her once and went to a female classmate's house after school. We spent a long time jumping on the bed of her absent parents. It was glorious, unforgettable fun. When I got home, two hours late, my mother made me strip naked in the living room and lay face down on the carpet. I thought for a moment: this is it; she's going to murder me; probably stab me in the back with a knife. Instead she whipped my backside with the small branch from a willow tree about 20 times. I couldn't sit. The welts took days to heal.

I never disobeyed her again. The humiliation that went with stripping naked, then being whipped did not make it easy for me to remove my clothes in front of someone for more than a decade. I did not associate it with affection or fun.

Of course my mother never explained anything about what physically happened between a man and a woman during sex. I learned nothing about it locked in backstage dressing rooms. I never heard four-letter words in those days. (I heard my mother say *merde* about twice in my life.) The nuns did not explain sex – only indicated or inferred that anything to do with *It* was bad.

That era was vastly different from the one we live in now. More than 50 years ago, sex was a hushed matter. There was no sex in the movies, on TV or in any books to which I had access. A kiss on the big or little screen was a Big Deal then. So I didn't know specifically what happened on the other side of the bedroom door for what is probably – these days – an inordinately long time.

When I was 14 and got my period, I thought I had cut myself. My mother still didn't explain that I was menstruating or why. Instead, she became upset and said she had to watch me every minute to make sure I didn't do Something Bad and the way she said it, I didn't want to know what Something Bad was. It just wasn't worth it. The subject came with fire alarm-type sounds and complicated feelings including terror. But I shall never forget that this ignorance – this blank page in my brain – and my fear of curiosity about sex was the source of repeated bewilderment in my childhood and adolescence. And it was accompanied by a great deal of frustration when it was assumed that I knew what sex was about.

When I was six, my mother said: Never show your wee-wee to a *leetle* boy. Never let a *leetle* boy touch you. What for? Why would he want to? The closest I ever got to a little boy after Dad left and I went to school and camp with only girls was on the other side of a television screen. I did not know what the big deal was when women took their clothes off in front of men, except that it seemed to make men happy. Later, when I heard the phrase, sleep with someone, or, take a nap with someone, I would wonder again – What for? I liked to sleep alone. Sometimes Mom and I shared a big bed in a hotel and I would wake with her leg like a log on mine. Who needs it?

I am sitting in a one-piece bathing suit – no bikinis for me – on the diving board of Blaze Starr's big swimming pool. She is passing around a platter of salami and cheese chunks stabbed with toothpicks and telling my mother that she, Blaze, and I are going to have a fun time, aren't we, Babe? She calls me Babe and my mother, Dan-yell.

My mother has designed an oriental act for her new dancing career which is set to Rimsky-Korsakov's *Sheherezade*; her new stage name, to which I object, is Danielle Dao Tien. In Vietnamese *Dao Tien* means peach from heaven. I doubt that my mother knows that Danielle comes from the Hebrew and means God is Judge. She does know that I have asked her to use someone else's name, anyone else's name, as she prepares to remove her clothes on stage after years of telling me not to do no such thing; but then she also has told me to do as she says and not as she does. Anyway, she's not going to take off all her clothes.

It's not allowed in many states. Dancers have to wear "panties" called a G-string and pasties – pieces of gauze covered with sequins or fake jewels – that are rubber glued onto the tip of the breasts or sewn into a beige net bra. If they don't there could be a police raid and the dancers could be arrested. But I don't have to worry about that because Mom is only going down to a bikini.

Blaze and Mom want to talk a little more about The Business, show business, before Mom goes to have a *leetle* operation. I'm supposed to stay with Blaze and then Mommy will be back from the hospital and everything will be fine. Mom says she's had her props made: a platform upholstered with *tatami*, some orange Chinese lanterns, a shocking pink paper Chinese umbrella, a gong. The act is to begin with her in a full-length lavender silk brocade Vietnamese dress. Her bikini is covered with several thousand tiny silver glass beads. Mom says she's only going to have pink lights because it makes the skin look nicer. Blaze agrees. Blaze has an act where at the end she's dancing in some phony fire or smoke, which goes with her name. She says real name is Belle. She insists her real last name is Starr, but I don't believe her. Blaze tells Mom she makes $2,000 a week, which in 1961 seems a fortune; she says Mom can get about a thousand for her oriental act, $750 minimum. Mom has repeated that it's very impolite to talk about money, so I'm getting uncomfortable.

Blaze sees this so she tells me about Chatty Cathy, that new doll that talks. I'm not sure I believe her, because the most a doll does these days is leak at the joints the water you give it with a miniature plastic bottle. She says you pull the ring in the back of the doll and it says, I'm hungry. I'm thirsty and I love you. Blaze has my attention now.

Mom has to go in a taxi now, down the long driveway in front of Blaze's house. She'll see me soon.

Everything in Blaze's house is pink. The walls, the wall-to-wall carpet, the curtains, the couches. There are no children and no books. It's TV or nothing. Why didn't I bring a book? I didn't know I would be staying this long. Mom doesn't tell me stuff in advance, in order to avoid discussions, should I dare to think of resisting her plans. It's always a no-choice situation for me.

I do not sleep well here. I'm worried about Mom.

The next day I watch *Queen for a Day* on Blaze's big TV. She says: Come on out to the Buddha-rock garden, Babe. Blaze lost her diamond ring out there. If you find it I'll buy you a Chatty Cathy doll. My agent's coming and we're going to take a nap. Now don't peek, hear?

Peek at what? Two people asleep? Who cares about that? I want the talking doll. The sun beats down on my neck as I examine the dirt, the rocks and Buddhas. After a long time I lay down on a chaise lounge and wake up with a sunburn which with freckles is normal for me. I too am very fair, having been blonde in my younger years, but fairness is about the extent of what I have in common with Blaze.

I have the key to our apartment and let Blaze in. I run and kiss Mom who is in bed and show her the Chatty Cathy doll that Blaze bought me even without finding her diamond ring. Mom looks a little puffy in the face but happy. At the edge of the sheet you can see her new cleavage. She now has huge breasts. Blaze is quiet. After she leaves, Mom says Blaze is mad that

Mom's breasts are bigger than hers. I am thinking this is a stupid competition. Mom can't get out of bed for a long time 'cause she has stitches and so I have to cook TV dinners and bring her tea and tea and juice and go to school and come back and clean the apartment and bring her tea and do laundry in the Laundromat where the tossing clothes behind the dryer door glass look like a turning globe, what the world must look like from a space ship, where I can go in my head whenever I want, and get away from breasts, pasties, The Business, Bon Ami and Tide.

I decide that when I grow up, whatever breasts I get are the breasts I will have. I expect the nuns with whom I spend my days would prefer that, too. They never talk about private body parts. They especially don't like you to even touch yourself.

I know because of the summer before at Camp Merryelande on St. George's Island in the Chesapeake Bay. I am taking a shower. I see these black oxfords just below the curtain of my stall. I put on my towel and pull back the shower curtain and ka-boom, right there is a nun. She says: What did you wash yourself with? And I say: Soap, Sister. And she says: Where's your wash cloth? And I say: I forgot it. And she says: You touched your body with a bar of soap? And I say: Yes, Sister, and my hands. And she says: You touched yourself with your hands? Her face is tight and red and her voice is tense. So I explain: To spread the lather with the soap, Sister, I used my hands. She repeats: You touched yourself with your hands? It is as if she were saying: You stole something? I feel like I can't talk anymore. My face feels hot. I feel as if I have done something wrong – but what? I'm afraid she's going to have me thrown out of the camp. Never do that again, she says, loud now. No, S'ter, never. Find that wash cloth. Yes, S'ter.

I have gleaned a false sense of permanence from Blaze's house, with its front lawn that seems the size of a football field. Somehow I think that if Mom becomes a dancer like Blaze that we will live as she does, in a big house with a swimming pool. But Mom says Blaze doesn't want another burlesque star in Baltimore. There's competition from a dancer named Tempest Storm.

Mom withdraws me from Corpus Christi School, just like that and life becomes two weeks here, two weeks there.

Mom plays Toronto first. A whirl of planes and trains. Cincinnati, Cleveland, Toledo, Dayton, Louisville, St. Louis, Buffalo. Movers transport her props, which appear at the theatre by the time we get there. She has an agent named Sol Goodman, who also owns the Two O'Clock Club where Blaze works. When he calls he says "see" a lot. This is Sol Goodman, see? I need to talk to your mother, see? You need to take a message, see? He makes the theatres pay for everything: her act, the movers, the hotel, the taxis.

The first thing I want to know when we arrive in whatever hotel is if there's a TV in the room. The first thing Mom does is have me go downstairs to buy the newspaper so she can see if she's getting top billing in the ad for the theatre. She gets mad if she's not top-billed. Then she tries to get me into a Catholic school but after a couple of cities she gives up –they won't take me for only two weeks. I go to public school in whatever city we are in because they have to take me. I live in hotel rooms where she comes back and forth between shows with barbecued chicken and bread. On weekends sometimes she takes me to the Gayety or the Roxy or the whatever theatre and locks me in her dressing room with my Nancy Drews. She keeps me stocked with them.

Backstage I hear the music, ba-boom, ba-boom. Sometimes there is a movie starring a beautiful blonde lady named Lili St. Cyr who's on a poster outside the theatre, but I'm not allowed to see the movie or any of the dancers onstage. Sometimes I get glimpses of comics, men who dress up like hobos and make jokes I don't get to hear. Sometimes the comic gets hooked off stage. I hear the drummer do ba-boom, as if to cue the audience to laugh, and it laughs. Some dancers have weird names. One is called Baby Lulu-Will-Not. I ask: Will not what? My mother won't answer the question, and I am not allowed to talk to the other dancers.

One time I break this rule because the dancer who is talking to me has started the conversation and I'm supposed to always be polite. The dancer says I am precious and gives me a gold scarab bracelet that she says is good luck. But when Mom finds out about it she makes me give it back and sounds like an ambulance for ages and she slams for a long time – the door to the dressing room, the backstage door, the taxi doors, the hotel room doors. After I swear I will never talk to the other dancers again, she calms down.

There are three interesting things backstage in a burlesque house. First, there are no children to play with, never, and so I think that exotic dancers don't like children or can't have children. Second, it is rare to see a man backstage who is not a comic or a stage hand. The dancers treat the comics as if they are cockroaches; I don't know if it's because they make so much less money than the dancers, or because the dancers think the comics have no talent. They're polite to the stage hands because they don't want their props incorrectly set on stage. Once or twice I see a husband or boyfriend of a performer. Body language, snatches of conversation, certain looks say that most exotic dancers look down upon a husband who either allows or makes his wife do this kind of work, even though many of them, including Mom, think they are artistes. The focus backstage is make-up, costumes, music, and getting on stage on time. Facial expressions do not show that this is fun. Sometimes the dancers have a show at noon, then another at four, eight, midnight or one a.m. The other interesting thing backstage is the light.

There are usually no windows backstage, or they have been painted black. Without a watch or a clock, you cannot tell whether it's day or night, and so it is a world created by its occupants. The light is only from electric bulbs, eerie in its stillness. Outside, the sun, even through clouds, moves and there is life. The light backstage is hopeless, reminiscent of the Edward Hopper painting of the man and the woman sitting at the diner at night, and for some reason evokes for me the sight of a woman in a kimono playing solitaire, her dyed hair in curlers, sitting below a bare light bulb, hanging by a wire. Sometimes Mom says: who will take care of me when I am old? I say, I will, Mom. But I wonder who will take care of these dancers.

At the stage door some of the men from the audience want my mother's autograph. I walk by them, then turn around and see she's stopped with her big hairdo or wig and false eye lashes, gracious, saying, *sank* you *vay-ray* much, as she signs her name. Later when we're alone I say: Mom you don't know who they are; you said not to talk to strangers and she says, *Non*, it's okay. They are very sweet and and have respect. Their hands tremble as they give her their autograph books or a piece of paper, a pen. Like this is the biggest thing in their world, to have been able to be that close to a woman as exotic as that.

We leave them hugging her autograph in the street.

Not so long after I stayed with Blaze, she was attacked by a burglar who broke into her house. He slashed with a knife at her chest, arm and thigh. She survived.

I want very much for Mom to get out of The Business.

We go back to Baltimore and Mom gives me a white poodle named Phillippe who adores me because the first night we have no dog food and I give him hot dogs. She tries to dye his hair pink. He comes out pale orange. I think she likes him because he is chic. I love him because he acts like I am the biggest thing in his life.

One night she comes home at 4 a.m. and leaves her fur coat on the living room floor. Phillippe eats the mink collar. Off to Camp Merryelande I go.

This is a Catholic retreat camp where kids come for two weeks at a time, but not me. I am going to be there all summer, like the year before. This year I arrive to find that no other children are coming to camp for two weeks during which I get to be alone with fifteen nuns. I guess Mom paid them off. The nuns are not happy about this. Neither am I. They do not care to talk. They never want to talk about where they came from, who their parents are or were, or why they became nuns. I think they are escaping something, some part of life, but they only say they became nuns because they love Jesus. I sit around watching them pick the meat out of hundreds of blue crabs. I think nuns have much in common with many exotic dancers. Their general attitude toward men, including some priests, is that men are alien to their focus in life, to be kept at a distance permanently. I suspect they fear men; I don't know why. Very complicated people, nuns and burlesque dancers.

When I get home from camp, we suddenly live in New York. Phillippe has gone to live with a *fam-ill-ay* in *New Jer-say. Eet eeze* better for him. I cry for a while, then get used to the idea that everything is temporary. We go on the road again. It's trains, planes, taxis and hotel rooms. I have a nanny for about three weeks; she disappears like Phillipe, with no discussion, no notice.

It's backstage into a locked dressing room I go again. I stare at the many light bulbs surrounding the mirror. The makeup. The extra pairs of false eyelashes that I mistake for spiders sometimes when one escapes its plastic case. I read. I eat. I sleep. I read. I do not talk to anyone. For a while I don't even go to school. One night, Mom forgets to lock the door. I am dying to get out of the dressing room. Just to stretch my legs, explore. So I slip out.

I hear *Sheherezade*. I look around. There are no dancers about. Most of them have done their act and gone. Mom is the star so it's the last show of the night. I move towards the curtains. I stand in the wing and peep out at the audience, knowing that it probably wouldn't be so good if the men in the audience saw a chubby little girl with pig tails offstage. It might blow the theatre's image.

There is a sea of faces lit by the reflection of the stage lights. They look like they're concentrating, silent, like in an old film. I step over so I can see the stage.

I see Mom. It looks like she's not wearing anything, but I know she has to be wearing a g-string. She is down on her knees and resting on her forearms. Now she is sitting, knees bent, on her heels. She's kissing a rose.

I want to get a blanket or a coat and run out and cover her up and tell her she is wrong to do that. That she's supposed to be wearing a bikini. But I know that even in a bikini, this isn't good.

I look back at the men. They look like they're plugged into a live electric socket. I want to get a fire hose like in the cartoons and blow them away and say, take that, you cowards, hiding there in the dark and watching an almost naked lady, my mother, you don't know her, you don't even know her.

And then I feel hands on my shoulders and I look up at the face behind me, a woman, a dancer, with old eyes, sad eyes. And she says, this isn't good for you. You shouldn't be seeing this. Come away.

And so I go. I am stunned. She leads me by the hand. Backstage is a blur.

I can only see myself yelling at them, the men, in my head: You don't know her.

I want to shout: She's not like that. She took me to the Bolshoi Ballet in Washington. You don't even know the Bolshoi. Or that she bought me a white muff that looks like ermine even though it's probably rabbit. You probably don't even know that rabbit is the cheapest fur or that mink is warmest but lightweight. You probably don't even know how to make *crepes suzette flambé*. She's an artist. She paints portraits. She makes things. She can go to Central Park and find a tree branch and spray paint it white and put pink flowers on it; make a Japanese cherry blossom tree, just like that. So she can feel at home, with Asian things that she grew up with. She's the daughter of a French colonist. You, you peasants probably don't even know who Edith Piaf is. You probably don't even know who Rodin is or Debussy. Creeps. Go home. Take the money you spend here and give it to your wives and children. Or your mothers. There is beauty in the world and it's not here, before these dusty old curtains, go home.

So this is America, I think. This is what's outside of New York, resplendent with the Metropolitan Museum and Bloomingdale's and Central Park. So this is Ohio. Texas. Missouri. Kentucky. Pathetic men who live to see women they don't even know with almost no clothes on on a stage. And they do it on Saturdays at noon even. That's how desperate they are, for *this*.

The dancer who found me is serious sad. She's not mad at me. She acts like there's been a death. She opens the dressing room door. Go in, she says. Go to sleep. She doesn't lock it. She knows I won't come out again.

Because I don't want to know anymore. A curtain between me and *this*, anything to do with this, comes down in my head and stays there, for years.

I don't think Mom ever knew this happened. I never mentioned it. She never mentioned it. I just knew this was not a good way for her to get back together with Dad.

Chapter 5

The period of true danger in our lives arrived in a yellow Cadillac convertible. Of course I didn't know this at first, about the danger. And it wasn't about someone replacing Dad who I still thought was my father. It was far more insidious, too sophisticated for me to have seen coming.

As I began my eleventh year, I saw that Dad had been gone for so long that I had to accept the idea that he might not come back and Mom might be better off with another husband, so she could stop dancing, settle down. I decided if someone suitable came along, I could be nice to him, polite, for her and keep Dad as my Dad in my heart. Actually, I had no choice; she was five feet eight and I was five feet one, and she had unforgettable long red nails that could dig into your arm, leaving scabs and immediately end any behavior that was not what she wanted, without saying a word.

She was stressed, trying to have a romantic relationship with a little girl around. And being a little girl in the way could get complicated. Methods to survive this kind of situation included keeping one's mouth shut at the right times and being ready to wear different hats, or, rather, masks – ones with no holes for eyes would have been ideal. Trying out different attitudes to see which ones could work best at the time and in the long run also helped. Watching your back was important because things could get kind of political. You couldn't be dishonest and you couldn't intentionally hurt people; otherwise you'd be stuck with guilt. But you don't have to love everybody, you know, although this is opposite to what I was being taught by the nuns, daily. You just have to keep your allegiances separate – like to the person you believe to be your father at the time or to your mother's beau – and if you can do that, you will get a certain not-usual education.

Mom gets tired of the road so we go back to New York. We find a corner penthouse apartment with a terrace on two sides of it at 205 East 77 Street. They take me back in fifth grade at St. Monica's on 79th Street. We get more uniforms 'cause I outgrew mine. I unpack the stuff the movers have brought from storage.

After I've lemon-oiled the furniture and polished the silver and jade demitasse spoons and the brass cutlery from Thailand, washed and folded the laundry, picked up the clothes at the cleaners, packed the refrigerator with the food I got with my rolling cart at the supermarket, I think maybe we can relax for a while. Maybe I can go roller skating in Central Park. I can walk there, it's so close. Kids are allowed in this building, although I don't see any, so maybe I could invite a friend from St. Monica's.

Non, non, non, non, non, non, she says, as if singing down the scale. *Non*! I don't like, she says. We are *vay-ray* busy. It's time to go down to the garment district and buy a few thousand gold coins with little holes in them, some rhinestones, other false jewels, a little stapler-like device for imbedding them in fabric and some sheer cloth – aqua and shocking pink – to make belly dancing costumes for Mom. Must wash her wigs, set them, dry them, tease them, style them, spray them and inevitably, whenever we are stationary for a while, answer the phone. This I do gladly, in hopes that Dad is calling.

Usually she takes it off the hook when she goes to bed so it doesn't wake her before she gets up at noon or so. Sometimes she leaves it off the hook until I get home from school so I can do the routine, which is, Hello, Who's this please? Then I look at her to get the signal of whether or not she wants to speak to him or her. She always wants to talk to her French girlfriends who are usually dressmakers. But the men thing is different.

If she shakes her head I have to tell whoever it is that she's not home; then I have to tell the priest in confession that I lied. Sometimes she gives me a name beforehand or while the phone is ringing and says if so-and-so calls, tell him I left town; and so I have to tell the priest in confession that I lied. But usually I have to say to a particular person that she's not home every time he calls until after many calls, he gives up. Sometimes a guy figures out I'm screening her calls within a couple of days, so when I say who's calling please, he repeatedly asks if she's there instead of telling me his name; I look at her; she figures out what's going on from listening and shakes her head. Some guys are a pain in the neck. Like talking to her is a matter of life and death. They know she's not going to call them. She doesn't call them.

I know why some of them want to talk to her and she won't talk to them. Because they had a date and they were stupid enough to indicate somehow that they wanted to sleep with her, just like that and now they're sorry because she's dropped them off her globe. She comes home from a date and I know right away if this is the case because she's mad and or laughing at them or she's in a combination angry-laughing mood and she says: Can you *eee-mag-eene*? He want to sleep *wees* me for a dinner, or a fur coat or a trip to Paris? Hah. (Then she slams something, like her clutch on the table, throws off her fur coat and kicks off her high heels. Then goes on.) Are *zay crazee*? *Ainh*? *Tiens.* As for me, I'm thinking: Why can't they just take her to dinner and the theatre or on a picnic and have a good time? Why do they need to sleep with her? What's the problem? They're afraid of the dark?

If she's really mad at them, she starts her speech about All Men. All Men are bad. All Men lie. All Men just want to sleep with you. All Men are animals.

I don't believe her. Can you imagine Jimmy Stewart being bad or lying? Or acting like an animal? It's guys like Jimmy Stewart and Johnny Carson who give me hope about men. And then there are the good guys in fairy tales, which I believe have to be based on some in real life.

But in the meantime I feel I should watch out for her. Sometimes I get suspicious about a gentleman's intentions even before he takes her out. I mean, I figure you can save a lot of time by finding out if someone is good enough to go out with your mother early on. For example, if they're educated and well-traveled, I think they're less likely to be afraid to sleep alone. So I tell the doorman when he calls on the intercom to let the date come up. Then I ask Mom who's been getting ready for hours, whether I'm her sister or her daughter, so I can arrange my brain. (She says if some people know I'm her 11-year-old, then they will think she's old. The guy arrives. How are you? Very well, thank you. Would you like to sit down? Can I get you a drink? Scotch and soda? Gin and tonic? Coca-Cola? With ice? Would you mind pouring it please? I'm not sure of the amounts. We sit down. I ask: So what do you do? A lawyer? Really? What law school did you go to? Really? My sister's divorce lawyer says Columbia has the best law school. Where did you go to college? I hear Johns Hopkins has a good medical school. And where are you from? What does your father do?...

I don't get to do this many times. After a while Mom decides it's better that she's ready when they come for her and I should stay in the bedroom until they leave. It doesn't matter to me, really. I just want to let them know someone else is watching. No one lasts too long with her. They're not good enough to marry. Or they're boring. There's always something.

Some days, when there's no school, are special. It's just the two of us and I can be her little girl, which I miss when I have to be her sister. Mom always sleeps late even when she's not being a belly dancer. I am quiet on my pullout couch in the living room. Am reading *The Borrowers*, a novel about miniature English people who decorate their tiny hole-in-the-wall homes with borrowed items from humans: thread spools for chairs; matchboxes for chests of drawers. I worry about what to do when I've read the whole series, because I'll miss the characters so.

Every ten pages or so, I get up and tiptoe to the bedroom doorway, to see if she is awake yet. But no. Not yet. I watch her breathe in, breathe out. How many mornings have I spent like this, waiting for her to wake up? Three hundred? Five hundred? I slip downstairs and get *The New York Times* and croissants or French bread so Mom can have breakfast on a tray with coffee. I will make it for her, with milk, no sugar. When she wakes, she calls me. Nanine, Ni-ni, Na-na, Nickette or Ni-ki. These are my special nicknames. She is the only one who knows them. She made them up. Ni-ki, she says, and then she smiles when I appear at the bedroom door and life begins anew full of happy possibilities.

I jump into her big bed and get under the covers, fold the edge of a pillow case, rub it on my cheek and suck my thumb. I know I am too old to be doing this but it is my greatest pleasure. She pulls my thumb out of my mouth. Your *teef*, she says. I put my thumb back in my mouth. She tries to pull it out again and I resist. It makes me feel safe like nothing else; I don't know why; I don't care. Finally she gives up and dozes. I make a cave with a pillow on my head and peer out at her bedroom. The saintly studio photograph of her mother in the brass filigree frame. The reflection of Chanel No. 5 and Miss Dior perfumes in the huge mirror with the gold frame over her dresser. The smell of Chanel No. 5 permeating her special top drawer holding several pair of kid leather gloves and her mother's white embroidered handkerchiefs. I gaze at the dozens of dresses hanging in her closet beneath the row of wigs sitting on Styrofoam heads, like people standing on line for subway tokens. Hats are tilted every which way on a rack.

Na-na, she says, I need some coffee. She will dip the buttered bread or croissant into the coffee. Her eyes will disappear into her eyelashes as her high cheekbones rise and she smiles, munching, her mouth closed. Na-na! she says. Get me some marmalade. I do. It makes me feel important to do these things. To take care of her. Then she will tell me to draw the blinds. Light floods in. She looks in the hand mirror she keeps by her bed, says she looks terrible and old. She studies her eyebrows, tweezes them and puts on her sunglasses to hide the smudged mascara and eyeliner around her eyes. I say she's beautiful. She says I'm sweet and what shall we do today? I say, Can we go to Chinatown for dumplings? Maybe, she says. She sinks back in the pillows and selects some strands of her dark brown hair to twirl around her fingers. She is daydreaming I know. I have seen her do this so many times.

I want to ask her what she is thinking about but I don't dare. We don't talk much. We never have. Partly because it took her a while to learn English and partly because I am afraid of her. But just being quiet with her is fine. Her daydreaming and twirling her hair is the quintessence of her languidness. I wish I could be like that, so relaxed; you can see it even in the way she saunters. But I'm not like that. I wake up worried about what's going to happen next. I don't think she knows this. I am glad when she says, put Piaf, because it is reading and music that calm me. I go and put Edith Piaf on the turntable. I put the side on with the songs I know she likes best: *I Love Paris* and *Sou le Ciel de Paris.* She likes to hum up and down the notes. I know she's getting up for the day when she takes off her sunglasses and says to run her bath. It will be at least two hours, unless she has a date which takes more time, before she's done her toilette and sat before her mirror with light bulbs around it and put on her make-up. The last thing she does before getting dressed is to put on a special net hood with a zipper in front, so that when she dons clothes that go over her head, her hair and make-up don't get messed up, and so the make-up doesn't get on the fabric.

We take the Lexington Avenue line to Canal and walk, past stores with diamonds in dusty windows, to Chinatown. These are amongst the happiest times we have. When we get to Mott Street we visit the Buddhist temple. On the outside it's a storefront with white paper in the windows. Inside a Buddha painted gold and bigger than we are sits cross-legged. I expect lots of people must come in here to pray and give money, like at St. Monica's. We go across the street to the dim shop with the ducks hanging high above the counter; the smell of spices rushes at you in the doorway. Mom walks around the store as if it's hers. She buys by the quart soy sauce and *nuoc mam*, Vietnamese fish sauce that we eat with lime, chopped fresh raw garlic and crushed chili pepper; we have that with meat, rice and Boston lettuce. She buys dried bean threads and mushrooms. I carry everything. I want to help her. I want her to be happy with me. She buys me little coconut candies and dried salted plums and laughs at me when I suck in my cheeks over the plums' tartness. I feel special from her attention. We pass a shop playing Chinese opera out onto the street; I think it sounds like screaming cats. She stops at outdoor displays, examines embroidered pink silk Chinese slippers for wearing around the apartment, then buys them for me. She says when you go shopping you need a *leetle* Japanese man to follow you and carry what you buy. You're supposed to point at things and he's supposed to bargain, pay for them and get the change – because talking about money is low class and touching it is dirty; you could get germs from thousands of people.

Finally, we arrive at number 46 Mott Street, a tiny cafe with a counter and little Formica tables where we order coffee with cream and sugar and *char siu bao* and other *dim sum* she points at. The *dim sum* arrives behind the counter in a little elevator with a sliding glass door that's covered with steam. I love *dim sum* and number 46 Mott Street even though it's not fancy because we're happy when we go there and also to the Hamptons. Some Saturdays, after I have finished cleaning, doing the laundry and shopping and I don't have to defrost the refrigerator or sew or do something that takes all day, she says, let's go, and we get in her red Camaro and drive to East Hampton.

We see signs for a town called Quogue and she says Quogue and laughs at the word. Or we buy French bread, scallions and Genoa salami, sliced very thin, and dark chocolate. We eat salami sandwiches and then the rest of the bread with the chocolate. It's a picnic at the beach. I spread big towels on the sand. We put Bain de Soleil on each other's back. We lay down to get tan, though I know I will burn first, but then it starts. Someone finds her. What do you expect with her in a bikini?

We feel his shadow blocking the sun or we hear the voice: Excuse me, please. Do I know you? She takes off her sunglasses and squints at him. *Non*, she says and puts her glasses back on. Oh, he says, you look just like someone I used to know. Or he asks what time it is and she says she doesn't know, even with her watch on. She also says things like: I am just waiting for my husband. Or, my fiancé is just arriving soon. Or else she says, oh *pleeze, dun't baz-zer* me. Or we get up and leave.

I get an unpleasant view of men on the loose in public places. Don't they know you're supposed to be properly introduced through your family or a friend? I know there have to be some men like Dad who don't act like this. I figure gentlemen are rare, like people who have silver or golden wedding anniversaries. But I have hope, because there are people who have silver or golden anniversaries. I don't know any, but Emily Post writes about what to do when they happen. In her book, on pages 262 and 263.

I respond one Saturday morning to an unusual request by my mother. I am reading on my couch. She comes out of her bedroom in her silk robe and sunglasses at a shocking early hour like 9 a.m. and shuts the door behind her without a sound. I stare at her polished red toe nails as she whispers. She wants me to fold the pull-out couch and go downstairs and buy myself some breakfast at the coffee shop down the street. She gives me five whole dollars. I say I need to go to the bathroom, which is entered through the bedroom, and she says, please go to the bathroom in the coffee shop. She says buy *The New York Times* and read it and don't come back for two hours. I say, Why? She says, tilting her head towards the closed bedroom door, I have someone here. I say, Who? She says, Never mind, just do what I say. And so I go, wondering.

She's in a good mood when I get back. She's humming Piaf. I clear the plates from the black and white marble dining table and wash the dishes and frying pan. It looks like they had an omelet, toast, juice, coffee. I'm thinking it might be better if she does get married again because I am tired of men chasing her.

But it doesn't matter what I think. Right away I know that her guest is a potentially serious contender, not only because he slept over – a first – but because the phone stops ringing so much. She's changed the number. Not only that: she tells me she told him I'm her daughter and not her sister, which means he can figure out that she's not 22 and probably not 28, like he is. Though she doesn't look it, she is letting him know she is older than he is, actually seven years older. She's been saying she's 29 for years. So I know she means business. She's saying to him: Take it or leave it now, early on. Finally, I know our lives have changed for sure because she says to stop calling her Mom or Mommy. She wants me to call her Mum. And they only do that in Veddy-Veddy movies.

I hear more about him than I see him. He comes and goes. He has a yellow

Cadillac in New York and a Bentley in London where he has a flat in Knightsbridge which is very chic. He is the cousin of Lord Antony Lambton, the Earl of Durham, who sits in Parliament and lives in Lambton Castle. His name is Michael Lambton and he is *vay-ray reeeshe.* He went to Eton and that's chic. Mom says he doesn't have to work, but he does, sometimes, in publishing, a family-connected business, but she says he doesn't need to. He is all she talks about: He laughs at people who have to work; he looks down upon people who work in general; he is *vay-ray* snob and this, being snobby, she thinks, is his right and her right. He is high class but it's low class to use the phrase high class or low class or, of course, to talk about money. He is Church of England and disdains Catholics, who are low class; also the Irish, Jews and Negroes whom he calls *niggas*, although he likes to listen to Shirley Bassey, Lena Horne and Josephine Baker constantly because it's chic to like them, even though they're Negroes. It seems Michael also thinks it's chic to constantly use f--ing as an adjective, which I think is a curse word that means shit. He doesn't say this to me. I hear him speaking to Mom sometimes. He never speaks to me. He speaks to her and she says to me, Michael says this or that. This happens sometimes while I'm standing right there, as if I'm not there. I am never sitting right there because I am not in their presence long enough to sit.

He doesn't eat with children you see; they are supposed to eat early and evaporate. In general, he and Mum live on different time cycles than I do. He gets up at noon, like she does. He says it's very low class to eat dinner before 10 p.m. and 11 p.m. is best. He is a gourmet and only drinks champagne. He likes to make onion soup from scratch very late at night when I am told to go sleep in Mom's big bed until she wakes me up to move me back onto the couch in the living room. For the next two years when I am around the cuisine is shepherd's pie, lamb with mint jelly, broccoli with white sauce that requires that I tear up the white part of bread into shreds so that it blends well, goose with dressing of sausage and fresh chestnuts, that I have to spend hours peeling, and plum pudding which has to be steamed. The breakfast favored by him is eggs with bacon, sausages, grilled tomatoes and toast fried in lard. *Crepe suzette*, which had been a rarity, becomes a frequent dessert, but it must be *flambé* with orange liquer, or else it's crepes with cherries and Kirschvasser or Courvoisier. Crepes are Michael's one concession that a non-British national might make one thing well. England is the only country in the world. A good English accent, not cockney or something working class, is paramount, though a good Parisian accent like Mum's is considered charming and *de rigeur*. Mum says Michael says so.

It doesn't matter to me that I don't see much of him. Mum says he doesn't like children and that even the Queen of England only sees her children a few minutes a day, when they're not in boarding school, which is where high class children are supposed to be, like Mum was and Michael was. So I don't take it personally when he never speaks to me. Children seem to come from the informal part of life and he's rather formal. I never see him kiss my mother hello or goodbye. I never see him in pajamas or casual clothes. He always wears a suit and a silk kerchief in his left breast pocket. She says they go to the most expensive restaurants. She especially likes *La Toque Blanche* and *La Cote Basque*. I can tell because she has a collection of matches in a big Chinese dish and many of them have the white top hat on them.

The match collection grows. She goes to the hairdresser every two or three days now. She never wears a wig anymore. She doesn't dance. It seems that getting ready to go out to dinner is their focus in life and that starts around four o'clock, unless she goes to the hairdresser around two.

This is around the time I have science projects to do. The one I've chosen involves driving a nail into a piece of wood. I go down to the lumberyard on 14th Street and get the wood cut to the right size and go out on the terrace with some nails and a hammer with my dreams of being a brilliant scientist. I'm going to make a light bulb glow from batteries mounted on a piece of wood. Mum says she and Michael are going to take a nap, don't wake them up. That's fine with me. I don't care because I'm going to discover some scientific thing that's going to improve the world. I drive the nail into the wood and the wood splits in two, I don't know why. I wish Dad were here. He would explain it to me. I realize I need to go down to 14th Street again and get more wood. But the terrace door to the apartment is locked.

The blinds on the living room windows are up but no one is there. The blinds to the bedroom are drawn but I don't dare to knock on the window. Mom said not to wake them up. But the lumberyard is closed on Sunday and I need to bring my science project to school on Monday. I worry and worry. I'm going to get in trouble with Sister. I can't explain this situation to her, I don't know why, but I know it's unusual because it's not the kind of thing that happens on TV. I wish I had a book, but then I didn't know I was going to be locked out. I lean over the railing around the terrace and study the roof tops of the lower buildings. The view is north and west. I wish it were south so I could look at the Empire State Building, or east so I could at least see the river. There is no furniture on the terrace. Only soot from the incinerators below. My broken science project. I sit down on the tiles and wait. The sun begins to drop behind the buildings in the west. And I have to be excused.

For a long time I have to be excused. After a while I don't think I can hold it any longer. What shall I do? If I go on the tile, she will see where it is wet and she will say I am like an animal. If she doesn't see it, she might smell it and really get mad. There is a drain in the corner where the water goes down when it rains. If I aim just right she won't know. But what if someone on the next terrace, divided only by a piece of fiberglass, sees me peeing in the drain? They might tell Mum and she will sound like an ambulance or not love me anymore. I don't know what to do. I look around the divider. It doesn't look like anyone is home. I better do it fast but there is no paper. And what if Mum sees me peeing. She is allergic to children who do not pee in a toilet. I remember. Because one of my sisters peed in her bed one time and Mom made all three of us stand with the wee-wee sheet on our heads so we could smell how disgusting it was. What shall I do? And then I can't hold it anymore. Better the drain than in my pants. I never tell her I did this. But this situation is a problem whenever Michael is here.

Mum says Michael loves his mother in Ipswich, England, a lot and so he has to go back and forth to see her though I never know when. I know he is coming back because she teaches me how to iron his shirts, there in the light living room. I am impatient when I also must iron his handkerchiefs instead of reading or doing homework, but, Mom says, Michael says tissues irritate his nose.

Sometimes I do not know if he's here or there but usually there is some indication in the morning: his suitcase, an empty champagne bottle, dirty dishes. I only care to know because I love to be with Mum and when he is here, I do not see much of her. On Saturdays when he is here, she gives me a list of things to do. I go to the cleaners, the supermarket, the hardware store, the pharmacy, the bakery. On Sundays I go to Mass and in the afternoon she either sends me to the Met or I go out on the terrace. I take my book and a chair. She locks the door. I hope that I do not have to be excused before they wake up. And I hope it doesn't rain. One time when I am out there, it does start to rain. I stand against the wall in hopes that I'll get less wet, but I get wet. Finally, she lets me into the living room.

One day I come home from school and let myself in with my key. The apartment is quiet. If he's not here, she's usually up by this time of day, but sometimes not. The bedroom door is closed. I do not see his coat or suitcase around so I guess Mum is sleeping, so I don't call out, because I don't want to wake her up. But I have to go to the bathroom and you have to go through the bedroom to get to it. So, quietly as I can, I turn the knob, so I won't wake her up as I tiptoe through to use the *loo*. I push the door open. A gasp. *Ainh*! A flurry of blankets billowing in the dimness. I shut the door.

I walk backwards in the living room. Terror. I am standing against the far wall. What will she do? Oh God. Please help me. The last thing I want in the world is to make her mad. And then the door to the bedroom opens. She is wearing her new white Christian Dior negligee. She closes the door behind her, then flies at me. I am trembling. I do not bother to put up my arms to fend off a slap.

I do not care if she hits me. I figure: just get it over with, so she isn't mad anymore. And then she stops. She hovers over me.

Sor-deed, she says.

I realize she's not going to hit me because he's there.

Sor-deed, she says. You are *sor-deed*. Michael says you are *sor-deed*. Get out.

I don't know what sordid means. I run out the door. Forget waiting for the elevator. I race down the stairs. Thirteen floors. I get to Third Avenue where the rest of the world is doing afternoon things. Thank you, God.

I am no longer alone. The city is here. The man over there is selling fruits and vegetables. The guy in the corner newsstand is selling newspapers and magazines. They make me calm. People are walking with their shopping bags and briefcases, determined, on their way home. They will make dinner and watch the news and take their baths and go to sleep. In their own apartments. One day, I think, I will have my own apartment. Like them. I will have a regular life, like them. I go to the coffee shop and use the bathroom. Then I walk to Central Park.

It is still light enough to go in there. I know you're not supposed to be there in the dark. Something Bad might happen. I make my way in at 72nd Street and go down the paths to the bronze Alice in Wonderland statue. She is my friend. She knows what it is to be a kid and be bewildered and that you do not need things that say "Drink me" and "Eat me" to get that way. I watch the children around her, the nannies, the mothers. The children climb on Alice, as if she were a giant nanny herself. It starts to get dark. I fear I will be in more trouble if I don't go back.

I ring the doorbell. She opens the door and lets it fall against me. I push it open. I can tell from her tirade that he's not there. She slams pans in the kitchen. I try to tell her I had to go to the bathroom, that I didn't see his suitcase or coat but it's useless.

Why didn't they just get a lock?

Soon thereafter I am living on another couch. It is speckled brown and orange. Stuffed with foam. I say I am living on it because I spend all my non-school time there, except for taking my bath. I do my homework there. I eat dinner there, the same thing almost every night – filet of sole with lemon, mashed potatoes and peas. Sometimes I get a TV dinner. I get to watch TV after my homework is done. I know she lets me watch it so she doesn't have to talk to me. I mean, what are we going to talk about? Corn Flakes? She must be in her forties.

She is my new governess, Marta Uckert. She's also a seamstress. She is from *Shermany* and she says *vissss* instead of with when she speaks which is not much. She almost never smiles. She is serious about patterns, chalk, stitches, thread and fabric with which she works on a big table before a large window overlooking some backyards in a building not far from St. Monica's. On the weekends I watch TV on the couch. I do not have to make the food list, shop, sew or clean anymore – a relief. All I have to do is put my folded couch bedding away in the morning, fold my laundry, bathe, dress, braid my hair, brush my teeth.

I figure Mum is paying her a lot of money because there is no indication otherwise that Marta wants me here. I wish Mum/Mom would call or write. I guess she's not the letter-writing type. Or she doesn't have time. She said she had to go to Canada to dance. I know life is hectic on the road. So I wait. A month. Two months. I wish I could invite a kid from school to come over, but I am sure Marta would not like it. And I don't want to explain at school where my mother is or why I'm living with this woman.

I don't know how Marta can stand it. We never go anywhere. She never seems to go anywhere. She sews. I watch her working her mouth, pressed closed, in different directions as she stitches. Beyond the big window snow is melting and little spring things are coming up, major events for me.

Gradually, in silence, Marta perks up, like the buds on the bushes and trees. She changes her hair. A flip instead of a pageboy. She looks a little younger, even though she has some gray in her blonde hair. Curious, I watch her.

She goes to the window more often. Once in a while she waves. Then I see him. Kind of bald, in the window across the back apartment gardens below. He waves. She waves.

Then he points at her and points at himself and puts a fist near his ear. He puts his phone number on a big cardboard sign. She calls him. They chat. She starts talking to me. She's interested, but she doesn't want to go over to his apartment alone. She starts smiling and asking me how I am when I get home from school. In the morning she wants to know if I slept well. I think she is suddenly nicer because she wants me to go over to Harry-the- Furrier's apartment with her for tea sometime. I might because I feel sorry for her, being so old and all, with no husband.

Harry-the-Furrier's apartment is clean. It feels like he's been there a long time; lots of books; furs on the floor; drapes. He has a pet ocelot and a fur shop on Lexington Avenue. He has a way about him, smug, very comfortable with himself and his life as a bachelor. He makes me suspicious; because he is so comfortable with us being there and Marta is not. I mean, it would seem more normal if he was a little excited or nervous too, like the guys who used to come to pick up Mom on a first date. But he's not; he's acting too smooth, as if he thinks that if he acts smooth, we should act smooth. He is giving us cookies and tea.

He puts them down on the coffee table before us. My gaze falls on a big book there. My face and ears feel hot. Am embarrassed. What will happen, I wonder, if I say something? It's a big deal to challenge a grown up. But what do I have to lose? Lemon cookies and Marta's non-affection? I feel it coming, what I have to say, welling up inside. I blurt.

Me: This isn't nice.

Harry: Oh? What's not nice?

Me: This book. It's not nice to put a book like this in front of a little girl.

Harry: Why! What's wrong with it?

Me: The lady on the cover isn't wearing any clothes.

Marta is wide-eyed, silent.

Harry: But it's erotica. It's art.

Me: No. I've seen art. This is a photograph of a naked lady. It's not nice.

Harry: My. I didn't realize you were so sensitive.

Just because I'm 11 I'm blind? And no, I did not want to know what erotica meant.

Marta has a different attitude after this. She used to ask if I liked my dinner but now she doesn't. She sighs a lot. Then, behold, within a couple of days Mom comes back from wherever she was. She appears in a flurry of smiles, short laughs and fur Cossack hats. She gives the nicer, white one, tipped in black to Marta, like a peace offering. I get the yellowish one. It's springtime, so a fur hat is not too exciting. Mom asks what happened, why I got so fat. I pack my Samsonite in a hurry. She takes me home to the penthouse, which does not seem dusty for a place that has been unoccupied for months.

I know Michael is still around because his shirts need washing and ironing. Also Mum is wearing a new ring. She says they're engaged to be married. It's a nice ring, heavy and gold with leaves overlapping each other. But it doesn't look like an engagement ring. There's no stone. I wonder, because he's supposed to be so *reeshe*. She says that he says that you have to buy the most expensive of everything, or else what you buy will have been made cheaply and fall apart. Sweaters need to be made by Pringle. Her suits need to come from Jaeger. I wonder if this ring came from Tiffany's or Van Cleef and Arpel. I shrug. She's happy. They're in love. You can tell because he doesn't seem to see anyone else in the room but her when he's here and vice versa. It's fine.

And I'm happy to be on my own couch. Maybe Mom and I can go to Chinatown or the Hamptons. But no. There's no time. I can feel it without her saying so. She is on the phone, calling summer camps in the classifieds in *Vogue* magazine.

I can feel the breeze coming in through the open terrace window. The weather is sunny and cool but not enough for a sweater. I know that many stories below, Manhattan is blooming with people ambling about the park and the museums and the galleries on Madison, but I want none of it, though ordinarily I would. Because of the package on the red lacquered table. There is a small card propped against it that says, For Danielle, and I know right away that it's something magic. Because the bag says Doubleday. It's on Fifth Avenue; it's one of the most beautiful stores in the world.

I know the package is from Michael because Mum only buys books for me at Christmas and who else around would buy me half a dozen brand new hardback books from Doubleday? The *Japanese Fairy Tales* were probably Mom's idea. I think he chose the one called *Hero of Trafalgar*. How would Mum know about Lord Horatio Nelson, whose mother died when he was nine, who went to sea when he was 12 on his uncle's ship and who in battle lost an arm and the use of an eye? This is an Englishman's book. Michael is trying to make me appreciate an English hero, not French, not American, English, like him.

That's okay, I think, once I start it. Because it's so exciting I don't want to put it down. Even after a few pages I wish I could be like Nelson, stalwart and brave, heroic. I guess that is what it means to be English. But I was born in French Indochina, Dad is part Irish and Mom is mostly French. But I can dream. Maybe one day I shall go to sea and be a girl Horatio, full of honor and valiance.

Mom gets some coffee from the kitchen. I am a little annoyed because I have to stop reading long enough to fold up my couch but after I do it she leaves me alone. Michael comes out of the bedroom. He's dressed to go to the St. Regis to get *The Times* of London and Mum is in her negligee and hovers, watching. I stand up and say: Thank you very much for the books. Michael nods. He's embarrassed about being thanked. Actually I want to rush at him and hug him 'cause I do get mushy when I'm grateful but I don't dare because he's *veddy* reserved. And then he's off, which is my cue to use the bathroom. Then I'm on my couch reading, happy. He comes back with his paper and goes into the bedroom. Mom comes out, dressed in a suit and wearing a hat, so I know she's going to the hairdresser. She says Michael is taping a letter to his mother so don't use the bathroom because the tape will be interrupted if I knock. But I don't have to go.

A couple of hours later I am in the Battle of Trafalgar. The doorbell rings. I look around for something to mark my place, because I don't want to bend down the corner of the page, it's so precious. I tear a corner of the Doubleday bag and use that. I ask at the door, Who is it? and she says, Mum. I open the door, wondering why she didn't just use her key. She has a new beehive hairdo, which is the fashion now, with little spit curls in front of her ears that go backwards.

Oh, Mommy you look beautiful.

I told you not to call me Mom-my. Call me Mum.

Yes, Mum.

She stands by the front door a moment and looks at me a long time.

What? I say.

You took a long time to answer the door. Why?

I was looking for a bookmark.

Oh, she says.

She looks at the closed bedroom door. Where is Michael?

In there.

I notice she didn't smile when I told her she looked beautiful. I figure she doesn't like something about the hairdo. She says hairdressers run a racket. If you don't watch out, they'll do your hair so you have to go back to them or else you look like a mess.

The light coming through the living room windows fades. I turn on the lamp, sorry, because I am moving towards the end of the book, but there are others to read on this Easter vacation. Mom and Michael go out. I make a TV dinner. I pull out the couch and fall asleep during Johnny Carson. They will turn it off.

Michael leaves around noon the next day with his suitcase. Mom goes in her robe with him out into the hallway to the elevator, which is unusual. Then she comes back and goes into the bedroom. I can see her eyes; she did her makeup before he left. Something's wrong. I don't know what. I wonder if he's going to England, but that wouldn't make sense right after taping a letter to his mother. Maybe he's going to New Jersey where, Mom says, a factory makes books for his family business.

She leaves the bedroom door open. I slip in and on the way to the bathroom, see her sleeping. I go back to the living room and my Horatio.

She gets up and makes coffee. I hear her stirring the milk into it, then the metallic tap-tap of the spoon on its rim. She is standing in front of me in her robe with the cup in her hand.

Why, she asks, did you take so long to answer the door yesterday?

I look up at her.

I was looking for a bookmark, I say, I didn't want to bend the page.

Non, non, non, non, she says, her tones going down the scale. You took a long time. I heard zee bedroom door close.

I'm confused.

From the hallway? I didn't hear the door close from inside the apartment. The bedroom door was never open. Whatever is the matter?

I repeat: the doorbell rang and I was looking for a bookmark and then I tore one from the bag. That's why it took time to answer the door. I didn't want to bend the page. It's a beautiful book.

Non, she says. You took a long time to answer *zee* door. A long time. Tell me where you were.

I was here on the couch reading.

Non, I know. You were in *zee* bedroom.

No. I wasn't. You told me not to disturb Michael making a tape.

You can tell me. I am your *muzzer*. You were in *zee* bedroom. *Wees* Michael. Yes? *Ainh*? What did he do?

Nothing.

So *eet eeze* true, you were *zere*.

No. I wasn't. I was here.

He touched you somewhere.

No.

You can tell me. If you tell me, every-*sing* will be okay. *Uzer-wize, non*.

But there's nothing to tell.

Ah, *non*. I know. I know *some-sing* happen.

Nothing happened.

Did he give you *some-sing*? Some candy?

No.

Some *prom-ize*?

`No. We didn't talk. I was reading. He was in there.

Do *sumi ma sen*.

But I didn't do anything.

My eyes are full of tears. It has been a long time since she made me do *sumi ma sen*. I hate doing *sumi ma sen*. And there's nothing to be sorry for.

Do, she says, pointing her index finger with its red fingernail at the place in the carpet in front of her feet, *sumi ma sen*.

I am afraid. I wonder if she has a willow branch somewhere. I get down on my knees, bow my head and fold my hands in prayer.

Say it.

Sumi ma sen, I say. The tears spill.

For what? she says. Tell me what you did.

Nothing, I say. I get up and step backwards. I dare to raise my gaze from the carpet. I realize I have made a mistake to do *sumi ma sen*, out of fear, in hopes she will stop this. Am so tired.

Tiens, she says. She paces the living room. I am crying hard now because she doesn't believe me, which is humiliating and insulting. I get an idea.

Ask Michael, I say. Why don't you ask Michael?

Tsk, she says, and gestures away from herself with the back of her hand.

My face is hot and wet. My nose is stuffed up. My eyes hurt. I'm scared. For hours she keeps interrogating, cajoling, saying everything will be okay if I tell her what happened. Then she gets tired. I am exhausted, relieved she is tired. She goes away, into the bedroom, into the kitchen. She gets dressed. She goes out. She comes back. She doesn't speak.

The next day I wake up with eyes more swollen than when I went to sleep. I am drained. Slowly, I make coffee. She comes out of the bedroom, stands by the front door and watches me in the kitchen stirring the Instant Maxwell House.

You have to tell me what you did.

Nothing. I didn't talk to him. He was taping a letter.

So you heard him taping the letter?

No, you said he was taping a letter. Not to bother him.

I may be a little girl but I can tell something is really wrong here. She is acting too strange. I need to tell someone. Who can I tell? I want to call Dad, but I have no phone number. This is scary. Who can I tell? It's probably not against the law, this questioning, so I can't tell the police. But I know it's wrong. Even criminals have rights. I saw it on TV. But I'm not a criminal. What shall I do? Who can I tell? The doorman? What can the doorman do? What would he think? That I am weird, to say my mother is blaming me for something I haven't done? It's not normal to tell the doorman about personal stuff. And it's too complicated to explain. It doesn't feel like a mother thing, what she's doing. It's a jealousy thing. But there's nothing to be jealous of. How can I tell anyone? Who would believe me? A priest maybe. But confession is for sins and I haven't sinned. Who can help me? What do little girls do when something like this happens?

Who is there for me? God, please help me.

Every day, for all the days I am on vacation from school, she continues. I cry until my eyes are swollen shut and my head throbs. I wish she would hit me if that would make her stop. Surely her hitting me would hurt less than this. But she's not going to hit me. She would have done it by now. She wants to know what happened in this imaginary scene in her head. But I can't tell her. Because I wasn't in it. She keeps questioning, as if she thinks that if she outlasts me, I will tell her what she wants to hear. But I don't know what she wants to hear. If I did, I might make it up, just to make her stop.

Finally, I have to go back to St. Monica's. I am in sixth grade and grateful for every whiff of incense at Benediction, every mournful strain of the *Kyrie Eleison*, every boring moment of religion class, every torturous minute of math. After school I fear I may have to endure more interrogation. But at home things are quiet until she comes at me with a burst, saying: Here is a curse upon you for all of your life: I wish upon you that your daughter do this to you – what you did to me – that she sleep with your husband, the man you love.

And I wonder: What for?

Though my return to St. Monica's somehow caused a cessation of this experience, it became for me eternal. It matched in importance the day I got married, the days my children were born and the days people I loved died. This was the Easter the closeness between my mother and me disappeared. Though we had some good times after that, she never called me one of my nicknames again, never treated me like a little girl again. Something was gone, replaced by distance so substantial, it almost felt tangible.

Still, I loved her.

Chapter Six

You would think that with her belief that something happened between me and Michael in the penthouse bedroom, she would have at least cooled toward him. But no.

They continued in their strange love. It seemed like a disease that bonded them like Siamese twins desperate to separate and to be together. Something was preventing peace between them no matter where they were I could sense it. She could sense it and I could sense the fear in her. This was inconvenient for me, since how things went between them dictated how things went between me and Mom, when I saw her. How things went with him, whether he was in New York or London, dictated her outlook on life. It made me ponder romantic love and wonder whether or not it would ever be worth catching.

I keep dreaming that Dad will save me, like Dudley Do-Right in the cartoons. Wishing goes a long way when you need breaks from reality. I think it's not likely that Dad will find me in this summer camp because it's not near a town. It's far into the woods in one of those states where the summer weather is cool enough to need a blanket at night and warm enough during the day not to need a sweater, Maryland maybe, or North Carolina; I don't remember. Campers are not allowed to make or get phone calls, except in emergency, because if all the campers made phone calls it would be disruptive. They can write and get letters, but most campers don't because most of them are only here for two weeks. I am to be here for six or seven weeks. I have almost given up writing letters to Dad because I get no answer to the ones I send to APO San Francisco. Mum did not write to me when I was at Camp Merryelande all summer even when there was no Michael, so I don't expect any communications here.

After my duffel bag is stashed away, I think: Since I'm not going to have any phone calls or letters, this might be a good place to start over.

A new life. No one knows me here. There are no nuns. But the ones at St. Monica's have given me an idea. I have just taken Veronica for my confirmation name, after the woman who wiped the blood off Jesus' face; it seems appropriate, since I always seem to be cleaning. What will happen if I say my name is Veronica? I could be Ronnie for short. I could sound more American like the other campers. What will happen if I don't tell anyone I was born in Saigon and have a French and Vietnamese mother and live in New York? What will happen if I don't braid my hair each day? There is no apartment to clean here. The laundry gets sent somewhere. What will happen if I am not always cleaning? Will anyone like me anyway?

It seems like an interesting experiment. And so I run wild with my hair flying behind me. And no one gets mad, like Mom and nuns who are allergic to long loose hair. Between the swimming pool and the showers each day, my hair's clean, just messy. I sit around the campfires and eat all the S'mores – melted chocolate and marshmallow yummies – that I want and no one gets mad. I weave cloth loops into potholders in crafts and the counselor seems glad. I sing with others the song about Hiawatha... "By the shore of Gitchie Gumee..." I feel like I belong to a club, accepted.

In riding I am assigned a horse named Buck; someone has to hold up one of his hoofs while he's mounted so he doesn't kick you while you're trying to get into the stirrup. You have to watch out for a certain tree he likes to use to knock you off when he turns around it. But I manage until the day he does knock me off him. Since he is 16 hands high it is a long way down. The breath gets knocked out of me. I'm terrified lying in a field of tall grass, unable to breathe for a moment, until I realized I've screamed – that I'm not dead. I get up and run after him and take him by the reins back to the stable and ride him again the next day. I tell him I'm the boss, that we're not going near the bad tree. I am firm with the reins, the crop and my heels.

He obeys me, sometimes.

Early in the morning I am on time at reveille and having made my bunk I salute the flag, say the *Pledge of Allegiance*, and say yessir, nossir, yes, m'am and no m'am and everyone seems happy. On Sundays parents come to visit. That's when my counselor gives me donuts and chocolate milk and tells me she's going to adopt me, take me home to *Suth Caro-lein* with her. I hug her but I'm non-committal. Because I want to be with my real mother and my real father, like most people. But Mom is busy with Michael so I would be happy if I could just be with Dad, because I deserve to be. I can tell from the way these people treat me. No matter what my name is, I am still who I am inside and after weeks at this camp, I see that people like me. It's a relief.

And then on a Sunday Mom arrives. She's angry. When she got to the camp with Michael, who is waiting in his yellow Cadillac convertible, they said there was no Danielle Flood at the camp. Only Ronnie Flood. Who is Ronnie Flood, she asks, and why is my hair so tangled? I try to explain but it doesn't matter because she is combing my hair with her fine-toothed comb, tearing through it and pulling knots out of it in clumps. I am trying not to wince in front of the counselor who wants to adopt me but I can see the look of dismay on her face. I am deflated, or defeated, because I can't control the tears. Stop crying, Mom says as she weaves my hair into braids; your face will be red. *Arretes*. Pack your clothes. *Vite alors*. She is striding with her long legs. I am running to keep up with her.

I have the feeling we've forgotten something. Then I remember. She hasn't asked me how I am. I haven't had a chance to kiss her. I haven't had a chance to hug my counselor goodbye.

We are at the car. Michael is in the driver's seat and doesn't say hello, which is normal. She opens the door. I throw my duffel bag in the back seat. She looks at me and then at Michael and I know what she's thinking.

Before I went to camp I had to do the laundry and there were only a couple of his shirts and so I asked if Michael was coming back and she started again: Why do you want to know if he *eeze* coming back? *Eeze* it because you want to see him again? *Ainh*? *Pourquoi*? Do you miss him? No, I said. I thought: God no. I said I wanted to know if I should wash the shirts and she said if they're in the dirty laundry, they need to be washed and ironed and I said, of course. I am afraid the interrogation is going to start over again.

I doubt that she would start again with him present. She doesn't do anything unpleasant around him. But I worry about later, when we are alone. So I decide to act extra interested in the scenery – the sky, the trees, the highway, the other cars, their license plates – wow, California, wow, Idaho; I wonder what they're doing over here. Anything to show her that I am not even vaguely interested in him. I can see he doesn't have to make any effort to be the same way. He continues to be oblivious of me and since he is acting as he usually does, I glean that she probably didn't accuse him of having anything to do with me in the bedroom. I guess she figured out that he might be insulted by such an accusation. I would be if I were a man. I mean, you should see what I look like – I have a barrel for a torso, like Humpty Dumpty. The idea crosses my mind to tell him about the days of interrogations; boy, that would probably get rid of him fast – he would surely think she'd gone nuts or he wouldn't believe me and think I was nuts. But I know she would kill me if I did that and no one would ever find my body. You think the nuns at St. Monica's are going to come looking for me? When we were on the road, I came and went there like it was a bus stop. Who would find my body?

Chapter Seven

It occurs to me, more than 50 years later, that as my eleventh year continued, my mother's sense that Michael was hiding something about another female was acute – only it had nothing to do with me. He'd become involved in Britain's greatest cold war scandal of the 20th Century, the Profumo Affair. The United Kingdom's secretary of state for war, John Profumo, resigned after lying to Parliament about his involvement with a showgirl/call girl named Christine Keeler who was also involved with a Russian spy/Russian embassy assistant attaché, and others. At the time, despite headlines on our side of the Atlantic too, I didn't understand the significance of this, or that the scandal helped bring down British Prime Minister Harold MacMillan's Conservative government within a year. I only saw what it did to my mother, who was still treating me like a stranger.

I am relieved to learn that Michael has gone to England again to see his mother. I am wondering if it's possible for things to go back to the way they were before Michael, but I see I shouldn't ask.

Something new is going on. Mom is watching the news on TV every night; unusual for her. And every day now she says I have to go to the St. Regis Hotel to get the London papers. All the London papers.

I know the St. Regis because she has sent me there before. It's a walk from East 77th Street, but I don't mind. I like the crystal chandeliers there. The doormen are nice to me. They tip their hats and say, hello. They have seen me many times in my St. Monica's uniform. I feel important going up the steps under the marquee to the news/tobacco stand inside.

Back at the penthouse, Mom's waiting on the couch and pounces like a cat on the London papers. She studies them. I don't dare ask what's the matter. There's a grim look on her face. Later, she looks through them again. I wonder. Then one day, while she's reading inside one of the papers, she says:

You see? I knew *eet*.

She slams the paper on the coffee table and says again, I knew *eet*.

What? I ask.

A *scand-ale*.

What's a scandal?

Some-sing vay-ray bad. Vay-ray bad.

Who?

Michael.

Where?

Ici! She stabs the paper with her red-polished index fingernail.

Tiens, she says, looking at the ceiling.

I see his name. It says Michael Lambton. He's in *The Times*. He's also in the *Daily Express*, *The Daily Mail* and *The Daily Telegraph*.

Why is he in the newspaper?

Because he is in a *scand-ale wees zat* tart, Christine Keeler and *zee uzer* one, Mandy Rice Davies.

What's a tart?

Someone who sleep *wees* everyone!

Oh boy. I figure this Keeler lady has problems. It doesn't sound too clean to sleep in the same bed with lots of other people. I mean I can't even stand to sleep alone with dirty feet. If you get in bed with dirty feet, the sheets will get dirty and then another part of you will get dirty and it just goes on and on. What if the people she slept with had dirty feet? Or bad breath?

I pore over the paragraphs in the papers. It's a lot to take in all at once. I don't really understand what's so bad, except that I see that it says she was engaged, Miss Keeler, to Michael, and that he gave her money to take holidays in France and in America. And it says she's 21 years old.

She's about 15 years younger than Mom. This doesn't sound good.

And it says Miss Keeler and Michael had a long and respectable relationship and that he is rich, which is a curious item, since Mum says it's not polite to talk about money, and she says Michael says so. So how can anyone know if he's rich if he doesn't tell them so? This doesn't sound right.

In another paragraph it's says something about intercourse. It says Miss Keeler says "she had had intercourse with Mr. Profumo, the former War Minister; Peter Rachman, deceased property dealer; a man named Charles, who lived in Park Lane; a Mr. Eylan; and a Persian."

Mom, what's intercourse?

Ah, non! she says. She snatches the paper from me.

Wow, she's mad.

She was already in a bad mood before the London papers thing. A couple of days after Michael left, she took the lamb he made out of the refrigerator to eat the leftovers. There was something wrong with the aluminum foil covering the lamb. It became black in places and in one place it had little holes in it. Like something in the lamb made it disintegrate. Wine? Garlic? I don't know. How am I supposed to know? My life is devoted to *TV Guide*, 1963.

When she sees the foil, fear moves over her face. She says: He eeze trying to kill me. Her eyes look wild. I don't know what to think. I don't think Michael would be bothered killing anyone. It would be too much trouble. His major job each day is getting dressed and putting a silk kerchief in his suit breast pocket.

How can *some-sing* in *zee* lamb eat *zee* aluminum foil?

Maybe it's the salt, I say.

But she continues. I'm perplexed, because I've seen leftover food with salt in it not eat through aluminum foil. She goes into long periods of silence. She stares out the penthouse windows. I am remembering, as I watch her, that she told me one should always have white ivory chopsticks, or some with white ivory tips, because they will turn black if you put them in food that is poisoned. I want this new preoccupation of hers to go away. Eventually, she throws the lamb out. I wonder why, if she thinks Michael is trying to murder her, or us, she doesn't show it to the police. But then it's not my business.

I wonder whether or not this is the end of Michael in our lives. There must be some explanation for the problem with the aluminum foil. Maybe there's even an explanation for the Miss Keeler stuff. I wish everything could just be quiet and happy. But then, probably, Mom would get bored and start re-examining me and everything I do, more than she normally does. So, better Michael and Miss Keeler get it than me.

For a long time, Mom is in a bad mood. She doesn't want to listen to Edith Piaf. Forget Chinatown – that was for when she trusted me. She doesn't relax and daydream while twirling her hair. She watches the news and doesn't let me see it. She sends me a few more times to the St. Regis. I don't dare ask for anything or about anything. I used to think I saw little of her when Michael was here. Now he is gone, there are shirts to be ironed, and though she's visibly present, poring over the London papers and slapping them around and pacing in the living room high over the east side of Manhattan, she's not here either.

Chapter Eight

So I'm not miserable when I hear I'm going away to school. What's the difference between an angry absent mother and an angry mentally absent mother? Besides, if my own absence is going to promote true love with Michael forever and make her happy to be with when I do see her, I'm for it.

I need to be measured for new uniforms. I have to try on fancy uniform loafers for every day – I need two pair of these – and some uniform pumps for Sundays. Why, they're like high heels. What is this? And I need nylon stockings. In seventh grade? I'm not even twelve yet.

Oui, zay are on zee list. It's a long list. There are blue and green plaid wool skirts, matching navy or green weskits, white blouses, a black velvet tam, blazers, sweaters and seven spring uniforms: cotton shirtwaist dresses in pastels with matching cloth belts. The white one is for Sundays and we get to choose the colors of the others. I need fourteen pairs of underwear, some full slips, nightgowns, another robe and slippers. Multiple items so I have plenty to wear when the laundry is being done. Someone else is going to do the laundry and deliver it to me. Why am I suddenly so special that I get all these clothes, this service? But then I understand: it's part of the price of her freedom.

The taxi goes up a long driveway past an apple orchard to a palatial cream-colored building with a cupola, stained glass windows, many arches, marble floors and others that shine. The Academy of St. Joseph, founded in 1856, smells like floor wax and furniture polish, except in the mostly marble chapel, which smells like beeswax candles and incense. There is no dust. For the next year I never see dust at St. Joe's. I see girls, a few priests, nuns and nun-like women: postulants, who are taking the first step to becoming a nun; novitiates, who have graduated from being postulants but haven't taken their vows yet; real nuns, who have taken vows of poverty, chastity and obedience; retired nuns, some rolling around in wheelchairs - one looks half-dead with her head lolling above her shoulders - and truly deceased nuns, buried in the nun cemetery there. This is not only a boarding school for girls, most in high school, four of us in seventh grade; there are also day students who get their lives back when they leave around 3 o'clock on weekdays. It's also the Mother House for the order of the Sisters of St. Joseph set on an enormous property in Brentwood, Long Island, a/k/a Holy Women Central.

Of course I miss the Mom I used to know. I learn that you can love someone even though not much seems to be happening in return, or the love that's there is simply on hold, like a subway paused between stations. I figure that if Mom could change her feelings toward me like this, with this idea that I had somehow betrayed her, then perhaps she could change back to the way she was. So I have hope. In the meantime I wait, and try to make friends at school. She had been my world.

I try to please. I go to Mass and kneel and bow and pray and pray, and try to get out of it by saying I have an upset stomach, or the flu, or that there's something wrong with my knee. I try to study, but my mind wanders so it sometimes feels hopeless. I set my hair every night and try to sleep on the curlers with tiny plastic teeth digging into my scalp. I polish my shoes for the nun's inspection and buff buff buff them with lambs wool, spit on them like soldiers in movies and buff them some more. I smile and look cheerful, even when I don't feel like it.

I hope that the nun who is assigned to me and three other seventh grade boarders, Sister Mary Margaret, could be my friend maybe. She is our teacher for all classes and the boss of every other minute we have. But she has a nasal Massachusetts accent, a haughty attitude and is most prone to not speaking to us whenever possible. If you accidentally or on purpose have done something wrong, it is likely she will not speak to you for up to about ten days, but usually a couple of days is the norm. The problem with this is that once the other boarders get the idea that she isn't speaking to you, it is not likely that they will be brave and try to keep you from being more isolated than you are by communicating with you. Sister Margaret wouldn't like that. You can tell. Her dirty looks go a long way.

This treatment is called being put into Coventry. Only a kid who wants to be put there is stupid enough to talk to a kid who is already there. Coventry is solitary confinement without walls. It isn't written down in any handbook. It doesn't work for day students. You need to be encompassed by the boarders' life style at St. Joe's for it to be effective.

I suppose I should have figured out early on that this was going to be the preferred method of punishment from the environment at meals where we are served by novitiates in habits who are not allowed to speak to us even though neither we nor they have done anything wrong. It's part of their penance – some kind of suffering or discomfort. It's supposed to prove that they can be obedient when they take their final vows. Sister Margaret says that once they become nuns, on special days celebrating certain saints, they get to flagellate themselves, like she does, with a whip, three times over the shoulders against their backs; not so they hurt themselves, just lightly, symbolically, she says. There are also days on which they must fast and only drink water. Happy, it seems, is not in the curriculum.

And so I begin a more predictable life laced with confusion. Jesus says to love one another and we are taught that we must be polite, so when we are served food by a young almost-nun, it feels funny when we say, Thank you, Sister, (novitiates are called Sister), and she doesn't acknowledge this. In fact, after a while, if one persists in saying, Thank you or How are you today?, it is possible to detect a glint of alarm in her eyes as she proceeds to not respond.

Fearful is the desired disposition. A good way to maintain this amongst a bunch of adolescent and teenage girls is to discourage them from speaking during much of the day. This is done by tightly packing their schedules and by moving their population quickly from one activity to another by ringing a bell or clapping the hands twice. Other ways to promote the desired disposition is to let the boarders know there is almost nothing they can hide. The telephone is not available. There might be one on the property, but where it is is not evident. A certain mystery is the whereabouts of a person called Mother Superior, who is referred to once or twice but never seen.

Privacy is a remote idea. Boarders' desks, hockey lockers and bedside cabinets are to be ransacked regularly, with every piece of paper in every book or pocket examined and sometimes questioned. The envelopes of all outgoing letters are to be left open so they can be read by Sister, who opens and reads all incoming letters, too. Letters will be rewritten, if necessary, to reflect a mature and proper attitude. It is pointless to write a letter and ask another boarder going home for the weekend to mail it because any odd communication that comes in response could indicate that this sneakiness has occurred.

Weekends come and go and I do not go, like other boarders, which means Sister Margaret is stuck with me, seven days a week. Since she makes it clear through nonverbal communication, facial expressions in particular, and absences in general that people do need time off from kids, this situation makes the possibility of establishing with her some kind of bond or mutual appreciation remote. I miss my friend on TV, Johnny Carson. The only time we are allowed to watch TV is when President Kennedy dies. I do not remember anything happening on my twelfth birthday and if something had, at St. Joe's, I surely would have, because so little else went on, except classes and chapel. The turkey with stuffing and cranberry jelly is good on Thanksgiving, and the novices serving me seem to step a little more lightly what with minus a hundred plus or so mouths to serve. You should try having dinner by yourself in a dance-hall-size dining room with a mute almost-nun serving you sometime. It promotes use of the imagination. I pretend a handsome boy prince is sitting across the table. I wonder who sat here before us over the previous hundred or so years, and how they ended up. Dead, probably, some of them, with their bodies in the attic here, and their ghosts haunting the white marble Senior Steps in the front hall, which must be scrubbed with a toothbrush by any non-senior who is caught walking on them, or so the high school girls say. I don't mean to imply that the nuns would kill anyone – that would involve blood probably, or sweating, which is dirty, and the nuns we see have nothing to do with any activity related to sweating or being soiled, which seems to be Sister Margaret's favorite word. I think that probably, some students before me never got out of this place; some of them graduated from the high school, became postulants, then novices, then nuns, then expired, only to haunt the 200-acre grounds.

The emptiness of the chairs, the image and idea, seems to reverberate in my brain, even later, in bed or at my desk Except for the nun standing behind me as I eat, the message is clear: I should probably be somewhere else, or, I have been using the wrong calendar. I learn that holidays have more than one dimension. The one for me is the one in which they need to be ignored because they make me feel like an inconvenience, even at Christmas. Sister Margaret is annoyed because everyone leaves for vacation before I leave, finally, on Christmas Eve.

When I do get home to our new apartment on East 78th Street, Mom acts like I've done something – like appear – to make Michael go away. I discover there are no shirts to wash and iron.

Is this the end of the dramatics?

No. Michael phones from England almost every day. Mom tells me not to answer it, I think, so that he's under the illusion that I am completely out of the scene and they can be romantic, which is not far from the truth. I can tell it's him when she answers the phone because her mood changes instantly. She sounds happy, but when she gets off she is again sad. I can see the thoughts flicker across her face. She pines, then stares at me at length. I dare not ask what the matter is. I have heard her reasons why Michael is not here with her: because I have become such a big little girl so I remind him that she is older than him, and because, as she puts it, I'm always under their feet.

But there's something else, something in her eyes, a faraway sadness when she stares at me for a long time. I don't know what it is, but I know it's something of note because she usually tells me everything that makes her sad. The most frequent thing she says is: I am all alone. Who will take care of me when I am old? And I say, I will. And she says, *Yah*? And I nod, and she gets into a better mood.

We have a silver tree this Christmas with all red bulbs and white lights. It's an arty tree, but also the kind you fold up into a box. I wish it were a real tree with the pine smell, the kind of tree we had with Dad, Ev and Pat.

On Christmas morning I get a gold ring and a gold Infant of Prague medal. I wonder if Mom gave Ev and Pat gold rings and Infant of Prague medals, too. But I don't ask because I am afraid of the answer if she didn't. I miss them so.

I also receive a manicure set in a red leather case from Uncle Dany and Aunt Annie in Paris, which means I have an Uncle Dany and Aunt Annie in Paris. I thought we were all-alone-in-the-world. Who is Uncle Dany?

He's Mom's brother and my godfather from when I was baptized at St. Matthew's Cathedral in Washington, D.C. Mom says he's a mathematician. Can I go visit him? Someday, maybe. She has a way of becoming vague or drifting off when a conversation is heading in an inconvenient direction, like taking me to Paris. But he exists. I can dream of knowing him and his wife one day.

Mom says nothing about Michael this Christmas. I am wondering if he is with Miss Keeler, or his dear mother. I wonder if he is still engaged to Mom. I wonder when he was engaged to Miss Keeler, or if he was engaged to Miss Keeler while he was engaged to Mom or if he was engaged to Mom and Miss Keeler while Miss Keeler was sleeping with the five men. I wonder if Miss Keeler slept with those men one by one or with all five of them at the same time. If she did, how did she get any sleep?

Mom is still wearing the engagement ring. And Michael has sent her a dozen red roses. Soon, she tells me as I clean the apartment on New Year's Day – she says it's bad luck not to – she's going on the road again. So I don't know what to think about where she is with him, which is almost more comfortable than knowing.

I take a taxi to Penn Station for the train to school. I do the routine: I get a piece of paper and a pen, lean in the front passenger seat window and tell the driver to turn on the meter so he doesn't get mad about losing time on it while I get his hack license number and his name. I write it down in front of him, then bring the paper to Mom who is in the lobby with my Samsonite and blow her a kiss.

Back at St. Joe's, I still hope to have a great friendship with one of the girls, but there's not much time for it. Another boarder catches me sucking my thumb in bed, which ends my thumb-sucking forever because she is kind enough to tell anyone who will listen about it, with laughter, for days; the only kid who doesn't pay attention to this tells me she's at St. Joe's because her mother hides alcohol in her cologne bottles. So I understand, kind of, why she seems preoccupied much of the time. We are taken on a bus to the symphony. I fall asleep and Sister Margaret is disgusted with me because I missed everything. We go on another big outing, wearing our black velvet tams and white gloves, to Brentwood, Long Island, itself, to a stationery store where we may choose stationery to write letters that will be examined before they are mailed. We are not allowed to remove our white gloves until we return to school. We also must wear them during dance class so that our bare hands do not touch other bare hands even though we are girls dancing with girls. We learn the Lindy and the Triple Lindy, which in 1964 is imperative preparation for life, along with walking around The Bend every day.

The Bend is the driveway around the apple orchard in front of the school. The trees are like people who grow. I see their leaves change from green to red, orange or yellow and fall to the ground. The branches are covered with snow. One morning the snow is so deep that we are excused from walking The Bend. But I do, by myself. The snow is almost to my knees and gets in my boots but I want to show them, Sister especially, that even though I may not be the smartest kid in seventh grade or the best student, I have more stamina than the rest. I tell myself I shall win, some day – I don't know what, but I shall.

Apple blossoms begin to bud on the trees inside The Bend – a big deal because Spring means Easter is coming with the possibility that I will be able to get away from Sister Margaret. When this becomes a reality I run to the dormitory. I'm packed long before I am taken to the train station.

Michael is still not at the apartment and there are no shirts. The first thing

Mom asks is did I break my *teef* yet, then proceeds to tell me about being in England and France with Michael for some months. They were drinking champagne and forgot one of her fur coats on the plane between Paris and London, Ha-ha, very chic. She says he made her bring clothes for the beach, even though it was winter, and clothes for the summer, but she had to come back because of me.

She is still wearing the ring. She says he calls and says he misses her, but I don't want to hear it. She breaks the rule about talking about money and says she spent so much going to see him – he invited her – that now she has to replenish her finances. She is here and he is still there. She says she feels lost and sad, what should she do?

What do I say? Who should I be now? Am I her daughter or her sister or her mother or her imagined competition? If I say, Forget about him, go on with your life and find someone else, she is likely to ask, Why? Because you want him for yourself? And then she might start with the interrogation again. If I say, Go see him in England, and it doesn't work out, she will say it's my fault; she wasted so much money. If I say, Invite him here, I fear she will say, Why, because you want to see him? If I say, Be patient, she will say he is going to find someone else. If I say, He did that already with Miss Keeler, even though I'm not sure about the timing of that relationship, it's going to make her crazy with jealousy and fear. I want so much to get away from this subject but it's all she thinks about. Michael, the obsession. I'm tired and I want to sit on Dad's lap with his big arm around me. I want someone to tell me what to do and smile at me and tell me I'm good, because I am. I do not want to make so many decisions, to think about all these possible responses to her questions. It has been hard, ever since I learned to play chess, to think beyond four or five moves. It makes your mind tired.

She makes me want to go back to St. Joe's. I want to drown in Latin chants, holy High Mass hymns and repeated prayers that eliminate thought, leaving you rested, at least. I want to close my eyes, see nothing, think nothing.

The first thing I get back at St. Joe's is a cold stare from Sister Margaret.

She says: What did you do before you left for vacation?

Nothing, Sister.

You know what you did.

No, S'ter.

Finally, she tells me I left my soiled winter uniforms in my hockey locker before vacation; disgusting.

Raise hand in class. It's ignored. Catch up with her in the hallway ostensibly to ask a homework question but really to see what's the matter. No answer. Billowing black veil. Fall into step with other students, ask them how they are. No answer. Glances in Sister Margaret's direction.

I am in Coventry. The other girls won't explain to me why they won't speak to me because that would involve speaking to me. I know, for I was in Coventry once before, when I first got to St. Joe's, for leaving a basket of apples we were allowed to pick from the orchard in my hockey locker until some of them rotted. That Coventry lasted a few days. But it was different then. I got over it quickly because I was so excited at the time about my new life at St. Joe's, so many possibilities – friendship and freedom from the complications of grownups in love. This time, Coventry falls more heavily upon me. It is a shroud on a spirit worn thin. There seems no place to go, no one with whom to talk. But then comes hope.

A new nun, Sister St. Joseph, moves into our dormitory. She smiles at me in the hallway. She is younger than Sister Margaret, light-hearted, so I think she is not so angry with her life yet. Maybe we could be friends.

The dormitory is designed so that every click of a rosary bead in every one of its dozens of cubicles can be heard. Each cell has three walls, about six and a half feet high, about halfway as high as the ceiling and is fronted by a curtain, to be drawn open whenever one is not dressing. After lights out, the Nun of the Night paces up and down the carpeted center aisle, leading us in moaning our prayers, her head, her veil moving as her dark figure turns this way and that to check that we are in our beds. You can hear the breathing of the sleeping.

Sister St. Joseph's little light is on in her cubicle behind mine. I am so tired of Coventry, of fear, of yearning for Dad, of Mom's mistrust and distance, I surrender to weeping. If only one person would say, There there, like in the movies. But Sister does not come to talk to me. I cry the next night and the next. The boarder who told everyone I sucked my thumb complains that I am keeping her up. I apologize. But after lights out, when the no-place-to-go feeling returns, I am beyond caring what anyone thinks and I weep again, until the Friday I shall never forget.

It is a quiet time, late Friday afternoons. The day students have gone on buses. Cars come, girls are embraced, Mom, Dad. Bags are loaded into car trunks, engines start and fade down The Bend.

On this Friday Patricia Dupre is here. She stays for weekends more than the other boarders. I never ask why. You don't ask these questions in boarding school, because if you do, you come to the threshold of the same questions about you. We decide to take a walk around The Bend on this sunny day. Then we dress for bed early as we do on weekends. We eat dinner in our bathrobes, and pad in our slippers back to the dormitory to read before lights-out, prayers.

At breakfast, Sister Margaret arrives at our table, tells me to follow her. Unusual. Her veil billows as she walks towards the part of the building where the classrooms are. Ours is at the end of the long, shining hall floor. We stop far short of it, at a doorway with a closed transom. She reaches into the deep pocket of her habit and pulls out the dozen or so mostly old-fashioned keys on a long chain attached to her belt. She unlocks the door with a jangle, follows me inside and closes the door behind us. She turns towards me. Sit down, she says. I sit on one of two varnished wood chairs at a small table. The light streams in through a window with transoms that I know will be pulled open on warm days with a long wooden pole with a key-like hook on its tip. There is a small green vinyl loveseat. The inevitable crucifix on the wall. The standard frieze of the Virgin Mary. The room is otherwise bare. Easy to clean.

At first I feel privileged; I have never seen a student go through this door before. These are none-of-your-business doors. Their transoms are usually closed, so the nuns' lifestyle when they are not teaching, praying or clapping their hands at you remains mysterious. In fact, never having seen a nun sleep or eat, I have joked to myself that they probably never do. So I feel like a real insider, in this nuns-only room until Sister Margaret says:

Are you sick?

No, S'ter.

Because if you are we can get you a doctor.

Excuse me?

At first I wonder if this is about my crying at night, but then she says:

What did you do after class yesterday?

I tell her what Patricia Dupre and I did.

Sister Margaret shakes her head. No, she says. A little smile on her face.

Excuse me, S'ter?

You know what you did.

S'ter?

Why was your underwear in the laundry wet?

S'ter?

Why did you try to wash out your underwear?

I didn't S'ter. It just fell in the sink when I was washing my stockings.

No. That's not what happened.

S'ter? A wave of heat creeps up my neck. I realize she is saying I am a liar. Am stunned. My ears burn, tears come. Am not verbally fast. Am very proud. Am embarrassed that she doesn't believe me, then crushed because how, tell me, am I going to prove or disprove that what I am saying is true? Are you kidding? The word of a middle-aged stuck-up nun against a child?

I say I want to call my mother. She shakes her head slowly from side to side. She says I need to say the *Act of Contrition*. I say I have nothing to be sorry for. I want to say I need to call Dad, but I don't know where he is, which country. Frustration makes my mind blank. She says I am impudent and disrespectful. I say I haven't done anything wrong. She says I need to go to Confession. I refuse. She says I must tell her what I did. I say I've done nothing. She gets tired, puts me in a classroom with another nun who also seems angry with me. She too asks me why I tried to wash out my underwear. I tell her I didn't, that it fell into the sink. There was a brown spot, she says, on my underwear.

So there was a brown spot. I am supposed to explain this? I am silent.

My face is so hot. I stand, crying in the back of the classroom as she wipes down her bulletin board with a wet cloth. I note that, again, nuns have been going through our dirty laundry, like at camp.

Sister Margaret returns with another nun I don't know. The two of them continue to interrogate me. I refuse to tell anything but the truth. Finally, they let me go to the dormitory, where exhausted from crying, I sleep. I wake to see Patricia Dupre across the aisle.

What's going on? I say, Are they asking you questions like this? She says, No; where have you been? I say, In rooms with locked doors; they keep asking me what I did. What's going on?

Patricia says someone defecated on the shining hallway floor between the second and seventh grade classroom. An older kid told her. She has to go do homework. She doesn't know why the nuns aren't asking her questions, too. Why aren't they asking her if I was with her? She doesn't know.

I don't remember what happened after telling Patricia Dupre that a second grader must have had an accident in the hallway. I don't remember the rest of the school year. Maybe I was sent home. I do remember telling Mom what happened with the nuns. She stared at me, said and did nothing. I thought that she should complain. Then I wondered, since she didn't believe me about Michael in the bedroom and the nuns didn't believe me about their feces incident, if I was going out of my mind. I worried that no one was going to believe me in the future, about anything. But they did.

Chapter Nine

Mom is painting me again like in Washington, only this time I am wearing a linen dress with a full orange skirt with crinoline attached underneath, a brown embroidered bodice and puffed cream-colored sleeves. My head is tilted. My hair is in a flip. Sitting still for her for two hours at a time, sometimes twice a day, is boring but it's better than her starting a fight. She's tranquil when she's painting. I wish she would paint all the time – but not me, please. Why doesn't she paint Ev and Pat?

They're back, with Dad, from Korea. It is 1964. I am still 12, Ev is 11 and Pat is 9. We are with Mom in an L-shaped efficiency apartment on East 78th Street. Dad is in some Manhattan hotel. I have not seen him. But I am waiting. I am sweeping up the dirt on the floor from the planter from Thailand that I broke the night before when I was walking in my sleep. I wonder if I was looking for Dad. Mom and Ev say I went to Mom's bed and told her I had to fix her hairdo. Am sorry for breaking it. Was an accident. Will glue it back together. Also am sorry for blaming it on Ev this morning and having said so, she has forgiven me. I can't remember it. All I can think of is seeing Dad. I want to beg him to take me with him and Ev and Pat this time. Then Mom can be alone with Michael. I am anxious because I know Dad will be gone for a long time again. It's clear that that's part of his job. To be gone for years. Overseas.

I am attending St. Monica's again. I can't wait to get home each day to see Ev and Pat and maybe Dad. I have big energy. I clean everything, as usual without being asked. I make sure everything I own is clean and ironed, in case I have to pack quickly to go with them. Go anywhere with them.

But I come back from school and Ev and Pat are gone with Dad. He has been gone for a third of my life. I had plans to make a big scene in front of him before he left town because I am desperate now to go and live with him. I would go with him anywhere, even to Korea. But now there is only Mom to deliver my message to him. She's lying on the couch. I summon up a lot of energy to make this announcement:

I want to go with Dad.

You cannot, Mom says in her rare stage whisper. I become alert.

Why? I ask.

Because he might do Something Bad to you. Because he is not your father.

Dad's not my father?

Non.

Suddenly I have no right to insist that he take me with him. Suddenly, it seems I have no right to him at all. But I still love him, and the idea that Dad would ever do Something Bad to me is not believable; I dismiss that.

So who is my father? I ask.

She says he's a British secret agent named John Orr and that his cover name is John Van David. She says his cover was being a cabaret singer in Saigon when I was born. She gives me the photograph of him. He is thin and I am not thin and he is blonde and I am a brunette, though I was blonde as a young child. I ask her why the photograph is torn. She says it doesn't matter. I notice there is a woman's hand on his shoulder, but the woman is torn out of the photo. Though there is something unsettling about this particular missing information, I believe her.

I feel as if I have been hollowed out.

And then, one more thing. A little gasp. She says:

I am *preg-nyant.*

Excuse me?

I am going to have a baby. Michael's baby.

I say: You can't be pregnant. You're not married.

She crimps her face, cringes like a bad little girl.

No. I am not going to rush at her and give her a big hug like in some Veddy-Veddy movie and say oh dahling how sim-play mah-velous and what are you going name it?

Because the room seems more still than it is, as if it is a three-dimensional photograph, airless, a crypt for dreams.

Within a few minutes I have lost a father, gained a stepfather, gained a father but I don't know where he is or if he is alive, and gained a sibling-to-be but I don't know where he or she is inside my mother and I do not know when the sibling-to-be is going to arrive. This means the fear that I may never see Dad, Jim Flood, again may not be unfounded, which is not all right. This means I have a father somewhere and I have no idea how to find him. This means we may be connected to Michael Lambton for the rest of time. This means the five of us – Ev, Pat, Mom, Dad and I – will never be together again like before. This means Mom and I will never again have that intimacy of the two of us again, like in Chinatown or the Hamptons. This means she has managed somehow to entertain the entrance into our world of another child when it is clear – how much more clear can it be? – that she doesn't have the time or the ability to give attention to the ones she has. At least Ev and Pat have Dad. What will happen to me?

Michael doesn't call anymore. Ev and Pat are gone. Mom is glum. Maybe we should go to Puerto Rico, she says, where they can do an operation. What for? To make the baby go away, she says; it's illegal, but they do it there.

I do not know how someone can make the baby go away when it's not even here yet. With voodoo maybe. How should I know? I don't know where babies come from, only I'm not buying the stork thing plus: I kind of don't want to know; I sense a lot of complications surrounding the subject. The immediate problem is, from what I know on TV, things go wrong in operations sometimes. Sometimes people don't wake up after an operation.

I am scared. Mom buys us airplane tickets. We go to the San Juan Hilton where at night green lights play up from the base of palm trees. It looks like a fairy tale there. Lush and warm and relaxed.

I ask her: if it's illegal to have the operation, how are you going to find out where to have it without getting into trouble for asking where to do something illegal?

From a taxi driver.

Now I don't want her out of my sight for a minute.

We take taxis. You can tell the drivers' English is limited. They know where Old San Juan is. They know where *El Yunque*, the rain forest, is. They know where to get mangos. But I figure out Mom doesn't know how to say illegal operation in Spanish. And so I'm glad when she doesn't try to ask. The subject seems to be drifting away. I am more glad, because I know if she is determined, she will have her way. But she doesn't seem so determined. *Tant mieux* (so much the better).

I relax at the airport on the way back to New York.: she's been with me every minute, sauntering, window-shopping and I know she's not going to die in an operation; relief.

Dad, who is stationed in Washington, D.C., is getting us passports in three days. He can do that because he works for the government. Mom says this usually takes longer, a month or more, for people who don't work for the government. At least Dad and Mom are still connected enough for him to do something nice for her. The passports do arrive in three days.

We take Aer Lingus to Dublin. We get to a tiny hotel and sleep and sleep and have eggs and wonderful thick bacon and then take a taxi to see a school for me. It's called St. Mary's Dominican Convent in Cabra.

A thick, high stone wall flanks the entrance to the driveway on Ratoath Road. Cows graze in the pastures in the surrounding countryside. It is the most green land I have ever seen, deep, rich, full of life. The air is cool, moist and clearer than New York. Inside the stone walls a gravel driveway, framing gardens, sweeps up in front of the convent, a three-story red brick Georgian house. Wings connect to other buildings. The skyline is decked with crosses, one on each pitched roof and cupola, and on each spire of the connected church. This is a holy-looking place.

I want to think about this but there's no time. We go to a store called Gorevan's. Mom buys me a steamer trunk and makes someone put it on a dolly with a rope. I push or pull it around and fill it as we go from shoes to uniform skirts, sweaters and blouses to hockey shorts to thick wool blankets called rugs. One problem here is that for underpants my mother buys me bulky cotton rugby shorts, thick as sweatpants, that with my uniform skirt on adds 20 pounds to my figure; this is so that if a rapist or imaginary lover lifts my skirt, he truly dies of laughter before thinking of doing Something Bad.

Someone puts the trunk in a big black taxi that looks like cars in old American gangster movies. Back at the school Mom kisses me goodbye. The reality that she's leaving me in a strange place again sets in and I start crying. She says she'll see me soon. Then she's gone in the taxi. But Sister Mary Muiredach is there, the nun in charge of me and other boarders, and she is calm.

More: She's peaceful. You can feel it from a few feet away. You can see it in her blue eyes. Her skin is pale and clear. She is beautiful, always clean in her habit, a white gown, black veil. Her hands, with filed fingernails, are resting at her sides. She never fidgets with the long rosary hanging from her belt. She doesn't fidget. She does not cross her arms. She is never cross.

She needs only to come into a room, tall that she is, and we fall silent, our eyes on her. If we are not at desks or in pews, we flock about her. There are seventeen of us in second form, called eighth grade in America, but somehow she makes you feel like you matter so much that you feel she is in charge of only you. What can we do to please her, this poised and graceful being? She, our Mistress of Conduct.

We strive to get the round green or red metal pin of the week, meaning we excel in our academics. We are silent during the daily study hall for two hours. All of us work at one of more than a hundred desks there, before the carved oak shrine of Our Lady of the Study Hall, on our assignments after field hockey or before swimming. It is so quiet that if you dare to tear a page out of a bound composition book, many heads will turn and gazes fall upon you. Now there is nothing in our lives but religious knowledge, Gaelic,

English, geography, history, arithmetic, algebra, geometry, science, Latin, French and aural culture (elocution). I do not get into trouble with any prefects, older students assigned to supervise us when a nun is not around. Or I don't get caught. There are temptations and for me the worst is within the fountain pens we use. The urge, once in a while, to get someone's attention by flicking, or squirting the lovely blue liquid across an aisle is uncontrollable. How far? Over how many heads or shoulders do you think one can flick or squirt ink? And since our uniforms are mostly blue, how much harm is there in it?

We rise in the dark and pour water from pitchers into the basin by our beds and bathe in our curtained cubicles with soap and a washcloth. It is so dark that one morning I cover my legs with toothpaste instead of the cream for my little allergic bumps. It hardens and I need to explain why I am late for class. My prefect, Margaret, in the next cubicle, manages somehow to part her hair exactly straight and to produce two perfect braids each day; I hope in a few years I will have learned how to do it by feeling with my fingers. We are each given a half hour time slot to take a bath once a week. When I mention that I am used to taking a bath every day, one of the girls who hears about it says, Americans are sooooo hygienic, and the others say ach, it's true. But no one gets nasty about it. Because I want to be like the others, I sometimes skip the bath; we clean ourselves very well with our washcloths at our basins. None of the girls or nuns is unkind. Our lifestyle is too parsimonious, it seems, to be bothered with frivolous matters. At meals the staples are soda bread and tea, hot porridge in the morning. Mom pays extra for me to have some kind of fruit twice a week and two hard-boiled eggs a week, but I am unable to eat these in front of the other seven students at our table; some of them do not get eggs or fruit, and so we take turns eating mine when I say I don't want them. I also realize that some of the deaf girls working in the kitchen are not much older than we are; I feel sorry for them and so after dinner, I slip in and help, until I am told through much persistent nonverbal communication that I don't belong there. On special holidays we get a steamed fruit cake with heavenly hot custard to pour on it. Most all the girls stay at St. Mary's on the weekends so no one feels left out if she doesn't go home. On Saturdays it's fun Irish dancing for two hours and after hockey, we talk and read and write letters to the tantalizing smell of baking soda bread which so permeates the compound I would bet you could smell it in the precious chapel. No one reads students' letters to parents, but those to anyone else are examined, I heard, for spelling errors. The telephone is I don't know where but it doesn't matter since it's too expensive to call Mom in England and an operator has to place the call and call you back when the connection is made. But actually, I'm so happy I don't feel the need to phone her.

I do not miss TV. I doubt there is one anywhere in the convent but being a curious sort, I look around for it; better entertainment is the contents of what I consider to be a secret room up the stairs off the back of St. Patrick's Concert Hall. We are not encouraged to hang around there. This room, St. Dominic's Hall, is much a museum. Antonio Ciseri's life-sized nineteenth century painting of *Christ Borne to the Tomb* dominates it. It's a shock because, to someone five feet tall, it is so big, seems so real and full of grief. Jesus is dead and his Mother and Mary Magdalene and the others in it are beyond being upset. It's such a sad gruesome sight, it makes me wonder why anyone would want to treasure it; but then, I have encountered plenty of art works that are a wonder why anyone would want to hold them dear.

But also, it is full of reverence, this Ciseri. It and another painting at St. Mary's that has been treasured by these Dublin Dominicans – a very large Van Eyck crucifixion – and the chapel itself – a large mosaic and marble jewelry box – whisper a sure message: I am living amidst very much evidence of belief in God the Father, the Son and the Holy Ghost. I can see that if I get confused sometime, or my mind wanders toward loneliness, agnosticism or atheism, it would be impossible not to think again. Since I am faced with this artwork as frequently as a toothbrush, I feel connected to these dead artists and craftsmen, the Dominicans who started this convent in 1819, and their antecedents, persecuted hundreds of years ago. I live with prevailing spirits at St. Mary's and the drama of its history as I travel the halls of its seemingly winding interior ways that always do end up in some recognizable place. But the mind passages there are endless.

I share this hatchery for fancies with my best friend, Elizabeth Mullan, tall and dark haired, from County Sligo. Since I am short and chubby, I guess we look like Mutt and Jeff, cartoon characters. I dub her Silly Dilly and she doesn't mind, and calls me Silly Dilly, too. Like many other students, she is twinkle-eyed and generally in a good mood and I teach her how to jitterbug during Irish dancing sometimes. And I have another special friend, though I don't see much of her and when I do, she is discreet. Ah, that would be Mary Maguire. She is gray haired, kind of balding and somewhat in demeanor what I imagine a live female leprechaun might be like.

She comes into my life on the day that I am unpacking my trunk in the dormitory. My space is smaller than at St. Joe's, with each cubicle divided at night by pulled curtains. She watches me from a few beds away, hanging back behind a corner of gathered ones. I wonder who she is, this plump short non-nun, about sixty years old. She sees I see her. She comes forth and makes signs with her hands, pointing to herself and the bed. She starts making my bed. I work on my side, tucking hospital corners. She helps me unpack the trunk, shows me where to put things – without words. She is deaf, with dancing eyes.

She might have come to Cabra when she was younger, to the adjacent school for the deaf, and stayed on to work. But this is the kind of thing one does not ask, I told you, in boarding school. Why someone is here instead of at home. What a beautiful intelligent woman like Sister Muiredach is doing giving her life to God and the deaf and boarding school girls when she probably could have married a fine man and had children of her own. Everyone has their story, but in a convent, it's respected, private. Sometimes there is no story, for in Europe, it's normal for people who can afford it to send their children away to school. Some consider it a status symbol. In 1964 Ireland, it's not unusual for those who can afford it because there is no free secondary school. What matters in boarding school is making the most of the time you have together, and giving. She, Mary Maguire, teaches me this in her silent way.

I watch the other girls stand in line in the evenings to fill their hot water bottles at the sink set in the wall near my cubicle. But I don't have to, many nights, because Mary Maguire has already filled mine and put it down between my sheets when it is about freezing in the dormitory. There is not much heat in the school. And there is nothing like it to have someone do that for you at the end of a day so cold, you're wanting to be wearing gloves to class. But you wouldn't want to make yourself stand out, indicating that you're dissatisfied with anything. So you just giggle, when you try to see your breath inside a classroom, because 'tis nuthin, you know, the chill. You pull the sleeves of your sweater down over your knuckles and go back to work. What's something is a birthday cake with your name on it when you are 13 and candles and the singing of Happy Birthday and lovely holy cards from your friends; you tuck them into your leather missal between the fine thin gilt-edged pages with the Latin part of the Mass on one side and the English on the other. It is a huge flower in your life to wake up on St. Patrick's Day and find your wash basin full of shamrocks, complete with roots and soil, a rich moist soil that is not dirty at all.

I think I am the only girl Mary Maguire does this for. Maybe it is because I am from America and my mother is in another country. But after a while one learns there are no degrees of aloneness. It's a good thing to learn to handle, makes you strong, ready. For in the end, except for God, we are all alone. Kindness is the only antidote when being alone is lonely, along with prayer and the Mass which is always there, somewhere, no matter what country you're in.

I sleep deeply after a full day of classes, then raucous, glorious field hockey, then study hall, except when I have night business. There are nights when I manage to give Margaret, my prefect in the next cubicle, the slip. I go down a certain corridor that seems like an underground tunnel, though it's on the ground floor, because it has no windows. I arrive at the chapel.

It has two naves. One larger one for us students, and another smaller one off the apse, called the Nun's Choir – the pews there face each other instead of the altar. I creep into a front pew of our empty darker nave and see through the sanctuary the altar in candlelight, and the nuns praying in Latin behind the huge rococo wrought iron fence between their choir and the apse.

They sing in Latin as they move in procession, led by two Sisters carrying lit candles, through the wrought iron gate fronting their space, through the sanctuary and into our nave. All are sprinkled with holy water by one nun. Sometimes I venture to kneel before the shrine of the Blessed Virgin to pray and show them all how holy I am, so they will like me more than they might. I wait during the day for Sister Muiredach or someone else to say, You're not supposed to be there in the chapel at night, What were you doing there in the chapel at night?, but no one does. And no one catches me in the infirmary at night when I go there sometimes to wet my hair and stick my head out the window so I can get sick and get a break from studies. But I never even catch a cold at St. Mary's. We are a hardy bunch, we are, and we see that we can be happy with the barest necessities; that makes you fearless of being without. But we do get something that never have I been allowed to have on a regular basis.

It's candy. Joyous, sticky, chewy, teeth-rotting candy, called sweets. We get sixpence, which goes a long way, to buy it in a once-a-week dispensary.

Ach, sweets are the stuff of dreams, they are. They become an obsession at St. Mary's, where a cow, from the convent farm, getting stuck while trying to jump over the three-foot stone wall bordering our hockey field competes in newsworthiness with a High Holy Day. I never do get into trouble at St. Mary's. Probably some guardian angel hovering, the power of prayers. Perspective, probably. For this business of obtaining, hiding and sharing sweets is as devious as any of us bother to get. Otherwise, why should we be? We want naught.

At Christmas we get more than three weeks off. I am put on a plane to London where Mom picks me up. My eyelids flip up when I see her because her mantra has always been: Never get fat. *Grossi.* Fat, fat, fat. *Tien*, gargle, gargle, *tien*. Roll of the eyes. No fat. Stop eating. Drink water instead.

Well, she is fat, but not in the face, or arms, or legs, but in the belly. She is huge. She tells me The Baby is kicking and do I want to feel it?

No. I do not. I want to try and figure this out first. How The Baby got inside of her. But the more I think about it, the more I do not want to know.

I don't know how to feel about this until I get a cue from a man selling flowers on the street. Mom is wearing a heavy green suede trench coat that's obviously designed for someone in this physical state, soft brown leather boots and her hair is up in a French twist. The flower seller puts out a long stemmed red rose in front of her as she is about to pass him and says, Madam, you're the most beautiful woman I've ever seen.

I told you. Not even when she is eight months pregnant can you escape going anywhere without men noticing her. Not in New York. Not in London. It's not normal.

She's acting unusually nice to me. She takes me to Harrods and buys me wool things – a beautiful white wool suit, some turtleneck sweaters, a pale blue coat with a drop-waisted belt that's slenderizing and a big red coat. She shows me the big Food Hall at Harrods where she buys me fresh *marrons glace*, whole peeled chestnuts dipped in vanilla icing that I've never had before – so delicious. It's almost like it was before Michael, when we were close and went to Chinatown in New York. Then I learn I am going to Paris the next day. Christmas is three days away. We have been apart for almost three months and we get two nights and one day together and no Christmas.

She says she doesn't know whether or not she is going to spend Christmas with Michael even though we are staying in Michael's flat in Knightsbridge while he is staying with his dear mother in Ipswich. He says he is not the father of The Baby. She says she is suing him for breach of promise. I don't know how she is managing to stay in his two-story Knightsbridge flat while suing him.

His sister, Lorna Lambton, comes by. She dresses *de rigeur*, Mom says, especially in her taste of colors. She wears purple a lot, very dramatic, especially with green. She is an aloof woman, about five foot seven, with thick honey-colored shoulder-length hair. She glances at me, but doesn't say hello. I guess ignoring children is a family trait. Mom laughs a lot when she is there. It's not an embarrassed or nervous laugh. It is her *Who Cares What Zay Sink* laugh. She really is above them all.

I think she is very brave.

Mom takes me to the airport, I fly to Paris alone and the stewardesses act like that's something, since I'm 13. I meet relatives I never knew I had: *Tatie* Jackie, Uncle Alban's wife, picks me up at the bottom of the stairs off the plane at *Le Bourget*. I love her forever because she acts like I am precious and makes me steak and *pommes frites* (French Fries) for dinner and gives me rose preserves on my toast at *petite dejuener* (breakfast). My little cousin, Isabelle, 7, is sweet. We drink our *cafe au lait* from bowls and dip our croissants in them. I am given a gold watch and a gold filigree cross for Christmas. Isabelle, *Tatie* and *Tonton* Alban act like they are really happy that I'm there. I love being with them, but I can see they are a unit, and that the possibility of my living with them is not something they are considering.

They take me to Notre Dame for Midnight Mass where the coughs from the bronchitis I have suddenly acquired echo over the packed worshipers. I am taken to the city of Nancy where I meet three other cousins. One is six, the others in their teens. Uncle Christian is married to *Tatie* Nicole, Mom's older sister, a reserved lady, tall like Mom. She is not happy that I have brought bronchitis into her immaculate home, where hearing cowboys on the American TV show, *Bonanza*, speak French feels bizarre, where my cousin tells me that everything French is of the best quality and whose teenage friends laugh as they call me an *Amerloque*, a pejorative term for an American. I am generally silent throughout this visit since I have no idea what anyone is saying. No one speaks even a little English and my French is generally limited to counting to one hundred, the alphabet and the conjugation of *etre* (to be), in the present tense

I fly from Paris to London. I try to find a public phone to look in the phone book for John Orr, then John Van David. I wonder what I will say to him when I find his phone number. Maybe I will just listen to his voice first and then hang up until I decide what to say. But it doesn't matter, because I can't find a public phone with a book. Then I call Mom before catching my plane to Dublin. She is delighted to hear I have a French accent, which I got an ear for from her in the first place and which I have been using with fervor when I say anything in English in France, in hopes that if I speak English with a French accent, someone might understand what I am saying.

At St. Mary's the snow melts and we dance in a *ceili* on St. Patrick's Day. All of us, about a hundred and twenty or so, get to jig and reel for hours, until we are about ready to drop to the booming floor and then we dance some more. The weather is warmer and we are playing much field hockey now. It is thrilling to be a right half, and once in a while a center forward, saying bully one, bully two, bully three before trying to hook the ball away from the opposing center forward. I am fast. I am going to save the day; every game, I try. So I am not so great at it. I hear one of the older girls tell the others that she would rather have me on her team than a better player because of my spirit. Spirit? I am happier than any time in my life.

Then Sister Muiredach says I must fly to London:

Your dear mother is asking to see you.

I cannot help but study her blue eyes a moment to see if she's joking about how dear Mom is. Of course I haven't told her about Michael, Christine Keeler, The Baby (who prefers to remain anonymous in this book), Dad and my Secret Agent Father, so how would she know how wary I feel? She means it – your dear mother – and I say, of course. Then I say, I'll be right back, soon as I can, to finish my lessons and get better at field hockey. I am first in the class now in religious knowledge, arithmetic/algebra, geometry, Latin and French, and second in English studies, composition and geography.

Mom picks me up at the airport. She's slender again and holding the bundle. She places The Baby in my arms, shows me how to support the head. Tiny creature, not three months old. Sweet smelling. Born at St. George's Hospital, near Hyde Park corner. The Baby sleeps most of the time. A black gangster-type car takes us to Southampton and we board the *SS United States*. We have a big stateroom, several portholes. Mom says apologetically that it's not first class but the next class down from that. She puts The Baby on her bunk and shows me how to change the diaper.

The ship's horns blast, long and mournful. The passengers wave to loved ones on the dock. Mom says this reminds her of when we left Asia and took a steamship across the Pacific. She says it was customary to throw long streamers off the decks. Did the streamers tear when someone on the dock was holding one end and someone on deck was holding the other as the ship pulled away? The finality of what is happening does not affect me until we are on the open seas and I understand that we are probably passing Ireland, even though I do not see her. Then dismay takes over. I think:

Wait. Stop. I have to get off.

What about my studies? What about my trunk? My hockey stick? Sister Muiredach. Elizabeth Mullan. Mary Maguire. My other friends. I was doing honors work. No one could beat me memorizing theorems. I got the red pin. I was winning.

Doesn't matter, Mom says.

But I want to go back. When am I going back?

She says: I *dun't* know, sometime, maybe.

I know her. When she does this. She thinks if she's evasive I'll forget about whatever it is I am asking for. But this time I will not.

I have to go back. Mom, I say, I have to go back.

I have been unsure of many things in my life but I know this: if I go back to St. Mary's, I will be happy. I was happy. I could finish my education there, be out of her way. Then go to university. It's sure. Everything else is not sure.

She says: who will help me *wees zee* baby?

Hope is sinking, like I surely would if I jumped off the boat and tried to swim back to Ireland. She is looking at me with her big brown eyes, her face still. I look away at the carpet, the portholes, the moving sea. I want to throw up.

I am all alone, she says. Who will help me?

I still don't want to look at her, she, who is asking me to give up the happiest time in my life except for when we lived with Dad, Ev and Pat. But I have to, I know, help her, and so I say it – I will, Mom.

I start getting used to the idea of our family of three.

It is time for dinner for our class on the ship. The Baby is sleeping on the bunk. I put my hands around The Baby. *Non*, Mom says, the Baby will be fine like that, sleeping. Let's go.

But it doesn't feel right. I look at The Baby in the middle of the bunk. Tiny, swaddled, can't turn over. I say we should take the Baby. *Non*, we are going to go and relax, Mom says, in her don't-argue voice. But fear taps on my shoulder. Fear of what? I don't know. I know nothing about babies. But this feels wrong.

The reaching-out feeling stays with me through dinner and afterwards when we get back and the Baby is O.K. The reaching-out feeling is akin to ones that come with memories, of the times Ev and Pat and I are playing in the locked fenced-in back yard in Silver Spring, locked out of the house while Mom and Dad are taking a nap. Of the so many times Mom and Dad go out and leave us alone, Pat, being the youngest, locked in her room, and of Evalyn and I picking the lock with a hair pin to get her out one Christmas Eve because Pat said she had to go to the bathroom. Of the how many times Mom leaves me alone in Washington, Baltimore, New York, St. Louis, Cincinnati, Cleveland, Buffalo, Louisville, Toledo or Toronto saying, Don't open the door to anyone, even if they say they are the police, don't open the door. But this feels different. I don't know what could go wrong leaving a baby alone. But if something does, The Baby is helpless. The reaching-out feeling for The Baby never goes away. It is there in the morning and at night. Often, I wish I could shrug it off and be free, but I can't.

And now in the spring of 1965 on the *SS United States* watching the waters churn off the stern I see that feeling meld with another – that all seems unfinished. I have not been able to say goodbye to Muiredach or Elizabeth Mullan or Mary Maguire. I have not been able to tell them I loved them all and St. Mary's and Ireland. I wanted to say I wished that I was part Irish, so did they make me feel I belonged with them. Though I know I am part French, I do not know enough of what that means for it to touch me in a substantial way. I know I am supposed to be part English, but this does not feel genuine either, because until I find this John Orr/Van David secret agent father, he is not real, and so a part of me, who I am, feels not real.

Chapter Ten

Regardless of whether or not you have a father or a part-time mother around, is there any time when you feel less complete than when you are a teenager? You're not an adult. You're not a child. You're constantly reminded that you are neither one nor the other by signals like pimples or training brassieres. And then, for some reason, hormones probably – though we heard almost nothing of them in those days – everything seems magnified: the funny is hilarious, the sad is tragic, the embarrassing seems mortifying. And so, at almost 14, I found myself back in New York frequenting the statue of *Alice in Wonderland* in Central Park again, she having been oversized or undersized in Lewis Carroll's book and living with that in-transition feeling. I took comfort there knowing her creator was aware of how disproportionate matters can seem, or be, even without teenage angst.

The restful rolling of the *SS United States* is behind us. I have unpacked everything from storage and organized it in the new Manhattan apartment, in an old townhouse on East 64th Street off Park Avenue, an address that pleases Mom. She has bought for The Baby a huge navy and white enameled English pram. Every day after St. Monica's I have to take The Baby for a stroll in Central Park, two blocks away. Then I have to bathe, dress, feed, burp and change The Baby, who has cloth diapers that I have to hold by the corner and dip into the toilet until they're rinsed. I have to wash them every day or they smell too much. I do not have to iron them, for there's enough other stuff to iron, including sheets and pillowcases. I buy an array of baby food – the kid likes apricot – and carry everything up to our place on the third floor, then carry the garbage down again. A walk-up makes you plan ahead or you'll be exhausted by the stairs.

I don't think Mom was thinking ahead during her involvement with Michael. Or maybe she was. Sometimes I wonder if she thought she might have a better chance of keeping him by having his child, this child that he says is not his, which is ridiculous. You should see my mother now.

She's withered. If Michael had died, Mom might be less devastated than she is. If he had died, there would have been some finality to the situation, and eventually some recuperation from the grief. There are widows who survive and sometimes thrive after a husband's death. But no simple ending like that for Mom's affair. I know and she knows. He's there, in England, and she's here, wondering what he is doing, who he is going out with, being carefree, and years younger than she, his life ahead of him. I think she loved him, or loves him as much if not more than any wife would have. Her London lawyers and his London lawyers came to a settlement. But that is just about money. It's nothing, compared to what he has done to her, or to what she has done to herself by being with him. She pines, hardly speaks. I get the feeling it would be healthier if she cried, but she doesn't have the energy. She sleeps a great deal of the time or sits and stares. She could not take care of The Baby if she were alone. The Baby would starve.

Sometimes Mom gets angry. I am relieved because this indicates some of her spirit is returning. She says she is finished with men. She says she will never fall in love again. Men can never be trusted. To punctuate this she changed her name legally in England. She is now Madame Suzanne Clara Lambton. But I know the truth and she knows the truth. I say: But you're not married. Doesn't matter, she says; *Zee* baby is named Lambton and I am *zee muz-zer* and I am Lambton.

I told you. In perpetuity, it seems, he is always around.

I think: I will work so hard that she will see. We do not need him in our lives. We will be fine without him. I know I have to take care of her when she is old. My plan is to go to high school at St. Vincent Ferrer at 65th and

Lexington, two blocks away, and then go to Columbia University somehow and become a powerful lawyer. She says the best lawyers come out of Columbia and they run the world.

I don't want to run the world. I know you need really good grades to go to Columbia. But there is no time for homework when The Baby cries or needs to be fed, changed, strolled, bathed, dressed, changed again, fed again and cuddled. The Baby likes to be held and hear things like cutchie-coo, kaboom, whee. Between kaboom, whee and running the bath for Mom, or making rice or chicken or salad or shopping for food or washing dishes, clothes, linens and diapers, or ironing, doing Mom's hair, scrubbing the bathroom and kitchen, dusting and vacuuming the apartment, taking the garbage out and going to school and mass, my mind goes into suspension, which is not an unusual place for it.

I study the shape of a baby bottle, consider it, as if it were a Grecian urn, its shape, wondering who invented it, when and where, what they did to feed babies before it was invented, how they will feed babies in the future.

Someday, I think, I shall read fairy tales to The Baby. It will be more interesting than *Patty Cake*. My favorite fairy tale when I was little was *Cinderella*, but it's not any more. Life is too complicated to expect Prince Charming to fix everything. Anyway, I'm too young, not ready for boys, men. Look what happened to Mom.

I wish she would put her arms around my shoulders and pull my head to hers and let me rest there, like a little girl. But it won't happen. She is so angry she seems to want to stay that way, as if it gives her strength. This makes starting any kind of conversation with her fearful. But I must because at school, playing basketball is required but embarrassing. I need a bra.

I consider that Mom, too, at one time first needed a bra and so I hope that she might welcome me to this entrance to womanhood. But when I ask for one, she laughs. I don't know if she is laughing at me or laughing at life but it's unforgettable, this bitter laugh. I want to shrivel. A few months later, when I get my period, she gets mad, says she can't let me out of her sight for a minute. I hide in the bathroom when I change, not wanting to remind her of my development. I try to lose weight, so I will be flatter, like some thin girls. But it does no good. She acts as if I've done something wrong.

For a while I hate bras, because they make me look more curvy. I am pushing The Baby in Central Park near the *Alice* statue one day and a busybody lady comes over to look in the pram. She says, Oh, how adorable, and then she looks at me, in my St. Vincent's uniform and says, Is it yours? I blush, angry. A girl at St. Vincent's told me how babies are made. I don't want to go near the subject. I say, No, it's my mother's baby. This lady knows I might look old enough to have a baby but not old enough to be married. I want to spit at her but, I'm too polite and it's not worth it.

I understand now why Mom won't go to the park or anywhere with us. She didn't want people to figure out how old she was with a daughter when I was ten. Now that I have to wear a bra, I look older than I am and of The Baby, she says: People will *sink I am zee grandmuzzer*. She likes it best if she is seen without children at all. It's not part of her image. You don't see models on the cover of *Vogue* or *Harper's Bazaar* surrounded by kids, you know.

We move to a larger apartment on Second Avenue and East 87th Street. It's a tall new building. I am the one who goes in and out the most because I go to school, shop and push The Baby around. So I chat sometimes with Jimmy the Doorman, who tells me there's an old lady in the apartment next to us who is filing the wall between her apartment and ours with a nail file, so if I hear that sound, of filing plaster, that's what it is. This is marvelous, I think, so New York, possibly crazier than parts of my life. Mom supervises my construction of a room divider in the living room, creating a second bedroom: hers. I sleep in the real bedroom with its closeable door so I can get up and take care of The Baby in the middle of the night without waking up Mom.

She goes out more now. She has a friend, Igor, a Russian painter she used to know in Washington. He comes over to pick her up when they're going to a party, but they're not in love. She buys paintings from him including an almost life-size one of a pretty, seated blonde woman wearing a tight, low-cut pink silk dress that Mom keeps over her bed. The woman in the painting is elegant, relaxed as if she is above everyone, like Mom. Mom gets energized from Igor. She starts painting again. She paints a pretty good portrait of Michael.

At school it's dramatic, there's going to be a dance. This is the chance to see live boys who are invited from nearby schools, Regis or Loyola. *Ah non*! Mom says, no boys. I beg, implore. She relents. I go to two dances. After the second, she shouts from her bedroom: I am not paying for any *abor-shons*. She says a boy could touch me somewhere and I could become *preg-nyant*. Just like that. She makes such a scene, I give up.

The rattle, the teddy bear, and the mobile of dangling animals above The Baby in the crib. What can I do to relax, have a break from school, housework? The TV died. There's *The New York Times* columnist, Russell Baker, who makes me laugh. But once the experience of seeing through his eyes is over, there are twenty-three and three quarters hours left that day. The rest of the time the radio in Mom's stereo provides some entertainment. When she goes out, the apartment detonates. Oh!

I'm *Crying in the Chapel, Like a Rolling Stone*, with *Mr. Tambourine Man*, because (*I Can't Get No*) *Satisfaction*. The Baby likes *The Sounds of Silence* and gets very excited when *I Got You Babe* comes on, and we dance. Just as The Baby is encouraged to be happy when we do *Patty Cake*, I am given permission by the blessed music explosion of 1965, 1966, to feel, to be transported into other people's joy, sadness, silliness, inanity, rebellion and peace, to be connected finally to the rest of the rocking, rolling, reeling and slow-dancing world.

The most trying time I have being left alone with The Baby involves a fever. The Baby is about a year old. I come home from school. Mom goes out, saying The Baby is sick. I take The Baby's temperature every couple of hours. I get nervous because it always seems to get higher at night. Now it is a hundred and three. I don't know where Mom is; she never leaves a phone number. I'm afraid to go to sleep even though it's midnight. I give The Baby the baby aspirin on time, crushed in apricot baby food. But then I go to the bathroom and when I come back The Baby is shaking. I have never seen someone have convulsions before, but I know this must be them. I am afraid to touch The Baby while jerking like that. I'm terrified that The Baby will die. What to do? The Baby stops jerking and starts screaming. I call Lenox Hill hospital. I tell the nurse I don't have the money for a taxi, I don't know where Mom is; what shall I do? Should she send an ambulance? She asks how high the fever is and I say a hundred and three. She says hurry and get some trays of ice and break them into some cold water in the bath tub and soak a towel in it and wrap The Baby in the ice-cold towel and another dry towel on top of that. She says do this while she is on the phone and I do. The Baby screams more when I put the ice-cold towel around her. I hold The Baby in my arms and keep saying, it's okay, it's okay, but I'm thinking: Jesus Christ Almighty, will you do something? Then I figure if The Baby is crying The Baby is not dead, so it's good. I carry The Baby back to the phone. The lady says be patient. After a little while The Baby starts to quiet down. The lady says to take The Baby's temperature again. I do and it's down to a hundred and two. The lady says go get another cold wet towel and do it again but it doesn't have to be icy cold, just cool. The Baby hates this, screams again, then after a while settles down. I go back to the lady on the phone again. She says take the temperature again. I do. It's down to a hundred and one and a half. She takes my number and gives me her name and a direct number and says to stay awake with The Baby until Mom comes home. I do. Around 2 a.m. Mom arrives. I tell her what happened. The Baby seems fine now. Mom looks at me as if to say: What are you talking about?

In the morning she takes The Baby to a doctor. I don't go to school because I feel almost dead. When Mom comes back she wakes me up and says The Baby was dehydrated and the convulsions were my fault. I tell her I fed The Baby and gave her her bottle and the aspirin and kept taking the temperature. But Mom is indignant and acts like I'm the enemy. I know I did everything the best I could. Maybe I saved The Baby's life but it doesn't matter now. The Baby is well. I love The Baby.

I am hovering near the bottom of my class at school. It's not that I can't do the work. After taking care of the baby, shopping, cooking, cleaning and doing our laundry in the basement, I want to go to sleep, though that's probably no excuse, because American pioneer stories are full of kids who walk miles to school in the snow, pitch hay, feed pigs, help with the young'uns and then study by candlelight. I do not do my homework a lot of nights. I am so behind in school, catching up seems impossible. Some days I don't go to school because The Baby has kept me up all night or because I have a test for which I didn't or couldn't study. Mom says nothing as long as I take care of The Baby. I'm tired. But I get a lot of energy one day when the announcement comes over the public address system that the school is having a contest. The girl who sells the most raffle tickets for the parish fund-raiser wins a transistor radio.

I have a chance to prove myself, maybe, if Mom lets me. It's for the church. I can tell she's trying to figure out what's wrong with the idea. She doesn't work anymore, just paints, so she could spare me for a couple of hours a day. I tell her I'll feed The Baby when I get back. The Baby just won't go to the park every day. It's for the church. Mom thinks, then allows it.

Oh, glory. For two hours a day for many days for about six weeks I am free beneath the Manhattan sky. In my gray and green school uniform, I seize a part of my time – for me.

I start on our old block at 64th Street at the chic Alrae, an apartment-hotel-type place with a lounge called the Henri IV. I ask for the manager and, amidst the upside-down chairs on the tables, I tell him we used to live two doors down, that I go to St. Vincent's, the school for his parish and I'm selling raffle tickets. He could win a television. The tickets are only a dollar each, a book of six for five dollars. He could help the church, the nuns, the school. We look eye to eye and lo, he takes out a clip thick with money and gives me a five-dollar bill. I say I'll fill his name out on the tickets if he wishes and he says not necessary. I say, Well, thank you so much, Sir. God bless you. I almost skip out the door.

Back in the daylight, I notice the Wildenstein Gallery down the street. I think: If they sell paintings for thousands of dollars, they can afford a raffle ticket. The Wildenstein people are my old neighbors. I point that out. The lady says to come back tomorrow, the right person is not here. There's a drug store with a soda fountain on the corner of 64th and Madison. I think the manager bought a ticket just to get rid of me. I ignore his attitude and keep moving up Madison Avenue which is mostly galleries and boutiques. I visit each gallery and each boutique, including Jaeger, where Mom buys her suits. I do feel guilty because I'm acting nice to strangers only so they will buy tickets, which feels hypocritical, but then what harm is there in being cheerful?

It is work. You have to memorize things you're going to say. You have to act pleasant so no one's afraid of you. You have to be ready to be rejected and be oh so nice anyway. I keep a notebook for places like Chase Manhattan Bank on Madison in the 70s because it's not open after school, so I go back on a High Holy Day when school is closed. I have a savings account there with $2.63 in it. That's a bona fide connection.

I work Madison all the way up to 86th Street, then down on the other side of the street to 59th, then back up to where I started. I skip Fifth and Park Avenues because I figure doormen are poor. I work Lexington and Third Avenues. In my own building I explain I live on the second floor. The bonus to selling tickets here is when I notice children, I can also offer myself as a babysitter, then I can buy real albums that I can play whenever I want.

As soon as the raffle is over, whenever Mom will let me, I begin to babysit for $1 an hour. Before I am able to save enough for a record, however, the winner of the contest is announced (draw in breath). Having sold some $350 worth of tickets, it's me.

The nun in charge of this is nice to me when I go to the office to get my transistor radio but remains reserved. I understand why. Because we know: not only are my grades not good, but in this my sophomore year, I have been late 25 times and absent 24 days. At St. Vincent's, this is tantamount to being a juvenile delinquent. But I feel better now. Because I know that even if my grades never go up again, I will survive somehow. And I have shown the nuns that I am worth something.

But more: I learned there are people who will take you seriously even if you are a teenager because you are persistent or because – it's in their eyes – they admire you because you work hard and mean business and that's New York.

The transistor radio does not impress Mom. But I can play it to and from school. What does get her attention however is that I start making money babysitting when she doesn't go out.

I save enough to buy my first album – *The Beatles* – which I play softly if she lets me. I decide to collect only The Beatles and Simon and Garfunkel, who are important because most their songs are gentle. They calm me down when I am nervous, tired. I am about to buy my second album but am set back one day when Mom says I can pay for my lunch now.

So I do. I need to work more, so I tell my babysitting clients. People refer me. I buy my lunch and my second and third albums. I'm doing okay. Then one night when I return from babysitting, Mom says she wants me to give her my babysitting money to pay for the food I eat at breakfast and dinner.

If she was broke and there was no food for The Baby, I would have given her everything. But she has just bought new clothes, a couple of new fur coats, which she collects, and two new paintings from Igor have just arrived. She says she commissioned them.

One is almost life-sized, of her sitting on the couch in a low-cut short white dress, her long dark hair pulled up in a big sweep of a ponytail. Her slender legs are positioned as if she is just about to get up. Between them, the crotch of her white panties is evident. I do not know what to think of this, but then, remember, she is an artiste. Questioning a Bohemian's life style can elicit ire: Who do you *sink* you are to question how I live life?

The other painting is of The Baby, now two years old, whose hair Mom has lightened with peroxide. The big painting of Mom is hanging over the couch that is in the painting. The other painting, she says, is being shipped to England, to Michael's mother, so she can see The Baby is indeed a Lambton.

By the way, she says, Igor wants to paint you nude.

I'm 14, I say, incredulous.

So?

No.

He says he pays his models very well.

No.

Now she's embarrassed. She says: I had to ask you. He *eeze* my friend. He ask me to ask you.

I give her a dirty look and go into the bedroom and take The Baby in my arms. She won't slap me with the baby in my arms. The Baby is my pal. I know this Baby loves me.

There is only baby food, cereal and milk in the apartment. No peanut butter, no bread, but there's jelly. I ask Mom what's for dinner. She says she's going out. I say there's nothing to cook; what shall I do? She says to eat cereal.

I am grateful for the babysitting clients who say, Help yourself to what's in the refrigerator. This is especially meaningful when I work for them for five hours or so. Though I am often able to buy lunch at school, babysitting is not regular work and sometimes lunch is a cup of coffee, like breakfast. I am sometimes unable to buy the albums I want for long periods of time.

They are my freedom, what connects me to other young people with whom I am not allowed to socialize. The albums give me choice in my mostly no-choice world. The songs I choose to listen to become a part of me, who I am, the mood I need. They let me be the editor of my feelings; with my albums I can go from sad to dreamy peaceful. They give me control over a little of my life.

One day Mom tells me to go to the apartment of one of my regulars. The mother leaves me standing amidst such a mess of toys, clothes and papers, it's difficult to chase her disobedient toddlers. She comes back, kisses the boys and looks at me as if to say: Why don't you go home now? I stand, embarrassed, but ask: Did you forget to pay me? She says: I already paid your mother.

After school Mom says I should go baby-sit for this lady again. I say: I'm not available. I go in the bedroom with The Baby, turn on soft rock and wonder what to do. The situation is not too bad because I have other clients she doesn't know. But when I get home from school the next day I go into the bedroom, dreaming of listening to the *Help* album, but I can't find it.

I can't find any of my albums. I go into Mom's little bedroom, which is brave. She is lying in bed, in blue jeans. Her feet are crossed. Her arm is over her head. She is twirling her hair with her fingers, relaxed. I ask her where my records are. She says, I *dun't* know. I'm scared. She's acting smug. My heart is beating fast. I look under her bed. No albums. I start opening all the drawers in her dresser. In the living room I pull the couch away from the wall. I look under its pillows. I look everywhere. No albums.

I consider that the albums might fit through the incinerator hampers. I look in the incinerator rooms on our floor and other floors. I run downstairs to the incinerator room in the basement. – locked. Maybe they are now some big glob of melted vinyl in the bottom of the incinerator.

I wonder what more Mom could do to hurt me but I can't think of anything, not even the humiliation I felt when she tried to see if I was still a virgin with a Tampax; I shut my eyes and told myself it wasn't happening; I couldn't fight, she would win; she's so much bigger than me. Now she is giving me the same message: You are nothing, no one; I have no respect for your body, your possessions or your mind. She is oblivious to the possibility that I have feelings, that I am someone.

I stand in the dining area near the apartment door. She's on the living room couch, feet up. I face her. I seethe: What did you do with my albums? She laughs. I keep my distance.

She took what I love most besides her and The Baby. I realize she must hate me to laugh while I am so upset about losing something that means so much to me – almost everything.

I see we have nothing now. I lunge at the dirt-filled planter from Thailand on the table by me and throw it on the floor a few feet in front of me in her direction. Her mouth drops open. I grab my coat from the closet behind me and flee. You think I'm going to wait for the elevator?

The stairs are still my friends, the stairwell my haven, ever since Washington in the building where children weren't allowed. It's a good place to hide temporarily because if you sit quietly you can hear someone coming; there is potential escape on every floor. But I'm too scared to be stationary. I might cry and I don't want anyone to hear me. I run up the steps, then realize she might hear me if she follows. I need a place to rest, think. On the fourth floor I go into the hallway and take the elevator to the penthouse. There I take the stairs to the roof. Out the door to the right is a small flight of stairs to another door. It's unlocked. Thank you, God. A room. Windows, a bare concrete floor, a cage structure with elevator stuff in it and a big cable. Behind the door a giant wooden spool holds more cable, something to sit on. I dare not turn on the light. It's cold, even with my red coat on, but by the window there's a heater. I can't believe it. A heater. I sit on the concrete in front it and consider everything. It feels like all the furniture in the world is being hurled at me. Feelings tumble like clothes in a dryer. I do love her more than anyone in the world. Don't people who are loved love people back automatically? Maybe not. I know I have been bad, throwing the planter on the floor. I cannot undo it. Am sorry. Scared. What to do? A rushing in my chest, my head. I explode.

I cry. Doesn't matter; no one can hear me.

It's dark when I wake up. Must be ten or eleven. I want to walk. Don't know where to go. Where can a girl go, walk at night alone in Manhattan? Central Park? Something Bad might happen. The library is likely closed. But I could find out if it's open. It would give me a place to go while I walk. Walking will make me feel better. I go to the penthouse, take the elevator to the lobby. The door slides open. Jimmy the Doorman is standing in front of the glass front doors. He hears my footsteps and turns. I get to the glass doors and face away from him. I fear he will see my eyelids are swollen, then I don't care.

He says: Your mother called the police.

Oh, God. I look back at the elevators. I say: Are they still here?

No, they left.

Don't tell, I say. Please don't tell anyone you saw me.

He looks at me, then faces the street.

I push the elevator button, then look over my shoulder at him. Please don't tell, I say. I didn't do anything that needed police. I step into the elevator. He looks over his shoulder at me again.

I know, he says, they told me.

On the roof I take the stairs two at a time to the elevator room. I take off my red coat and curl myself in it, then lay on the concrete in front of the heater. She doesn't care if they take me to jail or put me in reform school. The girls at St. Vincent's say kids in reform school do bad things to each other. Mom cares so little for me she would let them put me with hoodlums, juvenile delinquents. So she doesn't have to give me food I guess. In reform school, I wouldn't cost anything.

In the morning I'm disgusted and starving. I'm so tired I don't care what happens to me. I decide to go back. She can call the police. They can take me away. Let her watch them put handcuffs on me, like a criminal. I will give her a look she will never forget.

I ring the doorbell. She looks through the peep hole, opens it, lets go of it. I push it open. She has cleaned up the broken Thai planter. Interesting. I can't remember her cleaning anything. Oh, I see. She's showing me she doesn't need me. Like it's a privilege to do what I do for her and The Baby, what I have been doing for years. I feel grim. I look her in the eye. I say nothing.

I go in the kitchen and get some corn flakes. I eat with my coat on in case. In her crib in the bedroom, The Baby is open armed. We hug. My coat is dirty with concrete dust but I go to bed with it on. I sleep. When I get up Mom is standing in the dining area near the front door – our place for confrontations. I am afraid to go into the living room. She could corner me there.

Standing in her negligee, she points at the floor in front of her with her long polished index finger.

She says: do *sumi ma sen*.

Excuse me? My mind is flipping through memories, looking for an answer. Do I say I'm too old for *sumi ma sen*? Should I say this is America, not Vietnam or Japan? And then, it comes. It's not the answer to give her. It is the answer that will draw the map, tell me what to see, how to feel. I wonder: What would Russell Baker think?

I know he would appreciate this scene. This puts it in perspective. I snap out of the brief daydream and say:

No.

Ainh? she says. She blinks. Her eyes are wide.

No, I say, I will not do *sumi ma sen*.

I brace myself for a slap. I suppose I've become insane.

Why? she says.

Why? I cannot remember her asking me why about anything.

I say: Because you sent me to Catholic school all my life; *The Ten Commandments* say Thou Shalt Not Bear Witness to False Gods. If I get down on my knees and kowtow to you, that will be like worshipping you like a god. It's wrong. There is only one God.

She stares at me.

It flashes in my mind that *The Ten Commandments* also say, Honor Thy Father and Thy Mother; but the nuns say that means respect, not worship. I can see that I am not being so respectful by challenging her, but there's no time to figure this out.

She steps towards me and raises her pointed finger above her head and stabs the air in front of her feet.

Do, she says loudly, *sumi ma sen*.

No.

I put my arms up to protect my face but she gets a few slaps in. Then she steps back, breathing hard. I'm gone. The ding-dong thing reverberates after the door slams. I take the stairs two and three at a time.

On the roof, the elevator room door is locked. But there is another structure there. Its door has no lock. I open it. A narrow tunnel follows a brick chimney wall that is very warm. It has to be the top of the incinerator. I look for something to prop the door open so I can see. I creep around the corner of the tunnel. My foot hits a bundle – it's an old, rolled up *Mad* magazine.

Only in New York.

Chapter Eleven

Mom says I'm impossible, *vay-ray* bad. She sends me to see her divorce lawyer, Ralph Goldman at One Liberty Street. It's down near Wall Street. Dark wood furniture. Law books. Big desk. I'm scared. Maybe he is going to tell the police I have to go to reform school, or reprimand me.

He smiles at me, shakes my hand. Sit down, he says. He's fair-haired, a little gray. Gold-colored wire-rimmed glasses. Well-modulated voice. He says, Tell me what seems to be the problem. Your mother says you threw a vase at her. I say, copying his even tone, that I did not; I threw it on the floor. I say: I was too angry; I'm sorry, but Mom did something with my records; they meant everything to me. I tell him about when I was eleven and Mom interrogated me because she was sure I had slept with Michael. I tell him she wants my baby-sitting money while she is buying paintings and fur coats. I tell him about *sumi ma sen*. I tell him everything except about her trying to see if I'm a virgin, because I can't talk about that with a man. He listens. I get quiet inside.

He says, Why don't you and your mother get some space? He says his brother-in-law needs a mother's helper for the summer. He has a baby boy and a little girl. Why don't you spend the summer with them? They live near the beach. It's nice out there. I'll talk to my brother-in-law. I'll talk to your mother.

I spill into the street and the natural light of day. The sky, the trash cans on the street corners, the subways – all feel glorious. I am a little nervous about going to be a live-in mother's helper with a strange family, but 'tis nuthin, I hope. Ralph Goldman, Esquire, a normal person, a lawyer, my mother's lawyer, has treated me with kindness and respect, like what I say matters, like I'm not the crazy person Mom keeps saying I am.

The house is a couple of blocks from where the dark blue Atlantic crashes onto the shore as surely as *The New York Times* hits front lawns in the dark of morning. Predictable becomes delightful. If it is a weekday, Lester Rosen, Ralph Goldman's brother-in-law, will get up and go to work as a lawyer. I will dress baby Jason and help little Amy dress, pack a bag with baby bottles, snacks and put them with pails, shovels and other plastic toys in the stroller. We will go to the beach at Duchess Avenue, while their pretty, relaxed mother, Marge, goes shopping. In the late afternoon, I will bathe the children and dress them. At six thirty, after Lester has his cocktail, we will eat together at the small dining room table. Jason will gnaw on a teething cracker and make a mess. We will laugh about it.

They are peaceful people. Content I think, with their organized life style. After dinner I wash the dishes. In the beginning Marge said I didn't have to, but I want to; I want them to like me. I want to make sure I earn my pay of $15 a week and my room and board. Marge makes sure I have plenty to eat, but I want to watch my weight, like them. After dinner, Lester will have a cigar in the den on his big foldout leather chair and listen to the classical music he loves. Once a week Margie gets her hair done. Once a week the lady comes to clean their orderly house with three small bedrooms and its neat small garden. On Saturday nights Marge and Lester go out. On most Sundays we visit the children's grandparents who live in a big house close by on the bay. There is never a conflict between the Rosens and their parents, not that I see. The grandfather is a tall man with the air of nothing to worry about. Lester acts like someone who doesn't have much to worry about either, or he never shows it. I never see Lester or Marge angry. We get along well. I do not ask for love. They are reserved. I am treated like I matter because that is the kind of people they are. They're fascinating in their consistencies. I want to be like them.

I sleep so well in this place called Atlantic Beach off the Long Island south shore. The air is softened by the sea, smells faintly of seaweed. I get a whole day off each week, all to myself. I choose to spend it on the sand, reading or watching the waves break. Lester has a bookcase to the ceiling loaded with books that he lets me read. I have my transistor radio. I am happy. The importance of having my records to calm me fades with my nervousness.

Since I take the children to the beach almost every day, I see the same lifeguard sitting on a high stand. He's handsome with big muscles. He nods at me after a couple of days. I nod back. After work he goes surfing there. He's good at it. I wish I could do that, but I am too shy to ask how, yet. The best I can do to communicate with him is to play my transistor radio loud when a good song comes on, then turn it down for the commercials. An invisible present.

Sometimes an attractive girl comes with her beach bag and spreads her blanket out near him. They kiss affectionately, but not gross. He talks to her while watching bathers. They are comfortable together. She brings him drinks, sandwiches. She reads.

One day on my day off when she's not there and he starts rubbing his surfboard with wax, I venture to see if we can be friends. He is Steve Tarter. He goes to NYU. He lives on the bay side of the village with his parents and sister. Through him I meet the other lifeguards and their friends. There's a clique. They're all college students or about to go to law school. Many of them surf. They let me hang around even though I'm too young to go out with them. Steve invites me to his house. The den is decorated with books, sea shells, driftwood and other items he scavenges from the beach. His Mom reads a lot and plays tennis with him. His Dad works for the village.

The neatest thing is that, like the Rosens and his parents, Steve is calm. He doesn't seem afraid of anything. I love being around these people. I hope one day I can be like Steve and his girlfriend, or married like Marge and Lester. I am so relieved, taken aback, as I see how these men behave, especially with women. They act like it's normal to treat women gently, to carry heavy things for them, open doors for them. They are gentlemen, not animals, like Mom said. This is the first time in my life I get to see, not only on TV, that some men besides Dad are lovely. So the future takes on a more auspicious hue. I realize this one morning while I watch the sun rise at the beach like a huge *Red Rubber Ball* as I listen to The Cyrkle sing their song of the same name on the radio. It feels mushy, but I'm allowed because I'm 15.

A big deal this summer plays out one day when the cleaning lady doesn't come while Marge is in bed with a virus. As a teen who enjoys drama, I seize the chance to do something heroic, to fight for regularity to return to the household. I plop the kids in front of the TV. I am all over the house, done cleaning in about four hours. Am thorough, thanks to Mom, who would make me wash all the dishes again if one was greasy. I know about cleaning the toilet inside and out. Marge watches me from her bed. I make her tea, bring her lunch, help with dinner. The next day Marge and Lester call me to the dining table. I worry that maybe I broke something and didn't know it. Instead they say I'm getting a raise to $25 a week.

I say I'm happy to help with some cleaning. They say it's not part of my job. I ask if I cleaned well. They say I did excellent work. They look at me. I start to understand. In their world kids aren't supposed to clean other people's houses. I still do the dishes.

I have been saving money. Now with this raise, I can buy my own used surfboard. It takes about two weeks for me to catch a wave. After that I am consumed by surfing in the morning before taking care of the children, in the evening before sundown and on my day off.

It is innocent almost instant joy. You have to be sharp, watchful to choose the right wave, the right moments and to avoid collisions with others. You have to work, plowing the water until you're going as fast as the wave you want to catch. To catch it you have to make precise dance-like movements that make you feel graceful, agile. Your timing has to be exact so that you become part of the momentum in the sea, part of its energy. Then you belong to it, to nature, to life.

At summer's end I am invited to Steve's house for a beach party like in the movies. The Rosens let me go if Steve or one of his parents brings me home. Great music blasts over a big open campfire on their bay side beach. Hundreds of clams are steaming in a new clean trash can. Something Bad does not happen even though I am surrounded by beer-drinking college kids having a blast.

I doubt that the Tarters or the others at the party know what it means to me to go to something like this. To feel part of a happy group – Steve, other lifeguards, their girlfriends. At some point someone asks where I'm from or where I live. I'm terrified of anyone knowing I am living and working at the Rosens because of a family problem. I'm afraid of being seen as a servant, because I'm not, maybe. I try to carve an acceptable image, so I might fit in somehow with this group of youths whose parents think putting them through law school is normal. I do not lie. Even though Dad isn't my real father, he is still my Dad in my heart. But I can't get into my complicated story in detail. It's too much.

I say I'm from many places because Dad works for the State Department. When they ask where I live, I say, Dad is overseas and my mother travels so I'm staying with her lawyer's family for the summer until I go back to school in Manhattan on the Upper East Side. More than anything, I do not want anyone to think I am needy in any way – that I need money, or parents or love. I'm fine.

It's a Sunday. I'm silent as I put my Samsonite in the car, kiss the children, their grandparents. As we go over the Atlantic Beach bridge, I look back at the house and the boardwalk. I get the plunging feeling in my chest and start to cry. Marge says, There, there… Right away I'm mad at myself for making her and Lester feel uncomfortable, so I compose myself. Then Lester says, Would you like to come back next summer?

Love to, thank you very much.

I'm home a day and a half when Mom calls me into the foyer area to talk. It is good to be with The Baby again. The Baby is glad to see me. And it's good to sleep in my bed, to be surrounded by familiar furniture, bric-a-brac. Much as I loved being with the Rosens, and wished I had parents like them, the reality is that I was their employee. The house in Atlantic Beach is their home, not mine. As I approach her I hope Mom will have forgotten the turmoil from before. She has been subdued since I got back. She let me kiss the air by her cheek when I arrived, briefly, as if I had been gone for a day or two instead of three months. What did I expect? A celebration? I don't know. But I still miss the closeness we used to have.

She shifts her weight, stands framed by the setting she created: The big painting of her over the couch, flanked by the life-size tempera scrolls of the empress and emperor of China in their elaborate kimonos, the Buddhas, the Chinese dolls, the eggshell-skinned geisha in her glass and lacquer case, the big round red and black lacquered tea table centered with the dark jade carving, exotic and familiar, like she is, always has been.

She says she has been thinking.

Yes?

Eeze better here *wis-out* you, she says. *Eet* was quiet when you were gone. *Eeze* better.

I say, Oh. I nod my head a couple of times.

What do I think now? How do I act? What does this mean?

She says, you can support yourself now.

I nod my head. I pick a Buddha to stare at. Then I say: how?

Like *zee* summer. You can support yourself like *zat*. Like a babysitter who live wees a *fam-ilay*.

I say, Oh. Okay, I'll find something. I nod my head. Sure.

I want to run out of the apartment and keep running, down Second Avenue, up Third, down Lexington, up Park, down Madison until I can't breathe, so all this will stop, go away. But it's not going to stop. It's happening. She wants me to go. Away. From her. The Baby. And where we, I mean they, live.

Right away I go buy *The New York Times*. Think later. I have to leave as fast as I can. Where can I go? Have to find a place to go. My finger moves down the domestic help column. Well, what else am I supposed to do? Beg? Do *sumi ma sen*? No.

I live in Manhattan. I have The City. It's mine. I belong to it. All the faces that I faced when I was selling raffle tickets – the looks on them told me: you're one of us now, working us, pumping us for your cause; you will make it with that stamina. You are us. The City. You are we. Never alone. Not on this rock. We are the rock.

I hear the traffic as I walk fast. It is always. Even at four in the morning when the garbage trucks groan, the dumpsters are emptied, the trash is crashing. It's constant, this city's energy. It pulses through me.

Like that slogan. I have been reading it, hearing it on the radio, like the hook of a song. It says: I got my job through *The New York Times*. Good ole pal.

In it I see two or three possibilities. Someone needs a mother's helper. I prepare what I'm going to say. I dial. The lady answers. She sounds nice. But she says I seem kind of young.

Oh no, I say. I'm not young. I'm almost sixteen, in two months and a fortnight. I've traveled a great deal, so I'm older than I am. I have a lot of experience with children. I have references. And I took care of my mother's baby for two and a half years.

She says to come for an interview. I decide not to bother calling the other possibilities, until later, if I have to. I'm going to get this job. I'm gone to Sutton Place in my white suit from London with my best manners. I shall be elegant and sincere. I know how to do it, from selling raffle tickets. I can tell her Dad is a Foreign Service Officer. Maybe she will think some of the State Department will rub off on her kids, make them worldly, sophisticated, more advanced.

It's a huge apartment, meandering rooms. We sit. I tell her about coming from Asia, boarding school, Ireland, England, France, babysitting. I give her a list of my clients' phone numbers. Mrs. Bertram says she wants to talk to my mother about this. Fine. She leaves me in her living room hoping. When she returns she says she's willing to try me out even though I'm young. But she wants to meet my mother when I move in. She shows me a small bedroom crowded by empty bookcases, a desk and a twin bed. There's a window overlooking a side street near the East river. I think: I can be safe here. I can walk to school even though it's far. I can do my homework on this, my first desk since boarding school.

She has three little boys. The oldest is six. The youngest is a baby who sleeps in the room next to mine, so I can hear him if he wakes up. The position pays room and board. I will make $5 a week if I clean their beach house in Amagansett if we go there on a weekend. I can go to school during the day while the maid is here but they need me the rest of the time. I need to wash the dinner dishes. Fine.

Mom says she needs the Samsonite. She gives me a duffel bag. My white suit from London and blue coat will get wrinkled from folding them into a bundle. Will hang them up soon as I get to my new room. Also, there's a big laundry room off the kitchen and maybe the people will let me use the ironing board. I know how to steam suits and coats, with a damp cloth and an iron.

Just before we leave, Mom says to give her the key to the apartment. She holds her palm out. I fumble, feel the heat in my ears as I try to get the key off the ring.

She says she needs the mailbox key, too.

I hand her the key ring. It only had two.

She takes me in a taxi to the Bertrams' on Sutton Place. She meets them, shakes hands, smiles, laughs and acts charming in her blue jeans and high heels. She puts her cheek against my cheek, kisses the air. Click, clack. She's gone.

Mrs. Bertram gives me a new set of keys.

Now there is time to think while watching the boys play, bathing them, dressing them, changing the baby, feeding them, stopping them from fighting or doing something to the baby. They are savvy about babysitters somehow, especially the eldest. He doesn't want to be friends or get hugged. He acts like there's no point in chatting with me or the maid; as if he already has known many who've come and gone.

I have to make the best of what I've got. I act cheerio in the family's presence. I see little of Mr. Bertram, usually at the office doing lawyer things. Bernice Bertram is busy, too. She looks younger than she is, maybe in her late twenties. I admire her style, her long dark hair and bangs, like Beatles' girlfriends, her short pleated plaid skirts from Bloomingdale's and killer designer loafers from Henri Bendel. She fluctuates between being aloof and trying to get me to talk about myself, but I want my privacy. You think she wants to hear about Blaze Starr or a secret agent father I don't know how to find?

I put up a poster of Michael Caine on the wall by my bed. Mrs. Bertram asks me if I like him. I say I have no feeling for him. She asks why I put the poster up. Because it was here, rolled up on the shelf. It's just something to cover the bare walls. I do not tell her he is my imaginary company. His eyes remind me of the billboard face with glasses in *The Great Gatsby*. He is a presence, albeit lifeless.

As I lay in bed at night, I wish I could tell Ralph, Mom's lawyer, or the Rosens what's happened, but they've done enough for me. I have a job with them the following summer. I do not want to muck it. I have to be grownup and not bother anyone. If I don't ask anyone for anything, they can't say, No. Not even Dad. The last I heard, Mom said he was in Laos, wherever that is.

I shouldn't feel sorry for myself. There are orphans who do okay, I guess, in orphanages. I don't qualify for an orphanage. I feel I'm in a lot better situation than orphans because I have a job. It does something for you to earn your own way and owe no one. Though I wonder, worry: What if I get sick with flu? Who will take care of me if I can't get out of bed to get tea or medicine? Will I get fired because my bosses fear I will give the flu to their children?

Sometimes I think of *Pollyanna*, the movie with Haley Mills. Didn't her parents die and she went to live with her aunt? But I can't approach Uncle Dany, Aunt Annie, Uncle Alban or Aunt Jackie in Paris even just to be pen pals. I do not have their addresses or phone numbers. Getting those would involve asking Mom for something and that thought comes with a horrified feeling. Even if she gave me their phone numbers – do you think she would? – how could I communicate with them? I don't speak enough French. They speak no English. I have saved about thirty dollars from summer work.

Until I get to clean the Bertrams' house in Amagansett for $5, I do not dare spend, except for necessary feminine things. Even if I could get my French teacher at school to help me, stamps cost money. And if she knows about this, she might report me and I could end up in reform school with criminal kids. Same thing if I ask for help with a phone call in French. A phone call to Paris would cost $12 for the first three minutes. Even if I could get by these obstacles, what would I say? Can I come and live with you? That would cost money. I do not want to cost anyone money. I was costing Mom a little bit and look what happened. It is now impossible for me to ask anyone for money, or anything burdensome. It's a problem, even with the Bertrams. Because they don't seem to mind if I eat breakfast and dinner, but no one has said anything about lunch, even bringing a peanut butter sandwich to school. Am too proud to ask. So I pretend, again, in the school cafeteria that I'm not hungry or decide I'm on a diet. Having no money is going to delay my search for my father. Even if I could find him I could never broach a new relationship with no money. He might think that's all I want, money, when I really want something else. Someone to talk to, to start with.

I don't want to tell kids at school that I'm not living with my mother but with people for whom I work. They might think something is wrong with me because even my mother doesn't want to live with me. Or they might think she's so poor that I have to work for a place to live. I would die before kids at school thought this, especially since it's not true. All the other girls I know at school live with their families. Someday, I decide, when I am not so poor, I will find my aunts and uncles and my father, and I will buy them presents and we will have lovely relationships. In the meantime, I have to make it on my own. At least, now, in this bed, in this room, I'm safe.

I wonder how The Baby is. I miss The Baby. Her absence hurts.

The weathered wood house in Amagansett is big. It's on the beach but I rarely get out there. I'm here to work. There are several bathrooms and bedrooms. No clutter, so it's easy to clean, but there is a lot of floor space to cover, at least six beds, lots of sheets, bath and beach towels to be washed. This house has mostly tile floors that need to be vacuumed, then washed; like cleaning two houses. When I'm done, I need to bathe and dress the boys, feed them, read to them and wash the dinner dishes. Still, the sea air reminds me of Atlantic Beach. It's soothing. I sleep well because I'm beat. Homework is for people with time.

I'm up early because small children get up early. I feed them, dress them and try to keep them quiet. This is fine except when you have to go to the bathroom. I have to wait until Mrs. Bertram or her mother gets up to watch the kids for a minute. You cannot leave three children under the age of six alone for a split second.

This family shows me there must be some kind of art to succeeding as a live-in. Once everyone is up, you need to try and be invisible but present. No one says to disappear. I almost never talk to anyone but the children. But the feeling is there: This is a family and you are not part of it. If you walk into a room where the family members are together, sometimes you blow the intimacy they have. It's embarrassing for them and you. It's hard to know when they want you around and when they do not. If you withdraw because you think that's wanted, you might be misunderstood as being lazy.

Back in Manhattan, once the kids are asleep, then you go to your tiny room. You don't dare sleep while the Bertrams are out or having a dinner party, in case the children need something. In Amagansett, there's no place to hide – only the bunk bed – so you lay there listening in case a child wants something until an acceptable hour to be asleep like eleven o'clock. No TV. No radio.

One time working for this family at their Sutton Place apartment, I get a phone call around eight thirty, not too late. The children are in bed, which is when they usually want seven glasses of water or to go to the bathroom every ten minutes, so no matter who it is, I can't stay on the phone for long.

Mrs. Bertram points to the wall unit in the kitchen. It's Mrs. Cohen, one of Mom's neighbors. She just wants to let me know how sad my mother is. She says, Why don't I call her? Your mother, she says, is so lonely without you.

Excuse me?

The years of running my mother's bath water, of bringing her tea, ironing Michael's shirts, washing The Baby's cloth diapers, of helping her because she claimed she was all alone in the world.

I am empty of empathy, sympathy.

The day off I was told I could have on some weekends turns out to be a day on each of a total of two weekends. I get a ride to Atlantic Beach and go surfing before it gets too cold. I catch a wave, jump up for the ride and coming down on the board I sprain my ankle.

The Bertrams call an orthopedist friend – I have no money to go to a doctor. He comes to the apartment and says I need to stay off my ankle. Mrs. Bertram is not happy about this. I have to hop. I'm using up valuable real estate on Sutton Place, lying in bed instead of going to school because I can't walk there and I don't have the money for a bus, subway or crutches. I manage to wash the dinner dishes. I am able to babysit but I can't chase children who don't want to be dried after a bath or who don't want to go to bed.

I am worried about getting fired because I'm not so useful hopping. There is no way to hop gracefully. It's disruptive when you enter a room. It makes everyone feel they need to do something for you, which is the opposite of why I'm here.

So it's a relief when Bernice leaves a present on my bed for my 16th birthday. Do you give presents to people you are going to fire? She says I can exchange it for something else at Bloomingdale's, if I want. It's a culotte jump suit, light blue with a white collar and cuffs. It looks like a servant's uniform.

I can't wear it. I can do the work of a servant, but I can't wear a banner saying I am one. Because I have dreams that get me out of bed in the morning. I am too young to give up the hope of getting a good education – and of having a career that matters, of having a nice husband who loves me and a family of my own one day, of having my own home, of being able to buy flowers for the dinner table and books and music for my children – in favor of a mind set to serving for a living.

At Bloomingdale's I return the blue thing with white cuffs and get a plaid, pleated mini-skirt, like what Mrs. Bertram wears.

School's out for the Christmas holidays. Mrs. Bertram goes with the children and her mother to Amagansett. Mr. Bertram says he has to work and will meet them there. I think: maybe I can have a little time off, a mini-holiday in the apartment while they're gone. No. Mr. Bertram says I'm too young for the job. He gives me taxi fare to my mother's apartment on East 87th Street. I give him their apartment keys.

Chapter Twelve

You have to watch out for Rejection Residue. I had no time for it, the way things were going. My feelings were not deeply hurt by the Bertrams. It had been clear there was no love or friendship involved in our relationship. So I never opened my heart to them as with the Rosens, therefore was not so vulnerable. But being laid off or fired was embarrassing – to me, by myself, and in front of my mother. It's part of life, rejection, even if you are sixteen. You think: 'Tis nuthin, you know; try something else. And then, plop, Rejection Residue shows up in your disposition, suddenly, like mud spattered by a car on your clean school uniform, requiring exorcism, or a trip to the cleaners; only the real thing is invisible and insidious. You have to get used to it popping up from time to time. After a while, you expect it, try to get ready before it comes, or you stay out of traffic. But that would be boring, even if you had a choice, maybe.

Even without too much Rejection Residue, I feel weary when I get back to Mom's. She's acting smug. She has an I-told-you-so attitude, as if the Bertrams had proven her right in her decision months earlier that I should live elsewhere. She repeats that I'm impossible.

I need rest. I would like a break from worrying about supporting myself in high school and trying to get into college with lousy grades. And I miss The Baby. I want to be with The Baby. It means more to me to take care of this Baby than any other because we share blood. It feels good to be connected to anyone at this point.

I say, as I have in the past: Mom, let's start all over. I'll give you my baby-sitting money. I'll help more than before, though I wonder what more I could do. I even made the drapes in this apartment, put up the rods to hold them. But she is saying, *ah non*.

She is *vay-ray* busy. She says she and The Baby are going out of town *vay-ray* soon. I have to find *anuzzer fam-ilay* to live *wees*.

What would I do without *The New York Times*?

Chapter Thirteen

Before Mom takes me to my new job, she opens the coat closet door, fingers the shoulders of her fur coats, then pulls out the three-quarter-length dyed black muskrat. It's a reversible raincoat. The raincoat side is greenish-yellow. I think it's ugly but at least it's short enough for me to wear. I know it will be warm. I thank her. I wonder what this means, this gift.

Is it a message to people that I come from money, though I have none? Does it say: I am not needy when I need a place to live, food and toiletries until I finish school? Does it say she loves me? Or does it simply mean she doesn't want me to be cold? And if I am cold, is this coat supposed to suffice? Then I think: Just take the coat. There are more important things to think about.

Her name is Rina Ruben, the lady who ran the ad for a mother's helper, and she's glad about my starting on New Year's Day, 1968. I am still in my 16th year. She's petite, light-haired, blue-eyed, around 35, and frequently holds a cigarette between her polished index and middle fingers. She's quiet, still, doesn't take her eyes off Mom until she leaves.

Mom is wearing a sheared beaver jacket over her sweater, jeans and high-heeled boots. She says hi, hi, hi, like Rina is an old friend. Rina does not show emotion much, especially to strangers. I put down my duffel bag. Shira, Rina's pretty, slightly overweight, adopted nine-year-old daughter, comes into the foyer-dining area and smiles shyly. Mom says she's adorable, so cute. Mom puts her cheeks to mine and click-clunks out the door.

I smile at Rina and Shira and act like everything is fine. Shira goes into the bedroom to watch TV. Rina stares at me as we hear Mom's steps on the outdoor concrete passageway.

I say: Is something wrong?

I have never, she says, seen a mother do anything like that.

What do you mean?

Drop her child off to live with strangers.

I think: We don't have time for this. I need a place to live, not to analyze Mom. But then I consider how different Mom is from Rina, who adopted. Rina wants to be a mother. The concept is interesting.

I say: I'm used to new situations, camps, schools; I've traveled a lot on my own.

Here I go again, editing my life so I am the worldly independent loner doing swell. No I'm not going to tell her about my bizarre background, at least not until she gets to see how much I work. I feel sorry for her; she's divorced, raising an adopted child alone. I remember the change after Dad left – how precarious life felt; it never seems to go away. But there's no time for fear now.

I glance over my shoulder at the small kitchen. I guess the laundry room is in the basement?

I have to sleep on the living room couch in this small one-bedroom high-rise apartment in Queens. The terrace overlooks the Long Island Expressway (LIE) and the Alexander's department store red neon sign. In between, there's a great deal of sky. Eyes closed, the cars whizzing by on the LIE sound like ocean waves.

I get $25 a week without having to clean a big beach house – I can buy *The New York Times*, coffee-to-go, diet soda and pay my subway fare to St. Vincent's. Rina says I can take what I want to school for lunch. She says I can work for the Rosens in the summer. I can have a day off a week, sometimes two if Shira's father takes her on the weekend. All Rina asks is that I take care of Shira after school, run her bath and see to it that she's in her pajamas by the time Rina gets home from work as office manager of an employment agency in Manhattan.

Run a bath? Oh I'm good at that.

You think I'm going to wait to be asked to do something? Rina is tired when she gets home at night, kicks off her heels and lights up a Salem. Even though she has parents who own a Ma and Pa store in Jackson Heights, and probably gets some kind of support from her ex-husband, she needs someone to take care of this child so she can make money. I try to figure out how long I could be here. Three years? Maybe five. I don't know when it's normal to expect kids to be left alone at home. To secure this position I need to make Rina get used to a new life. I need her to need me. It feels good to be needed.

I do everything I can before she can think of it. I'm making a list for the supermarket. Every Saturday Rina gives me about $75 for food for the week. To save money, I cut down on prepared foods by cooking extra. It feels great to bring her $10 or $15 in change; we can still afford for me to make chocolate and vanilla pudding parfaits for Shari. Rina notices this right away. I make dinner most nights, breakfast and lunch for Shari and wash the dishes. I clean the apartment once a week – everything, including the windows and laundry. Rina brings most of her clothes to the dry cleaners and picks them up. She never asks me to run her bath or do her hair. I do not feel as much like a servant as I did at the Bertrams', maybe because I do more than a housekeeper or babysitter. What I do makes Rina happy and that feels great.

Shira is a good kid, quiet. She's addicted to TV. Since this doesn't bother Rina, it's fine because I'm busy with housework, commuting to school and trying to get through my junior year at St. Vincent's.

After Shira's father comes to get her on weekends, Rina and I run into the bedroom, gleeful. Rina jumps into her bed, I get into Shira's bed, we draw the blinds and watch movies. Rina is Jewish and her favorite is *The Song of Bernadette*, with Jennifer Jones, which actually makes her cry. I make us Dagwood sandwiches with salami, my chopped liver or toasted bagels with melted cream cheese, onions and smoked salmon. I'm less scared of being without a place to sleep. Rina starts calling me *bubbelah*, a Jewish term of affection. I call Shari *bubbelah*. We call each other *bubbelah*.

We hug each other. We care about each other. I wish we could love each other, unconditionally, but we can't because I work for Rina. I do not let myself love her. It would not change reality. We need each other. I will never be her daughter. Why should she adopt me when she can get what she gets from me for $25 a week? It is not our fault that we cannot progress beyond employer and employee. It's the way it is.

It's a slightly sad situation for another reason. Her attitude is if I give you something, you should give me something: I have let you come and live with me and my daughter, now you owe me: You should tell me everything. But this is not because she wants to get closer to me; it's so she knows who is taking care of her daughter and how long I intend to stay. Remember, she's in the employment business.

I tell her only what she needs to know: Mom and Dad are divorced; Dad is overseas because he works for the State Department; I am working my way through high school and not living with Mom because we don't get along. But Rina keeps questioning.

Telling her everything about my life would be upsetting and exhausting – I could write a book about it. I do not want to tell her about my search for my biological father because I don't want her to think I would prefer to live with him and not work for her. Who and where my real father is has nothing to do with the quality of my work. Mrs. Bertram never probed my past. The Rosens would never push questions that would embarrass me. I don't think Rina is trying to embarrass me on purpose. She's just blunt. I don't think she could dream of the feelings she stirs in me with her queries.

Things go quietly for periods, then she latches on and won't let go: Where is your Dad now? (I don't know.) Why don't you live with him? (Maybe he thinks I should stay in the same school since I'm a year and a half away from college.) When she does this, my mind gets crowded. I am afraid to say this is none of her business. So I have to work mentally, skirting hard truths, because the fact is I live in the shadows of shame.

I evade when she asks why Dad took Ev and Pat and not me. I say: I don't know. In my heart, I believe Dad loves me, even though he is my stepfather. I don't know why he didn't fight to take me, too. When I was twelve and Mom said he wasn't my blood father, was I supposed to change my feelings for him, like shoes, fur coats? Should it have occurred to me that he wouldn't feel the same way I do? So what if I live in a dream world loving him? My thoughts may not make sense, but since when does love make sense? It is almost impossible for me to face the possibility that he loves me less than my sisters; so why do I have to?

I wonder what Rina is trying to accomplish with her digging. Is my personal soap opera her entertainment? I don't know. There's no way I will reveal that I do not know my real father. That would show her I am at the bottom of the human civilization scale, amongst the offspring of creatures who procreate without marriage; I need, in my relationship with Rina, the dignity of keeping this one thing private because it's enough that I am her help at my age.

I am touchy about the subject of my real father because I saw a Veddy-Veddy movie when I was a little girl, on TV. In it, as usual in Veddy-Veddy movies, everyone is running around in evening gowns, tuxedos and English accents. There is a lovely girl engaged to be married to someone prominent who loves her but she learns that her father wasn't married to her mother before she was born, and, wow, she kills herself. Not right in front of you on the screen; that wouldn't happen in a forties movie. This young girl. Beautiful, with manners, education.

I got the message from this movie, thank you, when I was little that being illegitimate is socially unacceptable. But I decided that I wasn't going to kill myself when I learned Mom wasn't married to my secret agent father. My plan is to tell my fiancé about it the minute he asks me to marry him, or as soon as we have rapport, so if he doesn't want me because of it, I can get over it and find someone who loves me anyway because someone might; you never know. Meanwhile, I am ashamed of being illegitimate. If I talk about it to Rina or anyone, it would become more real: that I am somehow in the eyes of society tainted, a lesser person, no matter what I do to be good, to make a contribution to the world. Day in, day out, I pretend all is well with Rina, Shari, kids at school. But inside, the true me, the daughter of a man who was not married to my mother, is imprisoned by pride and fear.

I know it shouldn't matter that I have no father in my life, but it does: to have someone stand up to the world and say: She's mine; I love her. Someday she's going to do something that matters and I care about it. The biggest luxury would be to have a father – or a mother – who says: I care about her even if she doesn't make a big mark in the world; I just want her to be happy. But it's not happening. It's best to try not to think about it and to pretend you don't need or want anyone. But sometimes it takes a lot of energy to deny who you are to the world, to be a living fraud, to live with secrets that are part of your identity. It makes you feel alone even when you're with other people. It's worse when you're with members of a family, happy at a gathering, like the Seder we made for Rina's parents, because not only is it a reminder that you are not in the family, you're the help.

I'm proud of working hard for Rina, but not happy with the reality of being a servant when my mother said she grew up with plenty of her own. When I was little, I thought I was supposed to have some, too, so I could spend most of my time becoming educated. So this, all this is a continuing shock. None of the kids I know at school are servants. Many people look down on servants – working with their hands rather than their minds.

But more than anything, it is the actual work, the years of scrubbing and dusting the same things, the washing and cutting of food, the choosing, packing and unpacking of groceries, the hours at the laundry machines, the folding and ironing of clothes, sheets and towels; it is this, years of this, that makes me despondent sometimes, despite my gratitude for survival, because it is so boring. The thought of doing this continually, indefinitely, or for the rest of life is terrifying. When I think of the literally thousands of hours I have spent doing housework since I was a little girl, and how many more thousands of hours I might in the future have to spend on it, I feel defeated. The prospect makes me speechless. Tick, tick.

What is the point, I wonder sometimes, in saying anything, to anyone, about anything? Who can I tell that I have a mind that needs feeding as much as my body and spirit do? To whom can I explain what a toll the housework takes on my studies? I can't tell Rina. Even if I didn't work for her and could, I don't think she would understand. The reading material in the apartment is limited to the Spiegel and Sears catalogs. When she brings home the novel *The Valley of the Dolls*, I think this must be important since I can't remember seeing her read anything else. I can't tell the nuns at St. Vincent Ferrer how frustrated I am. They might report me and I might end up in reform school.

So I proceed with my hope of escape by getting into college. This is supposed to happen even though I sleep through many classes at school. One unforgettable day, I sleep through each class, wake up, change classes within three minutes, and go back to sleep, my head in my palm, in every class I have – seven, I think. No one says anything. I do almost no homework. I have been late for school only 14 times during this, my junior year, but absent for 31 days (sprained ankle, flu, bronchitis.) No one seems to notice.

Alone. Oh cool. It is so cool to be a loner. I talk myself into feeling it isn't bad to be an island, untouchable, therefore invulnerable. The image is fitting for a teenager in 1960s Manhattan. Some school friends have been talking about how hip it is to be an existentialist. The loner role seems to fit into that mode. Everyone is reading *The Plague* by Camus. We talk about him and Sartre and atheism at dances at St. Vincent's or Regis, a close-by Catholic boys' school. To be an atheist in a Catholic school in New York is to be impossibly chic, along with smoking cigarettes. Salems are menthol, which is good for you. The message, on TV and in magazines, is that you will be thin and pretty if you smoke them. Thin and pretty and oh so like Greta Garbo, who *vants* to be alone. Forget about God and tomorrow. Telling yourself you need no one is some temporary haven.

At school I am given an envelope. Inside it is another envelope, addressed to Mrs. S. Lambton, 245 East 87th Street, N.Y.C., but it has been returned to sender, St. Vincent Ferrer High School. Inside the returned envelope is an invoice for my tuition. I need $150. It is PAST DUE.

I do not have $150. That would be six weeks pay. How can I pay for the subway to school if I put all of it toward my tuition? What do I do?

I knew that Mom moved from the East 87th Street apartment. I went to see her and the Baby at the new apartment a few weeks earlier. I wasn't asking to live with her again. I was just curious about something, but I didn't know what it was until I was there.

It's an unusual place for Mom to live. She usually likes new construction, a good address. This apartment is in an old building over a drug store at 96th and Lexington Avenue, a not-chic neighborhood. There are high ceilings. It's bigger than the other apartments we've had. There's a lot of sunlight. The Baby, she says, is in Central Park *wees* a friend who has *chill-drens.* I walk through the many rooms, wondering why she sent The Baby to the park when she knew I was coming. Mom spends most of her time on the phone speaking French. She is *vay-ray* busy. Painting again. Here is a gay painting of flowers in a vase, a life-size one of a black woman wearing an African print turban, a small one of two black and white Buddhist temples on a green background; storm clouds hover over them. I wonder if the temples are in *Indochine.*

Here is the same furniture, the Buddhas, the Asian scrolls. There's a warm glow to the place - mustard colored walls. The feeling is different from all the other places we've lived. It strikes me, why: I had nothing to do with it, finding it, cleaning it, painting it, hanging the curtains. I am not part of this home, their lives.

Now with the tuition envelope in hand, I call the number at her 96th Street apartment. It's been disconnected. I call information to see if she has a new number. She doesn't.

The next day, a Saturday, Shira is gone with her father. I go back into Manhattan to talk to Mom about the tuition.

The address of the new apartment over the drugstore is 1486 Lexington, a five-story red brick building. A bank of metal mailboxes is on the left as you enter the vestibule. Cream-colored tiled floor. White marble steps. Turn left. Another flight of steps, a tile landing, an apartment door to the left, another flight of stairs, a hallway. Mom's apartment is No. 6.

I knock.

The door has a frosted glass and wire-mesh window in it, perplexing since Mom has always been security conscious. I guess, as I wait, the wire must be pretty strong.

There's no answer. I knock again.

I step back. There's a transom over the door. It's closed, been painted over. I imagine there was a time in this building's heyday, when there wasn't much crime, when you could leave the transom open, let the air circulate, without worrying about what someone in the hall could hear. I wonder about life with open transoms as I continue to wait.

There's no answer.

I lean against the stairwell banister and look down at my jeans, considering what to do. I sit down at the top of the stairs.

Nothing to read. Hadn't considered that I might have to wait for her. I just know she's going to say, *ah non*, no *moan-ay*, I don't have. But maybe she could lend it to me; I would pay her back.

I have been preparing what to say to her on the subway: I know I haven't been doing well in school. I'll do better. I have a little more than a year left before college. I can't go to public school now. I have to finish in this high school. It's better for my record. More organized. Less flighty.

But I know the real reason I can't go to public school. It's because I'm scared. For years I've heard you need to know how to fight in New York City public schools. I can't. I will get beaten up like I was once by some bullies after school in an alley in Washington. I have to stay at St. Vincent's. I'm safe there. Sister Marialein, the principal, knows me. She knows I'm not bad. I sold more raffle tickets than anyone in the school, even the seniors and juniors. I have to stay in my school. It's a good school.

I stare at the apartment door at the bottom of the flight of stairs. It's a newer door. With no transom. I wonder about the building. Were some of the apartments bigger at one time, then converted into smaller ones?

No pictures on the walls. The bareness reminds me of me and Mom. I lean against the wall by the stairs. No, I am not going to go to sleep, like a bum on the Bowery. I'm so tired. How long have I been waiting? How much longer? Then the guy arrives.

I hear him come into the vestibule, up the first, then second flight of stairs, trudging. He puts shopping bags down on the floor in front of the door of his apartment, at the bottom of the stairs to Mom's, and fumbles with keys, then looks up the stairs, and sees me sitting there. I get up and dust off the back of my jeans, tuck my long hair behind my ears.

Can I help you? he says.

I, I'm just waiting for the lady in apartment six.

She moved. Week ago, maybe ten days.

Oh, I say. I nod.

I look at the apartment door that was Mom's. It has four locks. Always big on strong locks, Mom was.

I look back at the man. I begin descending. I sling my bag over my shoulder and glance back one more time at Mom's door.

There is a numeral, six, over the door. I'm looking for some meaning. Some coincidence. Some sign from God. There is nothing.

I wish I could see the apartment so the reality sinks in. Why is there this delay sometimes in absorbing information? In one part of my brain I understand the message and in another I feel confused. Maybe it's because of the type of information I have to absorb – *Jeem Flad eeze* not your *fahzer*; *eeze* better *wees* out you; live *wees anuzzer fam-il-lay*; she moved; week ago, maybe ten days. I think about asking the super to let me in. But then I am afraid of what might happen if I walk through the bare rooms. Maybe they're not bare. Maybe someone else lives there already. I don't want to know.

Thank you very much, I say, as I pass the man at the foot of the stairs. He closes his door. I go down the last two flights and out onto Lexington Avenue where the afternoon sun feels like a monstrous klieg light. I am thinking: Why? What did you do? Am grateful for the cool dimness of the subway tunnel. The train roaring toward me to race me in safety back to a more orderly milieu.

The subway ride back to Queens seems much longer than usual. I feel numb as I walk from the stop at 63rd Drive to the apartment, Rina, and Shira.

Well, it's not something you tell your friends about, at school or anywhere, this kind of scene. It embarrassed me. It made me embarrassed for Mom. It took me thirty-five years to tell a couple of people about that time in the hallway. And when they heard how long it was before I knew where she lived again, they said: You were abandoned. I cringed inside, and said, well, I was working my way through high school; I was on my own, kind of; and I was almost seventeen, almost grown – but not really. I have known for years that that was a special day. The day I waited for Mom in the hall of her apartment building was a monument to the confoundedness in my youth because I realized that to try to understand why Mom had done so many things was pointless.

And The Baby. Where is The Baby? I love The Baby. I do not see The Baby again for many years.

Chapter Fourteen

On the way back to Rina's apartment, I decide to act composed so our lives proceed smoothly. Except for the tuition problem, what difference does it make that Mom is gone with The Baby? All this time that I have been living with other families, she hasn't had anything to do with me. She hasn't called, except once through Mrs. Cohen at the Bertrams', not even on my birthday. I learned she moved to her new apartment on Lex by calling her number and by having to ask Information for the new number. She hasn't written. So what does it change in my daily life that I don't know where my mother is?

But I do have to tell Rina about the tuition thing, in hopes that she might lend me the money, though I am too proud and professional to suggest she do so. Therefore, I have to tell her that the neighbor says Mom moved. And lo, Rina has a different opinion about this.

Rina doesn't like it a bit. She smokes Salems non-stop while pacing in the living room. I'm on the couch, staring at the parquet floor. Every time I look up she is looking at me with her blue eyes, as if something in my face might reveal at some point that this is a joke. I start smoking Salems, too.

What about your Dad, she asks. What about Jim Flood?

I told you I don't know where he is.

Well, she says, someone knows where he is. Doesn't he have a family?

A family? I'm thinking. Family is not a concept that comes to my mind as some kind of solution to anything.

He has a mother, I say.

Your grandmother.

Well, yes. I guess.

What do you mean, you guess? Don't you talk to her? Write to her?

I'm looking at Rina now. She knows I get no mail. What is this concern? Then, I think, well, she probably never thought of this because it didn't matter before.

She says, Why? Why don't you write to your grandmother?

I don't know her address. When Dad took my sisters we never heard from her again, me and Mom.

Do you know where she lives?

Pittsburgh.

So call Information in Pittsburgh.

What for?

To find out where your father is.

What for?

So you can ask him to help you with your tuition and to tell him you don't know where your mother is.

Oh.

Rina is looking incredulously at me. I'm trying to think. To Rina, it seems, all people stay in touch with their children, no matter about a divorce, like her husband does with Shira. I can't explain why Mom and I never heard from Grandma after Dad took my sisters. I know I understood why I didn't hear from her after Mom said Dad wasn't my real father, but I can't explain this to Rina now. It's too much to explain.

I think about calling Grandma. Probably she knows Dad isn't my real father. But does she know that I know? I can't be any more embarrassed now than I am. Could I pretend nothing happened, that Mom didn't tell me anything about Dad not being my real father, at least until I get to talk to him? (If I can talk to him.) Could it be that Grandma knows where he is? Do mothers always know where their children are? I don't know where my mother is. Why should I expect that everyone knows where their son or daughter is?

Thinking out loud I say, do you really think she knows where he is?

Of course, she says, his mother knows where he is.

I wonder why I couldn't think of this months ago when I had to go work at the Bertrams'. And then I remember. About not wanting to bother anyone for money. Uncle Dany. Uncle Alban. Dad. I do not want to cost anyone anything. Look what happened with Mom.

I'm afraid, I say.

Why?

Because I haven't heard from Grandma for so many years. Or Dad. Maybe he's forgotten about me. Maybe he doesn't care anymore.

Rina's eyes get wide. She raises her voice, for the first time in the months I have lived with her. She says: He cares.

I consider: I've dreamed that he still cares as much as I do. But what if he doesn't?

I say, I'm afraid to ask for money. I can't look at Rina.

He's your father.

I don't know what to say to him. What will I say?

Say: Dad, could you see your way through to helping me with my tuition?

See your way through?

Yes.

See your way through, I think. A nice way to ask. He loved me when I was little. He has to love me now, still. Love doesn't go away, does it? Maybe it will go away if I ask him for this money, or even if I ask him to lend it to me. The solution pops up: I can still love him even if he doesn't love me anymore. Someone doesn't have to love you back if you love them, do they? Why not? Why can't you love someone even if they don't love you back? You still have the pleasurable feeling of loving that person. If it doesn't work out, I will still have that. I can love him from afar.

Well, Danielle! Grandma says. Well, Danielle. How are you? How's your mother? She can't give me Dad's number but she can take mine. She says when she talks to him she'll give it to him...Thank you so much, Grandma. Thank you very much.

About ten minutes later the phone rings. My eyes meet Rina's. She answers.

Hello? She listens and says, Hi, Jim.

It's Dad, I think. Oh, my God, it's Dad.

Rina explains everything, then says: She's right here.

She hands the receiver to me, sits down finally after pacing, pacing, and takes out another cigarette.

Dad?

Hello, Kiddo. How're you doing. Eh?

Oh, to hear his voice again. To picture him sitting or standing there, somewhere. The rushing in my head.

Oh, Daddy. I explode, crying.

And Dad? What does Dad do?

He says: Hey there, Kiddo. Take it easy. Heh. Heh.

I stop crying to catch my breath. I hear him. He's laughing.

Then my crying becomes laughing. Because I understand. He's on another level, you see. It's one of the reasons I love him. He sees much of life as absurd. All this, this news, is to him completely absurd. And so very Mom, so very Suzy. Suzy the unpredictable, Suzy the self-absorbed, Suzy the coquette. It is as if he is watching her from above somewhere, like from the branch of a tree. Suzy the self-indulgent. This, what she has done, is to him just another scene in the grand comedy.

Rina hands me some toilet paper. I blow my nose.

I feel a lot better. I realize I wasn't feeling so good about Mom having left, without a phone call or a note, even though I was telling myself it didn't matter.

Dad is magic, having taken me with him to this viewpoint. And I never want to let it go, this light-hearted stance, his sense of humor. His calmness. His intelligence. His quietude. I want it. Could I have more of it if I get to spend time with him? Could I learn it?

I tell him I missed him so much, where did he go? He says he had to work, Kiddo, overseas. I tell him I have this job and I'm okay in general, but I have this tuition problem. I make $25 a week. I tell him about how I can't go to public school. I tell him I only have another year to go before graduation...See your way through please?...Or borrow it? Please, Daddy? I blow my nose again. I wait.

He says he'll send the money to the school on one condition:

His tone is serious now. Don't tell your mother where I am.

I say: I don't know where she is.

Don't tell her I'm in Washington. Don't tell her I'm stateside.

How can I tell her anything? I don't know where she is.

She may try to contact you later. If that happens, don't tell her you've spoken to me. You do not know where I am. And don't tell her I gave you any money.

I won't, Dad. No problem. I promise. I swear. Never.

He says he'll call me. He can't give me his phone number or address. Could I go see him? Could I come and visit? Could I see Ev and Pat? I would be so happy if I could see them, and him. Please?

You have school, he says. You have a commitment to Rina and her daughter, who has school. Maybe in the summer, for a few days. Right now you have to do well in school.

I wake the next morning wondering if what happened was real. It takes a few minutes to believe, and then, I'm off the couch, folding my sheets and blanket, putting them in the linen closet. I'm making our cereal for breakfast and bologna sandwiches, writing Shira's name on her lunch bag and feeling like I weigh as much as a piece of loose-leaf paper, like I could float off the terrace, all the way to the subway, all the way to school.

As soon as I get there I go to the office and say, feeling like a general with a chest covered with medals, that my father, who works for the State Department, is going to send them my tuition. It's coming, so sorry for the inconvenience, very soon.

My Father. A father. I have a father again. Okay, he's my stepfather and he's stepping back into my life. Step this, step that, oh two-step! He's saving me, making me feel much less afraid, making me feel like a princess.

He's a poised man. Affable, polite. With an even disposition. He is not one to display emotions, save those connected with laughter. When I tell him anecdotes about life with Mom, he responds with a sing-song up-the-scale "oh-oh?" whereas someone else might say, really? It is his non-committal way of saying: this is interesting (but not why it's interesting) and, tell me more. He appears self-confident while purporting to know very little about life for someone who by the age of 42 served in the army in the Philippines, with, he notes, a nine millimeter up his leg and a Thompson down his back; worked in Indonesia as a reporter, at 8 cents a word "to keep the old rice bowl filled," and worked for the U.S. government in Saigon, Hanoi, Saigon, Fukuoka, Bangkok, Washington, D.C., Taipei, Hong Kong, Seoul, D.C., Vientiane, and D.C., in that order, and in those vicinities. He picks up languages like he puts on a fresh shirt in the morning. I can see him tightening his bow tie, looking unflappable, after having been married to Mom for eight years, after having been divorced from her and raising his two daughters for almost 10 years, mostly overseas. Oh no, he doesn't know much about life. *Ching jing wu wei*, he quotes the Chinese philosopher, Mencius, saying to the polygamous husbands of China: *Ching jing wu wei*: *Maintain a calm and tranquil spirit for only in this is there armor against the keening of shrews and willful wives.* He is especially fond of Asian quotations, and of ancient cultures in general. I hope that if I stick around him as much as I can I shall pick up some wisdom, for he is constantly educating and re-educating himself with immersion into some new culture in preparation for his next overseas assignment, in his quiet, fervent way. Yet he maintains his humility. His favorite author, he says, is Simone de Beauvoir, because she writes about women, and women he says, are the most perplexing subject in the world.

It's summertime. I'm visiting Dad, Evalyn and Patricia in their D.C. apartment. Am prowling to see if I can tuck myself into their lives; too proud, just yet, to ask if I can live with them. And they are in flux. Dad has married a Korean lady who lives elsewhere; it's not clear where, or if the marriage will last; it's none of my business. Dad, Ev and Pat are living in obviously temporary digs. Dad has the bedroom where he hangs out in an oriental print sarong, listens to various Asian music on his reel-to-reel or to lewd sailor songs that Pat despises. He's built beds into a very large walk-in closet or tiny second bedroom for Ev and Pat. The rest of the furniture is nothing special. The place smells of strong cigarette or corncob pipe smoke, sesame seed oil and peppers from Pat's Korean cooking.

Ev is talking about going off by herself to California. Pat is going to high school in Pittsburgh soon. She'll live with Grandma and Dad's sister, Aunt Sue.

It's good to be with Ev and Pat. But it's difficult to gauge where they are – emotionally, intellectually. They have become rather private people. I can't tell if they're happy, sad or indifferent. I say to Ev: What will happen if you go away to California; I may not see you again for years; it's been so long since we were last together. She says: It'll be like the last time we didn't see each other for years; we'll pretend that it was just yesterday that we were together.

And so, to the tune of the transient time between us, we dance, mentally, tentatively towards each other and then backwards, and then towards each other, again tentatively, as if we know ahead of time that it will hurt too much if we get too close before we will again have to part. We are otherwise polite, warm and respectful.

We go out to eat. As usual Dad orders in perfect Chinese. The waiter is pleased. We are used to eating with chopsticks, absorbing the ways of other nationalities. We are a private multicultural club and take Dad's linguistic proclivity for granted, like his deftness at tennis.

Off to the P Street courts we go with a six-pack of green Gatorade in the Sunday morning sunshine. He rallies from the baseline with his cousin Marjorie, who also works for the government. Pat is reminiscent of a slender, graceful bird – she and Ev have Mom's long limbs – when she serves. I am anxious to prove myself on the court, but I cannot hit. I don't have a tennis racket. I get to use one of theirs during breaks, but I am so bad Dad says I have to hit on a back wall for a year before I get on a court again. I decide one day I shall hit well enough to play with Dad.

I want to belong, to become. I want to be other than a servant-student. But what? Dad, in front of me in his tennis whites, sweating with a terrycloth band across his forehead, with his nothing-is-a-big-deal attitude, tells me of the great philosopher who spent ten years writing ten volumes and the next thirty distilling his advice to the world down to one volume, then to one page and finally to one word: Relax. But still, I want.

I want to be like him because of his respect for people based on their brains and behavior rather than their color or race or religion, because of his love of freedom, honesty, books, education, good writing and well-spoken English, because of his self-reliance and his pride that he was on his own at 18 when he went to war and never turned back, in favor of adventure, the exotic, the dangerous. Because he knows so much about Mom, my background and beginnings, I don't have to explain any irregularities to him. Even about Mom's dancing, he is either not judgmental, or doesn't reveal his opinion. And I love him because he doesn't indicate in any way that there is something undesirable about me because I am illegitimate – something we don't mention at the moment, though I know he knows it and he is kind enough right now not to find out if I know it. And because he gave me a name.

He took another man's child and gave her a name, told the U.S. government she was his, and took her out of Saigon, where French, British, American and other foreign nationals were increasingly not welcomed. He took her across the sea to safety, to America. He fed her, clothed her, educated her for a while and paid for her to have an operation to keep from having a space between her two front teeth. He spanked her and chased her, when she was six, naughty and ran naked out the front door of the house in Maryland, and gave her a quarter every Saturday morning to put in her glass piggybank. He was her father in every way for eight years and now, so that she can save face, or perhaps because he knows the need she has, he is playing along, letting her call him Daddy.

I am his little girl, still, maybe always will be.

He lets me be. He lets me tap him for information to fill the void in who I am. I have a long way to go before I am complete. (Do we ever become complete?) But I need a plan to get out of the situation I am in. I do not have the imagination to pull from the choices of who and how to be. I know this: I do not want to be like Mom. Why not simply be like Dad? I want to help people; I would love to be a doctor but I know in my heart that I'm a writer. How do you become a good one? Dad must know. He published a novel. He seems interested that I want to be a writer. It's a relief to have someone be interested in my mind.

On the way to the P Street courts where Pat and Marjorie will meet us later, he stops the car, takes me by the hand, holding it tight as we walk as if I am little - not almost 16 - to a dim downstairs lounge. He orders a martini for himself and a diet cola for me and we talk. You need to write in the active voice as much of the time as possible, he says. Keep it simple. Strive for simplicity. Read aloud everything you write. It will help you from garbling what you are trying to say. Keep asking yourself what you are trying to say. He says I need to know this book called *The Elements of Style*, another called *The Art of Readable Writing* by Rudolph Flesch, and Fowler's *English Usage*. Read, he says. Read Hemingway. Read Dickens. Use the dictionary constantly. Need *Roget's Thesaurus*. Use it. Fight to be precise...

I have to go back to Rina and school, I know. I don't dare cry at the Greyhound station. I want Dad, Ev and Pat to want to be with me, and so I act cheerful, which isn't too hard. Dad paid my tuition and didn't act like he disliked me because I cost money. I believe he will be watching from afar whatever progress I make. Now that I have an audience, I am going to show what I can do with my will power.

Dad studied languages and went to college but he does not have a degree; I am going to make him proud by getting one. And if I distinguish myself in his world, at least as a writer, we will have even more in common; he might take note. If I become more like him, it might make him love me more.

Can you make people love you? Does it hurt to try to find out?

The first thing I read when I get back to New York from Washington is

Dad's novel, *The Jing Affair*, published by Funk and Wagnalls three years earlier under the pseudonym, D.J. Spencer, Spencer being his mother's maiden name.

It's about the efforts of the Taiwanese people to remain free, despite the doings of a Chinese General Jing, who is trying to sell them out for $30 million. The first chapter begins in the Washington office of the Central Intelligence Agency. I wonder if novelists write about themselves, whether or not they are any one character or if they are all the characters in a book, or none of them. Is Dad Harry Retton, "until recently CIA's star performer in the Taipei-Tokyo circuit" tossing documents into the office safe? Or is he the newspaperman, Bud Riggs, in a clandestine meeting with the CIA in a Tokyo whorehouse? And what of Mrs. Cho, code name: Molly, and Lydia Green, code name: Alex, the chief American intelligence agent on Taiwan? And Johnny Hsiao, code name: Dagger? Messages decoded by using a certain formula and the Sanseido English-Japanese dictionary. Dad was telling me to write what I know about. Is this what he does at the office and overseas?

It's a lot for me to follow. It would be decades before I could catch up to Dad's knowledge of: the intelligence community; how its members go about causing insurrection and mini-wars that can lead to big wars; the inner workings of the U.S. government in Washington and abroad; the history of Taiwan, China; and of Chinese curses even. (Impertinent ape! Chinese pig. Daughter of a pig. You, too dirty to live!) For now, I decide, if I can just do well in my senior year, I might, by a punctuation mark, make it into a college where I can learn to write better.

Since my visit to Dad, energy emanates from some mysterious source within me. I am no longer sleepy in school though I am up late studying – I have to start late because of housework. My grades escalate dramatically. I'm proud to send Dad my report card, happy to have someone to whom I can send a report card.

I am able to save up for a prom gown with a matching coat from a discount store but after the prom I take the over-the-elbow gloves I wore, wash them, iron them and put them back into the plastic sleeves they came in with the price tag and return them to their department store home.

Because I need the $12 that they cost. Doesn't matter.

With an application weighted by flattering letters from my mother's lawyer, Ralph, and from Lester Rosen, I am accepted at Fordham at Lincoln Center. My grades go up again.

I qualify for a scholarship, something to do with the State of New York State Education Department, but it is based upon need. I cannot produce my mother's income tax information for the scholarship people. So I write to them explaining that I have not been living with my mother for almost two years and that "I am totally independent... as I support myself through babysitting money." This is ignored. I get the minimum scholarship amount based on the assumption that I have no need. I do not know how to appeal. A mental gauge says don't bother Ralph and Lester. So I give up and settle for the tuition loan from Fordham.

Chapter Fifteen

Long distance phone calls are expensive so I can't call Dad in Washington. He calls on holidays, and then I am euphoric for days.

One call is unforgettable. The way he laughs after every other sentence. It's not an embarrassed laugh. It's a laugh that is as close as he can get to admitting sadness, pain. He wants to know if I could do him a favor. He calls me Kiddo again.

Your mother, he says, is suing me for your child support.

I say, slowly, to make sure I have it straight: My mother is suing you for my child support?

That is correct.

But I haven't lived with her for more than two years.

We are quiet.

I am quiet. He is quiet. I am thinking: He's not even my blood father.

There's going to be a hearing, he says.

I wait.

Would you come down to Washington and testify? I'll pay your way down. Just tell the judge where you've been living.

I am flattered that this accomplished Foreign Service Officer and author is coming to me for help. I feel important, excited over the prospect of getting to see him, and of being able to tell Rina and Shira I have to go to Washington, D.C., on court business after swallowing the disappointment that Dad has not become indignant over my circumstances and invited me to live with him or whisked me into school in Pittsburgh with Patricia. Instead he's said to me: I'm proud of you, Kid. You're doing a good job where you are.

I accept the reality that he's not responsible for my welfare. I have to be a big girl. I know that's what he wants. I have no right to expect to be treated, raised, as Patricia is, in the security of Grandma's big house without having to work as well as go to school. I should be grateful for Dad's friendship and whatever kindness he gives. I know I mustn't waste time with any discontentment. I block it, pretend I am wearing the blinders of a racehorse with one sight that matters at the moment: to help Dad by telling the truth.

I am going to Washington the next morning. I am smoking a lot of Salems. I go out on the balcony. I come back in. I sit down. I get up.

Rina says, What's the matter?

I guess I'm just excited, I say. Excited to see Dad.

She goes into her purse, takes out a bottle of pills, opens it and hands me one. It's a capsule, black and aqua colored.

She says, take this.

I look at her.

It's nice, she says. You'll see.

I swallow it with water. In a little while I feel calmer. There's a light shield between me and the world, but I don't feel real, somehow. In the morning I am still jumpy about seeing Dad. So I realize it's a temporary thing, this pill. It's a fake feeling. It numbs feeling. I wonder about Rina. Is this why she never seems excited about anything? Because she takes this pill so she can feel less of life?

Round about Dad's shins, the pants of his suit flap a little. I guess it's because he's tall and slender. I am staring at them as he talks to me about the hearing the next morning. We are standing in the small living room of his Washington apartment.

He says to me, so gently: You know, Kiddo, I signed for you.

I say, I know, I know.

I stop him before he stipulates the truth that might kill the role playing between us as father and daughter. Quickly, I say:

I know you're not my real father. But I love you like you are. I thought for so long that you were my father, I can't make it go away.

I can't look at him. I push the top of my head into his chest and put my arms around his waist and stare at his black oxfords. He has been buying these shoes at the PX for years.

He says, oh, take it easy, Kiddo, heh, heh. I pull back and fake a smile he knows I am faking. Then we go back to acting like father and daughter.

The next day, I don't tell him I am nervous to be in a courtroom, like on *Perry Mason* on TV. Perry Mason can get nasty sometimes, pushy. I haven't done anything wrong, don't intend to. So what is there to be nervous about? Dad's lawyer, Oliver Ellis Stone, says he's going to prepare me for my testimony, which sounds odd. If I tell the truth, what is there to prepare for? He says to look at the judge when I speak. I should say my name and where I live with Rina Ruben. I should say where I lived and worked at the Rosens' the previous summer, and where I lived before that at the Bertrams' and where I lived before that with the Rosens. That's all.

He tells me to wait in the little room until he calls me into the courtroom. I want to hear what's going on in the courtroom. There's a big window in the little room, but I am too distracted to bother to get up and look out. After a while the door opens. Mr. Stone beckons me. I follow him into the courtroom. The masses of dark varnished wood are imposing, intimidating. He gestures that I should sit in the boxed-in witness chair next to Judge Atkinson.

I do. I look over the other people in the courtroom. Then I see her. It's Mom. Her open mouth. The pain in her dark eyes. The horror. I might as well be stabbing her in the chest, such is the look on her face.

What is she doing here? I didn't come here to hurt her, or anyone. Why didn't Dad's lawyer tell me she was going to be here? What else does he know? Does he know where she lives? I thought she didn't exist anymore because I didn't know and still don't know where she lives. But she does exist. She's sitting before me, here, in this courtroom with hate in her stare. Mr. Stone said he was preparing me. Why didn't he prepare me for this?

A man tells me to put my hand on the *Bible*. I swear on it. I sit down.

The room is a blur. I am asked to state my name. I do. Then Mom's lawyer rushes at me, shouting: Objection, objection.

The judge gives me a dirty look and says sternly: You're excused. I know he has seen the look on Mom's face.

Mr. Stone opens the door to the room where I had waited. I go in and sit down. I hear Mom's lawyer saying angry things until the door to the courtroom closes. I look up at the light streaming in the huge window, but all I can see is the look on Mom's face and her hair.

What did she do to her hair? It's pulled back now into a pony tail at the nape of her neck. It's dyed blonde. You can see the roots of her natural dark brown color in her hair's center part. What's wrong with her? Why does she look like this? This is not her. She has never dyed her hair blonde before. The Mom I know would never let the roots show like this. She is always perfectly groomed, her nails always polished before she goes out, even to shop. What's happened to her?

Am sad for her. I never thought about this, that coming here to tell the truth would hurt her so. How did I get into this? How do I get out? I can't. It's done. I can never get out. Look what I've done. To help Dad, and to try and make him love me more. By being a champion of truth. Look at this mess.

What a daughter. What a Mom. What a Dad. We're dangerous, we are, treacherous, all three of us. Only, I never meant to be. I'm stupid, I guess. And naïve.

Even as stalwartly composed as he usually is, I can see that Dad is feeling down. There isn't much to say as he drives us to a lounge except: Well, Kiddo, you did what you could. He has vodkas. I have a Coke. We eat sandwiches and go back to the apartment. In the morning it's back I go to the Greyhound bus, back to Rina and Shira, cooking and cleaning. It's summer. Shira's going with her father for a few days. I do not bother to tell Rina what happened in Washington. I do not want to go over this memory again. The look on Mom's face. Until now, I was an innocent. Despite all the things she had done, I had never done anything bad to her, except refuse to do *sumi ma sen* and break the planter from Thailand. Now I have betrayed her.

Of course I come to my senses from time to time, remind myself that I did the right thing.

But then, there is Right Thing Residue, which feels like Rejection Residue. I'm not ready for it. I do not know someone who has died, but I know death now. Finality is everywhere. I am going to Fordham in the fall, but I can't picture myself there. I cannot see time beyond now, the midsummer heat, the dishes in Rina's sink, the droning of Shira's running bath water and Mom's face in the courtroom.

I figure Mom and I are finished. Before the court thing, I was trying to get used to the idea that she didn't love me, and to trying to figure out why. Now, she has reason to despise me.

I reason: If your mother doesn't love you, why should anyone?

I think there is no hope, never will be, of having someone special, just for me. I mean: someone who thinks I am extremely important to them. Dad and I are friends, but getting to see him for a couple of days in Washington is over. I do not know when I will see him next. He does not need me anymore. So that part of our relationship is over. Anyway, he has his own problems with his Korean wife. Evalyn keeps talking about going to California. Pat is settled in her life with Aunt Sue and Grandma, going to school in Pittsburgh. We write but it's light stuff, as if she doesn't want to, or can't get into, the subjects that could pull us closer together – like Mom and Dad.

Grandma and Aunt Sue and I write, but they hardly know me. They are reserved, formal people. I cannot tell them how devastated I am about

Mom. They know Mom and I are estranged but explaining that I still love her, though I am afraid of her, might confuse them. If they told Dad, he might have nothing to do with me, for fear that I might reveal to Mom where he is. And sometime in the near future, I will not know where he is, at least for a while.

He says he's going overseas again, as soon as he can. He has lost the lawsuit to Mom. She cannot get his government salary garnisheed, but she can have him held in contempt of court and jailed until he pays her what the judge says he owes her. To do that, he says, she has to know where he is. If he goes overseas, he says it will be almost impossible for her to find him. And if she does, he will be beyond the court's jurisdiction. Anyway, he says, he prefers to live overseas. Life in the U.S., he says, is too homogenized for his tastes. Foreign Service Officers usually live well overseas; the servants outside the U.S. are usually much cheaper.

I say I want to go with him, but he says I have to stay at Fordham and get my education.

In the wake of the court case, with the thought of Dad going abroad again, every subway train feels like it's on the way to nowhere. This summer I am taking care of Shira and when she visits her father or grandparents, I work at temp jobs as a Gal Friday at Rina's employment office and others. In the morning I leave Rina's apartment with the terrace overlooking the whizzing cars on the expressway and in the evening I am faced again with the whizzing cars on the expressway.

Right Thing Residue hangs round like cigarette smoke, casting a gray tint on everything, making the loneliness tragic, not only because I'm seventeen, but because the philosophy I have studied at school has me facing many questions. What point is there in moving on with no one around to care? Where is God now? Is God dead? Is there a God? If there is, why does he allow so many bad things to happen? Why are we here? What is the point? I am reading *Papa Hemingway*, his biography. He tells of "Black Assed Days." I know what he's talking about. When I come back to the apartment from work now I am in a black hole, down a well with no walls. I can't climb up, can't get out. I can't tell Dad how I feel, because he like most people I know has a posture that discourages the entertainment of emotional subjects, including displays of weakness. When I think of what I've done in Washington and my life, which seems sometimes like some pathetic trawl for love, a trawl that I fear is ill-disguised, the idea that hope is a waste of time flickers like a light with a loose connection. Look at Hemingway, whom Dad and I admire. Hem was a smart man. Blew his head off. Why? Because he couldn't write anymore? Because of the black hole he calls being Black Assed? Why write at all?

This is my frame of mind one late afternoon after the courtroom. I think of Dad, in the white suit he wore in Indochina photos, sipping a cocktail at some faraway exotic sidewalk cafe. Shira is away with her father. Rina is coming home late because she's going shopping. I go into the bathroom.

I have never bothered looking at the pills Rina has, but I do now. She gave me a tranquilizer once, the numbing-of-feeling pill that fixes nothing when you wake up the next day. So I figure she might have sleeping pills too, the ones I'm looking for – little red bullet-shaped capsules. I read about them while skimming *The Valley of the Dolls*, which is boring except for certain information: "...beautiful little red dolls that take all your cares away..." There are more than a dozen of them in a bottle there, in the cabinet in the wall opposite the sink. I get a glass of water and swallow all of them.

I sit down on the couch to die, thinking of how inconsiderate Hemingway was, leaving a bloody mess for his wife to find on his last morning.

Half an hour later I am still not dead.

Seconals are sleeping pills. They should make you sleepy. The bottle doesn't say Seconals but that doesn't mean anything because I've seen Rina put pills from larger bottles into smaller ones so they fit in her purse. I figure they are Seconals because they look as they are described in the *Valley of the Dolls*. But why am I awake? Oh damn. Rina will be home soon. I do not want to deal with her reaction. Maybe I should just not tell her. Maybe I should start making dinner. But what if I fall asleep while making dinner?

What if I die while making dinner? I could burn something and there could be a fire. I don't want to create some hazard. I don't want anything to happen to Rina. What to do? Better wait.

I put my head back against the yellow couch pillows. Another half-hour goes by. I am still not dead. I'm still not sleepy. I am getting nervous about not dying before Rina gets home.

And then it's too late. The key in the door. She comes in with her big shopping bag. I tell her what I've done.

Poor lady. She's usually very collected. Now she's saying, I should walk in circles, get up and walk in circles, make some coffee. No, she says, I'll make some coffee. But she's not making coffee, she's on the phone, calling the doctor who gave her the prescription. I sit down on the couch. She says get up and make coffee. The phone rings. She is talking to the doctor. She's reading the plastic pill bottle to him.

I have taken a bunch of antibiotics, the doctor says. I'm going to be fine. She wants me to drink some coffee anyway. I bring her a cup too. She's on the phone again.

Jim? she says.

Uh-oh. She's talking to Dad.

She's pretty quiet while we wait for him to drive up from D.C. She keeps looking at me. Her glances say, are you out of your mind? I make sandwiches. I wonder if she's going to fire me. I wonder what Dad's going to do.

It's almost midnight when Dad and Ev arrive.

He comes into the apartment. I get up and hug him. He grabs my shoulders, holds me at arm's length, looks me in the eyes and says: Don't you ever do anything like this again.

He's mad. Rina is indignant. She says: I think she needs to spend time with you.

Nothing could make me happier.

We get to Washington sometime after 4 a.m. Someone has taken Dad's rented parking space. Unh-huh, he says. Wait here, he says. We get out and he drives off to find another parking space.

Ev and I walk towards the back entrance to the building when we hear the sound: shhhhhhhhhhhhhhh.

We turn and see him in the street lamplight, a huddle by a tire of the car parked in his space.

Shhhhhhhhhhhhhhh.

Ev shifts her weight impatiently but it's clear that Dad is going to have his way. He is letting the air out of the tires of the car in his space, all four. When he gets upstairs, he calls the 24-hour towing company to take it away.

I think about the way he handles this infringement on his lifestyle and about his sense of justice. And I know: He is never going to pay the court judgment to Mom. Intuition tells me this thing between them will be a *guerre de mort* and it has nothing to do with money.

Chapter Sixteen

The sojourn with Dad in Washington does a great deal for me. Dad and I talk for hours. The idea that I should become a reporter, like he was once, gets established. This gives me a direction that I believe would please him, even if he is to be on the other side of the world, sooner or later.

I guess this provides an adequate distraction from suicide, which is good, at the moment, since I have no idea what or how I should be thinking of myself. I would be grateful for a brain transplant from a sharp octogenarian, so I could skip future surprises arising from the teenage decision-making process in which consequences are a vague, often-underused concept and drama is inevitable and exhausting.

When I get back to the apartment Rina looks at me with a question in her eyes. I answer it with a phony cheerful disposition. Shira is back from her father's and doesn't know about my botched S-attempt. Rina and I need things to continue as they were, so we pretend nothing happened. Soon enough, though, I see things cannot continue as they have, at least not indefinitely.

There are vast student lounges at Fordham's Lincoln Center campus with new comfy chairs, couches and coffee tables with light fanning from many lovely floor-to-ceiling windows. Between classes you can study there, read, write, dream, hope. The courses are packed with answers and questions that make your mind somersault. The libraries are stocked with books not available in the public library; you can borrow all that you can carry; it's easy to go into a silent frenzy in there; there are desks you can use for free; you can research subjects to the nth degree, investigate, maybe even find the answers to the secrets of life and write world-saving papers, articles. There are activities after school – chances to create more of who-you-are amongst peers who do not know that you are a housekeeper/nanny in disguise, if you have time.

But I do not have time. Most of it belongs to Rina and Shira and their apartment. Some days I am sure I shall wake up blithering incomprehensibly about Tide and garlic powder, so frustrated do I become over the limits on the time that I need to be mine.

There's more work to do in college than in high school. I want to do more than required. But I need to know that I have a consistent block of hours when I can study, read, write. It would be ideal if I could be paid more than $25 for the 50 or so hours a week I give Rina and Shira. But I cannot ask, I know, because room and board is part of my pay. A deal is a deal. Only I have outgrown the deal.

Dad's sister, Aunt Sue, asks in a letter if I need anything for school. I say in a letter yes, I do, I need a place to live and time for my studies and for myself. I feel like I am going sideways instead of up. I worked so hard for college. Now I cannot give it my best. I want to work on the school newspaper. I want to run for the student senate, knowing I probably won't have time to serve if elected. I do it anyway. When I'm elected I manage to get to some of the meetings.

I try and reorganize the housework so it takes less time. One Monday, I decide the way to get out of cooking every night is to roast six chickens at once. Rina sees me basting them when she gets home from work.

There's an incredulous note to her laugh.

It doesn't occur to me that there is anything wrong with cooking six chickens for the week. My mind is so preoccupied with school, I wouldn't notice what we were eating.

I am playing jacks with Shira on the living room floor, because Rina would like it if I would play jacks and cat's cradle with Shira, when the letter from Aunt Sue comes with a check for $500. I'm astonished. I neither asked for nor expected this. Rina sees me exclaim. Then I see the disappointment in her face.

In that moment I know I must leave her employ. I spoiled her and Shira. Instead of being happy for me, she is fearful of losing what I do for her. She's not glad someone has tried to help me get ahead. I'm disappointed that I could not make her love me with the work I gave her; I had no right to hope for it. One should not give with the expectation of something in return. But I know if I stay, her interests will continue to trump mine.

The $500 is not enough to get an apartment and pay for the textbooks that I have just been informed that I need. (My student loan covers tuition, not books.) And I cannot leave Rina with no one to help her with Shira now that school has begun. So I use the money for textbooks and I make a plan.

I see a sign near the mailboxes for a dance being held by a group called Parents Without Partners. I make Rina buy some dresses and push her out the door. I can't change my life if she doesn't change hers.

I hear her key in the door. I look up from studying. He follows her. A big jovial guy, divorced or widowed. He has three or four kids who are older than Shira and a house in Connecticut. I don't know what he's doing in Queens on this night. I'm trying to get uninvolved, so I don't ask. Eventually, they have a lovely small wedding in Connecticut and Rina doesn't have to work as the manager of an employment agency anymore. She and her new husband want to know if I would like to go and live with them. And clean and cook and do laundry for all of them and their children.

Phase two of the plan comes with a refresher course in fear. I have finished freshman year with a 3.2 out of 4.0 average, decent considering limitations. Rina lets me use her Queens apartment during her transition to Connecticut. I have the summer to make the money as a Gal Friday to get an apartment that's cheaper than staying in the dormitories on the Fordham Bronx campus, to which I have transferred in search of more writing courses. Dad says he's going to India by summer's end. His plan is to build a steam-powered motor home and travel around Europe before taking up his next government post. I ask again if I can go with him. He says, again, I need to finish school, so I can become a reporter.

I find an off-campus apartment in the Bronx. But I need a part-time job for during the school year. Even with the money I made during the summer, I will not be able to pay the rent and utilities, even with a roommate, beyond about mid-October.

Nine-to-five temp jobs are unreliable and would interfere with my classes. After my time in the black hole, I'm wary of work in which I might be humiliated, like waitressing, which might also be unreliable. I'm too proud to ask Dad, his sister or his mother for financial help – am afraid of rejection. Then I learn that Dad still knows his old boss from when he was a reporter for the Associated Press in Singapore. Stan Swinton is now the head of World Services for the AP. I pounce on Dad for an introduction.

Mr. Swinton is a wide-waisted man who seems, to someone my age, to be very old with thinning hair that's dyed almost black and a penchant, like Dad, for cocktails. He and Dad are reminiscing about their time together in Singapore during the lunch we are having with Pat in a Greek restaurant in Manhattan. I listen to every word. I have to get this job. I will not be able to make it on the salary from working pizza shops near Fordham. Dad is talking about openings at the AP and Mr. Swinton is nodding and saying, he'll see what he can do. Dad is thanking him. I am thanking him. Mr. Swinton is saying I should call him next week. After he leaves I am jumping up and down. Dad is saying, Take it easy, Kiddo.

Dad is in New York to leave the country. Somehow I cannot believe it. Hearing about it for a year is not the same as hugging him and Pat for the last time in I-don't-know-how-long-it-will-be and watching them go up the gangplank into the the *SS Michaelangelo*; then watching the gangplank be removed and more than 45,000 gross tons of white painted steel move slowly out of its slip, like a long sleek moving apartment building, bound for Genoa.

Try stopping a cruise ship from carrying away people you love from going anywhere sometime. It is not like hailing a cab. The ship lets out its mournful blasts. It begins to move. You walk towards the bow with your eyes riveted to the upper decks, searching. You walk back towards the stern, eyes on the decks, then walk towards the bow again. You walk until there is no place to walk. You wave with the crowd when you really want to say to your stepfather whom you thought for so long was your father: Wait. One more thing. Could we talk about this? But the ship keeps moving. That plunging feeling is in your chest. There's nothing you can do. You want to wail but you can't impose discomfort upon the people around you. So you watch through the blur until you can get somewhere private.

I do not know where Evalyn is in California. It's astonishing that Dad's mother and sister write that they don't know where she is either. I have been afraid to say to Dad: How could you let Evalyn go by herself to California? She's a year younger than me and she has no job. How can you leave her stateside and go to Genoa and India like this? But I'm afraid to challenge him, embarrass him, or make him in any way reticent to communicate with me. I will help her, I tell myself, as soon as I get established, if I can find her. School is starting soon. I have to call Mr. Swinton in five days.

Mr. Swinton says I should meet him at his club on a very high floor at 30 Rockefeller Plaza. It has white tablecloths, waiters who bow and bring dessert on a rolling cart. I wear a gray dress with a jacket that Grandma made for me, stockings and heels. I tell him about how much I want to be a reporter. Won't he please tell me about when he was a reporter? He says he's mostly been an editor. In between he looks at me a long time in silence. I want to say, what is it? But my instincts say, don't. I use my best table manners and hope that he can see I'm a poised and graceful Foreign Service family kid, that I would be an asset to the AP. If I wasn't an asset then he could complain to Dad, which won't happen. After lunch he says I should call him in about a week.

School begins. I count. I have enough for food for about three weeks or so, but then the rent will be due. I figure I will be okay if I get this job at the Associated Press in a week when I call Mr. Swinton. I'm a bit in a daze. All I can think of is the phone call. I'm otherwise in a good mood. I get to choose most of what I want to study. My small apartment is a one-bedroom palace, though the view out each window is another window surrounded by red brick. No matter. I have plenty of Total Cereal; it gives you 100 per cent of the daily vitamins you need, so I figure you can live on it. I do. The apartment stays clean. For the first time since St. Mary's, more than five years, I do not have to cook, clean and do laundry for someone else. I am almost 19.

Mr. Swinton asks if I would like to have a drink with him and a well-known writer. Wow. I dress in my other professional outfit, a discount store white pique A-line dress with a matching jacket. I meet Mr. Swinton in front of the Associated Press Building on Rockefeller Plaza. His friend, another old man named Bill Brinkley, wrote a novel called *Don't Go Near the Water*, a military comedy that became a movie years ago. We go in Mr. Swinton's black limousine to a lounge. They order drinks. I order a Tab, smoke my cigarettes like a grown-up, act polite, nod, smile. I want to talk to Mr. Swinton about the job but Mr. Brinkley is there. They keep talking about people they know. Mr. Brinkley has brought a copy of his novel. Mr. Swinton says the pages haven't been cut. I ask, feeling stupid, what that means. He says sometimes a new book's pages are attached to each other because it hasn't been read yet. I'm impressed with this bit of insider publishing-type knowledge. I feel privileged by this meeting, but I don't think it will help me with my career. Finally Mr. Brinkley goes to the men's room. I ask Mr. Swinton when I could start working at the AP. He says we can talk about that later. I say, sure. I thank him for the Tab and say I need to get going. He says, We'll take you home, where do you live? I say, That's OK, the Bronx. He says, We'll take you there. I'm starting to feel uncomfortable because he has said earlier that he and his family have a big apartment over on Sutton Place. The Bronx is far out of his way. I say, that's OK, I'm going to my friend Nora Jean's. Mr. Swinton says, We'll take you there. I say it's not necessary. He insists. By now he and Mr. Brinkley are talking loud and acting too happy. I tell the driver where to go on the East side of Manhattan. I get out and say thank you very much. But then Mr. Swinton says, We'll come up with you. I say, Nora Jean lives with her parents; it wouldn't be right. Mr. Swinton says, We don't mind. We go up the three flights. Nora Jean looks through the peep hole and says, Dani? I say, Nora Jean, I need to talk to you. She says, Who's with you? Mr. Swinton says, Just a couple of friends. Nora Jean says, it's 9:30, I can't open the door. I am so embarrassed by now. Mr. Swinton says, Aw, this is no fun. We all go downstairs. I say I have to go. Mr. Swinton says, We're taking you home. I shake his hand and say, No, thank you very much and walk backwards. Then I turn and walk fast.

I am too embarrassed to call Nora Jean ever again.

I'm very worried. Mr. Swinton's secretary says he's not in. Can she take a message? I say, I'll call back, thank you very much. I call again in the afternoon. The same thing happens. I call the next day. He says I should call him in about a week. Again.

I think that if there is no job for me at the AP, why didn't he tell me this weeks ago when we had lunch with Dad? I could have tried to get something else: I don't know what. What jobs are at night? I can't be a security guard; they want big men for that. Why did Mr. Swinton make me lose these weeks? In about ten days I am going to not have enough money for rent or food. Why didn't I think of this earlier, that this could happen? I never thought an old friend of Dad's would do something like this.

I start going to classes hoping this problem will go away.

Probably I will have to find some kind of nine-to-five secretarial job and drop out of school. I was so close to the path to my dream. If I withdraw from school, I will have to start repaying my college loan for freshman year. There will be nothing left to save for living expenses to go back to Fordham in the future. Fordham might not take me back because I would seem unreliable, having dropped out after freshman year. I would lose years from trying to be where I should be if I had had a more conventional family scene.

I go to the journalism class I wanted to take most: A beginning reporting class. I listen as best I can but I'm upset – it's hard to concentrate, but I do because there is something special about the professor.

It's an evening class in the basement of St. Robert's Hall. There are about ten of us, sitting at a long table. The air is stuffy. The professor asks us if it's hot. Some of us nod. He steps on a chair, then on a table and opens a window that's high in the wall. Just like that, it's cooler. He's decisive, takes action, then moves on. He has energy, speaks with confidence and calm. His large bright eyes are clear and alert for someone who has put in a full day as managing editor of the Associated Press.

I am stunned. Excuse me? Did God do this? Make my first reporting instructor be with the Associated Press, after these delays with Mr. Swinton? Such a coincidence.

We listen. We take notes. Everything he says is pertinent to how to become a good reporter. He says accuracy and fairness are paramount. He tells us of the necessity of objectivity and keeping preconceived notions and personal opinions out of news stories, out of news gathering and away from editors, co-workers. He says if the expressions on our faces reflect our opinions, this could cause an interviewee to react to them instead of our questions. Opinions should also not be in our voices, which should be modulated. Interviewees should know little or nothing about our backgrounds, for they could react to that and if asked, we should say *we* are asking the questions. Try to be part of the wall. We are eyes and ears. Keep yourself out of news stories, unless the story cannot be told any other way. He shows us quickly, by giving us the details of a traffic accident and by correcting our stories, how inaccurate we can be. Never trust the memory, he says. Always take notes. It's best that whoever you are interviewing sees that you are taking notes; even if they are uncomfortable about that, they will forget the notebook after a while. There is a difference between taking material on-the-record, off-the-record – which means you cannot use it but it could lead you to another source who could maybe go on-the-record – and then there is not-for-attribution, which means you can use the material but must protect your source and you should be willing to go to jail rather than reveal a source. Professionalism is imperative.

There is not a wasted minute in this course. I am impressed and made more at ease by the man's sincerity and devotion to helping us learn to get the truth, or the facts, which if incomplete are not necessarily the same as the truth. The room begins to clear of students. The professor puts his papers in his briefcase. Click, click. What do I have to lose, I wonder, by being as sincere with him as he has been with us? I expect nothing but maybe he could make a suggestion.

I ask him if I could speak to him please. He says I can walk him to his car. I am shy and embarrassed, but there is no time for that. I impart the necessary information about Dad, Mr. Swinton and that I don't know where my mother has been for two years. I tell him I want to be a reporter more than anything, that I love his class, but in a little more than a week, I shall be unable to pay my rent. I say I will have to drop out of school. I do not tell him I am frustrated and scared. I don't dare. This man is so professional, anything but the same demeanor would put him off. I ask if he has any suggestions, if he could do anything to help please. Maybe he could talk to Mr. Swinton. I apologize for having to tell him this – there is literally no one else to turn to.

Who else is there to turn to?

He says I should call him at the office the next day. I do. He then tells me to call Hal Buell, the head of photos.

Mr. Buell says I should come in for an interview. He tells me to see Miss Yvonna Mundell in the photo library. She will work out my hours with me.

I become an assistant researcher in the AP photo library three days a week. In the beginning I file photos and negatives and retrieve them for editors on the photo desk. After a couple months I am able to take requests from AP members, such as *Newsweek*, and newspapers around the country. I order negatives to be printed, sometimes cropped, and prints to be sent. I work nights and weekends. I am able to continue fulltime at Fordham. It's not easy. I live on Salems, Total Cereal and Tab, coffee, the inexpensive food in the AP cafeteria when I can splurge and an invention I call College Soup: cabbage, chicken, carrots, onion, salt and water. It lasts about a week.

Maybe I shall never have to wash dishes and toilets for other people again. I decide that someday, so that I can spend my time on my work, it will be most efficient to put the dirty dishes in the refrigerator, until the cleaning lady comes once a week.

Chapter Seventeen

No one at the AP or Fordham asks me about Dad or my mother like Rina did. I have a new life full of dignity – a relief. For the first time since I was at St. Mary's, I have a chance to be appreciated for what I do with my mind, for how hard I work and how polite I am. This brings with it quietude. I can concentrate.

Meanwhile, the professor who has helped me get this job, Lou Boccardi, is unwittingly teaching me to cope with how I am to think of Mom, Dad, God and Richard Nixon – most people, I suppose. Because when he says to keep your opinions to yourself, I, who always have to do more than asked, try not to have opinions. I dwell in suspended judgment whenever possible, which is an emotionally safe place, most of the time. As a student reporter and as a journalist, I absorb quotes, behavior, facts and regurgitate them on paper. I behave in a similar manner in my personal life when a potential friend presents herself or himself. I listen, I soak, appreciate, nod, act as if I care, if I care, but deep down I am noncommittal. I am waiting to see how they will behave toward me. I cannot help but live in a state of suspended involvement and, perhaps, suspended love. I have to. I do not mean to be insincere or untrue. I need time to assess whether or not someone is worth trusting. One needs to trust someone to accept affection, so I wait, dipping into people's lives like someone testing water temperature, reticent to swim in it. Like a journalist who borrows parts of life and rewrites them without living through them, I borrow people, their time and attention, their kindness – for a little while – rarely asking for it, never taking too much of it, giving back whenever I can, as much as I can, and depositing these pleasant exchanges in a bank of happy memories that I need.

I am the quiet small girl in the photo library working late at night. I move quickly through files, mindful of the speed competition with the other major wire service, United Press International. I examine negatives through a German lens to the sound of the 24-hour drumbeat of teletype machine keys, endearing, like the distant pounding of a hundred Irish dancing feet. Over the years I meet other AP staffers, journalists being a curious bunch. I feel special because at age 18, 19, or 20 I am usually the youngest one around, save perhaps for a messenger. I am grateful to the glamorous older women in AP Newsfeatures for saying hello in the hallway and for never being condescending to me for not being as accomplished as they are, yet. They are feminists; I muse over how liberated we are as AP Wonderwomen, playing softball in our navy shorts, called hot pants, and our powder-blue and shocking-pink team shirts against female teams at *Time* and *Newsweek* in Central Park, games attended by male news executives. I win the doubles match at an AP tennis tournament because I am paired with an executive who plays as well as Dad; my prize is a brand new Chris Evert tennis racquet. The New York bureau chief, gray-haired Doug Lovelace, listens patiently as I pester him for a reporting job. When I finally get onto the city desk, I'm grateful that the bearded assistant night city editor, Thomas Harris, who later becomes a successful novelist, crosses out unneeded words in the stories I write on my own time. At Fordham, an old priest, Julius Hejja, S.J., encourages me in tutorials, says he looks forward to reading my papers. I visit an elderly journalism professor, Ed Walsh, in his dusty, cluttered office near where Boccardi teaches; Mr. Walsh seems so alone, doesn't teach any more. I bring him coffee-to-go. We talk about journalism articles he gives me. The chairman of the communications department recommends me for, and I win, the Joseph Medill Patterson Scholarship from *The New York Daily News* – $1,000, a huge chunk of money then for tuition. Vicki Singer, next door to my apartment, sends over a plate of steak and rock Cornish hen on holidays when I am usually working to take advantage of the overtime pay.

One Sunday she comes over. I am sitting at the pre-war Royal typewriter I was able to buy for $25. She knows I have the Rejection Residue blues, which come round when I am missing people I love, wishing I knew where my father is or that Dad lived stateside. She says in her mellow English teacher voice: Dani, I never see you so peaceful as when you're writing. I look at her, eloquent, determined but gentle, with her beautiful hands and big eyes, wishing she were my mother, but I don't say that; it would be an imposition. She has too much to do: she has Richard, who's about 11, and Wendy, who's 16, and her husband, Izzy, and almost every night she's grading stacks of papers.

These – at the AP, at school, next door – are my Borrowed People. Like Steve Tarter, the Rosen family, Allan Berlowitz, Dad, his sister and his mother, they do not know how much they mean to me, how they alleviate the loneliness, lessen the fear of what might go wrong, like losing work when I am sick or not being able to make the rent because I do not get sick pay because I work part-time. And I do get sick, with colds, flu, bronchitis and hives, dozens of hives. One month I am not able to pay the rent on time and I am phoning the landlord, pleading for another week. I worry a great deal about succeeding, about learning as much as I can, about making good grades when I am sometimes exhausted from studying all night and then, behold, in the morning I can't concentrate on the Latin exam. But all the Borrowed People, even the sweet phone operators sitting in front of the bank of elevators at the AP, make me mostly cheerful because they give me faces to smile at. They are my imaginary audience. My pride keeps me from failing in their eyes. They are a blessing when six months go by with no word from Pat or Dad, or when he does write and says:

stiff upper lip and hang in there swinging.

Another time he writes:

The only one on whom you will be able to rely for life-long security is yourself. Develop in yourself that self-confidence that comes with knowing that you can – whenever necessary – hack it on your own.

There are great stretches when Dad's mother and Aunt Sue and I do not hear from him. His mother – recently nicknamed Tex by Pat because she's tall and plays bridge very well – and Aunt Sue and I share whatever news we get from abroad and from Evalyn, though they hear from her only about once a year.

When Dad becomes a U.S. consul in India between my sophomore and junior year, Tex quotes his letter:

Life here in Madras is very pleasant. The job is nice and the boss is an old friend. Our house is far and away the most commodious, almost palatial place I have ever been in. Three bedrooms, four baths, big living room, dining room. I am not sure how many servants. I think there are five, including a guard, two dogs and a cat.

At Christmas, he sends a card with a photo of the Madras Club, where he plays tennis in the afternoons. I wish I could visit him, but the cost would pay for so much tuition. I must not waver from becoming a reporter. The presence of one person while I work for this helps me more than any other.

Mr. Boccardi, who continues to teach me and others, does not know how much his attention and respect matter to me. I am lucky to have him for beginning and advanced reporting before he stops teaching and becomes executive editor, then president and chief executive officer of the AP. I am in awe of this journalism tower. I cringe as I read his sarcastic questions and comments in response to inferior or nonsensical language in my stories. Doesn't matter. I learn so much from him I don't care that I can't get a B in his class. Even after he stops teaching and I am able to put journalism questions to him and we part, I stop on the street and write down what he says. I see him each time I look up at the giant Isamu Noguchi frieze of *The News* – reporters on the phone, at the typewriter, writing in a notebook, photographers taking pictures – over the entrance to the AP Building in Rockefeller Plaza that is home to me. There I can ignore Thanksgiving, Christmas, my birthday, grateful that no matter what hour of the night it is, someone else is always there. I do not have to speak to them to take comfort in the camaraderie of people working with the knowledge that every minute could be a deadline at some newspaper we serve, and that what we do matters.

It is because of Boccardi that I know some Borrowed People secretly mean more to me than they should. One day, on the D train to the Bronx, I begin to write a letter to him and his wife, inviting them and their children to dinner at my apartment, which I can ill afford though it is something I would love to do. Then I look at what I have written. I think of how strange it might seem to his family, how inappropriate it is. I feel foolish. I tear it up. My gratitude to him must be confined to what I do with the training he has given me.

Chapter Eighteen

Unfortunately, the fact that some people meant more to me than they should was not always plain to me when I was 18, 19, 20. I thought in those years that because I had reached those ages some miraculous thing was supposed to happen and I would know how to handle everything when, in fact, I was – like many teens – handicapped. The reason, Vicki says, is that young people don't put thoughts in the perspective of a totality because they don't have a totality like someone 40 or 60 years old does. A year means much more to someone at 20 than it does to someone of 50. A romantic date, to someone who has never had one by age 20 is a big deal; several dates with one person or a potentially serious romantic encounter take on colossal proportions in the mind at that age, for some at any age. For me, after years of inconsistencies with Mom and Dad and without my father-father of unknown whereabouts, possible serious romantic encounters meant one thing: Run.

I am 20. I peel two beaus away from me like elbow-length prom gloves; I don't know why. One, a pre-med student, proposes and gives me a diamond ring. Then I think I have fallen in love with an accomplished young Harvard-educated lawyer; so we make love. Right away, I tell my fiancé about this. (I just don't know how to break up nicely.) Izzy, next door, says to me: I heard a man cry out last night. Then I'm overcome, to my surprise, by post-Romantic Residue, murky and melodramatic. I feel too guilty to answer the lawyer's phone calls for four months, which is how long he keeps calling. I increase my workload to crowd out the mess.

Then the news comes that Dad is not returning to the states after he retires as consul in Madras two years from now: he's going to travel around Europe in his steam-powered gypsy wagon.

Will he be trying to escape Mom for the rest of his life? Part of me says his decision probably has nothing to do with me, but it crosses my mind that Evalyn and I might not be very important to him.

And that I might not be important to my real father, wherever he is. Important to my mother? – the thought makes me speechless.

It feels as though nothing matters now.

Meantime Tex writes that Dad writes of his philosophy:

...getting all the pleasure [*out of life*] *and never looking back on what might have been, or if-fing as to how it could have been lived to draw out better returns. It was as it was because it could have been no other way. What happened was what had to happen because the decisions made were made inevitably. Fated to be.*

I'm crushed.

After reading my reaction to this, Tex writes that I've put myself under too much pressure. She thinks I'm depressed. Vicki says I should go to the counseling center at Fordham. There, I am assigned to see a psychiatrist who is doing his residency.

I look at him, in his dark suit sitting back in his chair with legs crossed at the knees, wondering how hard he had to work to get where he is now and what we have in common. He finds something – tennis. He plays frequently. I cannot afford lessons but on my days off during the summer, I practice on the back wall at school. He does not want to talk about boyfriends. The thought of telling him about my life, which is what he wants, seems ridiculous. I promise you he did not have a mother or a stepfather like mine and an invisible British intelligence father somewhere. It would take years of an hour-a-week to explain it. I need to feel better now, not in a few years. I cannot change the past, Mom, Dad, how they are, how I love them; how I would love to have just one person who is there for me without my being afraid of rejection. I try to explain. He says nothing in response. Meanwhile, I have massive piles of work to do, finals to take, papers to write. I can't concentrate.

All feels hopeless. I feel overwhelmed. Why? I won the Joseph Medill Patterson Scholarship. I'm getting through college on my own. But none of my parents wants to share this with me and it's embarrassing; my boyfriend situation is zero; my stability is wobbly, to say the least; I think it's all my fault and I feel like I'm from another dimension, so bizarre does my past seem now as I recount it.

I can see it in the shrink's eyes: if she's not nuts, her history has to have made her so. I'm disgusted. I decide to illustrate how this meeting is probably a waste of time. I tell him what Mom told me when I was little, that when her father shot an elephant, the natives used to drink its blood, for strength. I don't know what kind of natives there were in the jungles of North Vietnam, but I tell him I have often wondered the following: (because I have) What do you do with a dead elephant, besides drink its blood and cut off its feet for wastebaskets? Really. When I say this, the squint in his eyes says I should probably be a mental patient for a long time.

The problem is that talking about my past is making me feel worse. What are we doing here? Why not focus on how great life is supposed to be? (Then how would this guy make a living?) I know I need attention, Fordham is paying him to do that; so should I dwell on depressing subjects, so I can be worthy of his time? From time to time he asks a question, directing my mostly monologue away from anything positive. I want to cry. I'm crying. He says, Our time is up now. A mental guillotine.

He says I need to take something called Elavil, an antidepressant.

Back at the apartment, I take the Elavil for one day, two days. More than a week later, on a Saturday, late afternoon, I decide I do not feel less sad. My mouth feels like it's covered with chalk. Food is last on my mind. I sleep, feel tired when I wake. Does the shrink really think a pill is going to make me feel better? Dad is never coming back. I can't write. I try to study and realize repeatedly that I'm rereading sentences three or four times. I have called my professors and said that I am ill and must request an incomplete in all four courses. I go to work at the AP, come back to the apartment, look out the window and smoke Salems. There is little or no traffic on my street; little to see but dingy brick walls and curtains over windows. I have no TV or record player to help change my mood, to take me away from the truth of my solitude. The radio makes me nervous. Murray the K with his excited happiness is exhausting.

Vicki says, you don't look well, Dani. Maybe Iz and I shouldn't go to the theatre tonight. I say, No. Don't be silly. I'm fine. Wendy, she says, will be home before us. I'm fine. The door closes. I face the aloneness again, the kindnesses of the Borrowed People that mean so much to me when I am actually on the periphery of their lives.

I think I'm pathetic, an embarrassment to myself. I am really down the well with no walls now. What if I call the psychiatrist, give him another chance, maybe he will know what to do. He said I could call, leave a message with his service. He's not borrowed. He's there. Fordham has kindly provided him to me. I have a right to call him without owing anybody anything. Doctors take a Hippocratic Oath don't they? So I call him. The service has him call me. I tell him the pills aren't working.

He says he's going to play tennis. He sounds annoyed. He says: Is this an emergency? Can it wait until Monday?

Sure. Monday. Fine. How should I know whether or not this is an emergency? I want to kill myself. I'm trying to think of the best most convenient way to not wake up in the morning without causing a bloody mess for anyone.

I do not want to wake up feeling this way again. That beats whether or not it matters to anyone else, including the shrink. You think I'm going to wait until Monday? Oh, please.

Ten o'clock, he says.

Fine. Thank you very much.

I spill the Elavil onto the kitchen table and count them. Seventeen. Who would notice if I leave?

I swallow the pills two at a time until I get to the last one. My eyes blur. I recall the sight I have imagined of barefoot children playing on the cobblestone streets of little Irish towns, an image from a poem we had to memorize at St. Mary's. The last lines are:

And I have gone upon my way
Sorrowful.

I blow my nose and lie down. Why, if I'm so sad about leaving, am I doing this? Too late. Never mind.

Then I am up and vomiting. It feels like my stomach is going to come up my throat. I do not recommend this. I vomit until green stuff is in the toilet.

This is a mistake.

I keep vomiting even though there's nothing to vomit. I move slowly down the hall from the bathroom, my shoulder against the wall guiding me to the front door. I unlock it. I leave it ajar. Wendy, I hope.

I can't be sick like this before I die. This is a mess. I take it back, God. I'm sorry. And then, Wendy is saying: Dani, what's the matter with you?

Pills I took.

What pills?

This time there's an ambulance. I am swaying by the driver's window, trying to pay him cab fare. Because I don't want to owe anybody anything. Really, I say, I can pay my way.

At the hospital they pump my stomach. I tell them there's nothing in it. They still pump my stomach. It's gross, with a tube down your throat. I'm amazed that I can breathe while they do this.

A doctor asks me some questions. I say something about glass houses. He seems satisfied by my answers, whatever they are. I know he knows I'm not crazy, or else he wouldn't be letting me go home. Vicki and Izzy take me home. In the morning Vicki says, Get dressed. I have to take you to the psychiatrist.

The shrink is really annoyed with me now. They called him in the middle of the night. I made him work on a Sunday morning.

Maybe there are some other pills that might make me feel worth his time.

Chapter Nineteen

Am sorry I put Wendy through this ordeal. Also Vicki and Iz. How stupid can you get when you're young, feel isolated and want someone to care about you without fearing they may hurt you? I figured out that that someone was not going to be someone who's paid to do it or in whose best interest it is for you not to get cheerful and peaceful. So I peeled the shrink out of my life, too. In the meantime, thank God, they didn't know about this event at the AP or at Fordham.

I wouldn't have wanted anyone to think I was unstable.

At Fordham I was afraid they would take the Patterson scholarship away. At the AP, I was afraid I might get fired if the attempt had been known, or at least, never be promoted to the city desk.

Vicki said that one day I would marry a lovely man and that he would have parents who would love me, too. I didn't believe her, though I had vague hope. I went back to work, having decided that suicide is just too much trouble. I finished my four incomplete courses, grateful for my new 3.5 average. I made it to the city desk in the New York bureau, at first one day a week, then more frequently. And I kept borrowing people.

June, 1972: Dad says that he hasn't written in a while because he spends his days being the consul in Madras and his nights preparing for retirement. He's still building the steam engine that's going to run his gypsy wagon. The boiler is being built in Bombay. Then, he writes:

eye will tootle off on the truck bed to Srinagar up in Kashmir...Because that's where they have all the teak that will go into the construction of the cabin of the wagon. It's gonna be twenty seven feet long by seven feet high by seven feet wide...Now in Srinagar they build house boats so eye don't see why they can't build gypsy wagons up there too. When the wagon is finished eye will mount it on the truck bed and off through the Kyber Pass eye'll go. Eye'll traipse back to Europe the way eye came gathering things like sheep hangings for the wagon's walls in Afghanistan, a Persian rug in Iran, maybe some leather upholstery in Turkey...

There are tuition and rent increases, though there is sometimes no hot water. I sell the fur coat Mom gave me to a furrier for $25 – I know I was cheated. But it put College Soup, Total and milk in the refrigerator until the next paycheck. And some Salems. I tell Dad about it. He sends $40 for my birthday and Christmas; I use part of this to buy Grandma and Aunt Sue a Chagall book, because am too proud to be empty-handed at Christmas. I do not tell Dad or Tex or Sue about the Elavil. Why should I? What could they do from such a distance? Other matters would prove to upset them enough.

It's spring. Only a few weeks left of senior year. Many papers to write, final exams to take. For several months I have been dating someone eleven years my senior. His steady personality and age are tranquilizing. I think, being 21, he is the love of my life. He becomes the fiancé who takes me out to dinner once a week, and to the movies, brings me roses and writes poems to me. I am accepted at the Graduate School of Journalism at Columbia University and awarded a scholarship that is about half the tuition. I get my dream job as a reporter on the city desk of the New York bureau full-time for the coming summer. Then I receive letters that make me afraid to answer the phone, fearful that something will interfere with my graduation.

The first is from my mother's friend, a French-speaking Hungarian dressmaker in Manhattan. She writes that my mother is ill in Boston, that she had an operation that left a 16-inch scar on her chest and is asking for her children. She writes that my mother is still very sick. She writes: *Hurry, Danielle, because my own sister in Budapest died only one year after such an operation.*

Hurry. The court case, the wait at her empty apartment, the fear of being on the street, the fear of the black hole.

I send her a get-well card. She phones and writes to Tex, who is 83 and has heart problems. She tells Tex that while she was having bridgework on her teeth, a wax mold accidentally went down her throat and lodged in a bronchial tube, which became infected. She says she is in pain and needs money, that Jim Flood owes her a lot of money and should wire it to her. She asks Tex about me and the "other ones," meaning Ev and Pat.

Dad writes saying he has sent $500 to the Dragon Lady though he was tempted to turn the money over to me in order to force her to ask me for it after what she had done to me. He surmises that I would not want to deal with such an encounter.

I don't have time for this. I have to study for the final exams of my senior year of college.

I am reading the same paragraphs repeatedly as I try to concentrate. I can't sleep. I can't eat. I think of her in pain and possibly destitute. Alone. My mother, who hates me. What will happen if we speak? Maybe we can come to some mutual peace. Am desperate for peace.

I call. She tells me she sent The Baby to boarding school in England and to her brothers in France during vacations. She says she is so sick. (She does not sound sick, but I don't know.) She says at least her first baby called her. She thanks me a dozen times for calling. She is pleased to know that I studied hard even with "difficulties."

I am quiet after I get off the phone. I tell Tex about this. She warns that I can only tolerate a limited involvement with my mother.

I don't listen to her. I feel more in control of life than I did when I last knew her. I'm older. College is almost behind me. I have a place to live, a job. Perhaps we can communicate by letter once a month, with the past behind us.

Here come two letters, two days in a row. She says she misses me so much:

No one knows how to take care of me the way you do.

The second letter says she is excited about my fiancé and wants to know about him and the wedding. She encloses a self-addressed aerogramme, asking me to write back to her as quickly as possible. I have exams, many papers to write and demands at my AP job. She wants me to run errands in New York. She wants me to call Blue Cross Blue Shield for her. She wants me to call an old friend of hers to ask him for money (not possible). My grades crash.

I write to her infrequently and carry on. Somehow, no notice is taken by Columbia of my final grades as an undergraduate. At the end of the summer I am married in a ceremony in Bermuda so small, the minister's wife is a witness. I borrow a wedding gown. There are no guests. No one sees there is no father to give me away.

I begin the grueling reporting-writing regime in grad school. One Friday night in mid-October, my mother calls from Montreal to say she's going to be at our Brooklyn apartment at 3 a.m. She does arrive then. All weekend she talks. I can't work. She wants to know why I didn't tell her *Jeem Flad* has been in India all this time, why I went to court for him and where he is in India. I refuse to answer. A few years later in Manhattan she comes to my apartment on short notice laughing and smiling, then stabs me verbally again about keeping Dad's whereabouts from her. She thrives on mental fireworks that start with a whisper, or a sizzle, and end up destroying all hope of a potentially loving relationship, leaving feelings strewn about and smoking.

I get my master's degree and for the better part of the next ten years I try but eventually mistrust anyone who purports to love me. My husband becomes an ex-husband. I take a lover, who becomes an ex-lover. Dad slips into the country to see his mother and pursue his steam engine plans. I am saddened because Dad phones only once while he is in the country. He is in Pittsburgh, Chicago, Pittsburgh, then Redwood City, before I learn that he has been stateside for about seven months.

From California, he writes to me and my soon-to-be ex-husband.

I have received [from Tex] the message loud and clear: you are unhappy with me, Danielle, that I have not kept in touch during my stay here in the United States. But it came as an unsettling surprise… I'm a rather solitary person, a "loner." I get along alone just fine and I tend to forget that not everyone does, that most people and no doubt you are one, need the warmth that comes of frequent and multiple contacts with the few friends they think and hope they have in this cold and hostile world. Well, be assured, dear: I am your friend, I think of you often and I wish you the very best. And the best thing…that a parent can wish for a child is that that child should grow up to be strongly independent. Of all three of the kids you always seemed best able…to stand on your own feet and make your way alone. You asked for help seldom…I simply have never felt any urgent need to "keep in touch" with any members of my family. If any should call on me for help, I shall try to help, but I will try never to call on them. To the extent that you are indebted to anyone you have in that measure lost your independence. I am not excusing myself in saying all this. I don't need to. I think there are many long-range merits in maintaining one's identity and separation and uniqueness in this increasingly homogenized world and in nurturing those qualities in one's children…

Easy does it! I'll promise you this: any time either of you care to write, I'll give you an address to write to and I'll give you a prompt reply; any time either of you or both of you care to visit with me wherever I am you'll be as welcome as I can afford to make you and when I'm in your neighborhood I hope you'll make me welcome to call on you.

I said I'll give you a mailing address. At the moment I don't have one, but I should have within a week. It'll be good until the fourth of October when I set sail for Taiwan, Hong Kong, Singapore and Madras aboard the good ship Taft from Seattle. So for now and until next week. Salud, amor y pesatas. Jim.

Taiwan. Hong Kong. Singapore. Madras. Why do these words resound like strokes against a gong? Or the toll of a sad old grandfather clock? I haven't seen Dad in six years and he's been here in the states, hiding from Mom. Now he's gone again.

After Madras, he travels in Europe again, hangs around for a while in Afghanistan. Eventually he settles in the Algarve, the southern belt of Portugal.

I get over the disappointment. Work, sleep and time help to organize files in the mind. The sun goes down for a thousand nights, almost two, and rises. I brush my teeth. Comb my hair. I accept the way Dad is, the way Mom is. There's no choice.

I burrow into work. I live through other people's stories that take me away from my past and whatever weighs heavily in the present. I see no harm in it. I do beat work for Westchester-Rockland newspapers, ending up as the city hall reporter in New Rochelle. I freelance for the *New York News Sunday Magazine* and five sections of *The New York Times*. It's fulfilling work.

But there is still something missing. After I divorce my husband, I think perhaps what's still bothering me has to do with New York. So I go work for *The* (Baltimore) *Evening Sun*, then two Florida newspapers. I quit jobs without having another to go to over matters of principle. (The insertion of inaccuracies or opinion by editors into my copy ignites me.) I become disillusioned with journalism. I go fishing on nine boats, in search of real life, where for the first time in many years I learn that people do behave differently toward you when you're not going to write about them. It's nice. I log the 365 days of notarized time on the water and get my captain's license from the U.S. Coast Guard. I learn that some people do like me. I trust an old fishing boat captain and stay at his deathbed to the end. Our friendship is respectful, we are a student of the sea and a mentor. But always, love is suspended. I'm skittish as a dolphin.

How many times have I thought of him, my real father, as I looked across the sea toward England while fishing at the stern of a boat with its soothing rock? How many ocean waves are there? How many times have I said to myself, be tough, there are orphans out there who never know their parents. Maybe he's dead. Saigon was a long time ago. But I do not know that he is dead; it's not the same as being an orphan, to know that maybe your father is living somewhere; it gnaws on you.

My mother has breast cancer. In the midst of the treatments I go to see her. Despite all between us, I want to stay for a while and care for her but I fear I can't get work at Montreal newspapers unless I am also fluent in French, which I am not. How can I support myself while caring for her? She lives by herself in a three-bedroom house in suburban Montreal. Big sunken living room, big studio. There is a life-sized painting of three of her family's Vietnamese servants, wearing loose black pants and white Mao jackets, in the kitchen. She says she painted them because she misses them, especially Bep, the cook. The painting she is working on is called Rock Festival; eight-by-fifteen feet; young people with long hair standing, sitting, laying in the grass, smoking; the dominant figure is a standing teenage boy; his back is to the viewer; he looks over his shoulder, his jeans are pulled down revealing a cheek of his buttocks; he smirks. Who cares what *zay sink*, Dani? she says. And when I leave she bids me: laugh at *zee* pain.

I turn, startled, and look at the little smile on her face.

What pain? I ask.

She repeats, with a little smile: laugh at *zee* pain.

Eventually she recuperates from the cancer.

I meet Jim Morin through friends at *The Miami Herald* where he is the editorial cartoonist. We date. I tell him about my mother's dancing – I am ashamed of it. He turns his back to me, bends over and shakes his derriere. I laugh. He laughs. I tell him everything. We fall in love. Later I learn he was impressed by my giving away all of my belongings except books and files when I went fishing. At the time it seemed a rational thing to do because the more you have, the more you have to take care of and I wanted to be completely free – and I was. But now he is telling me the sun from fishing is making my skin like leather. He reads my published stories and tells me I must return to life on land, and to writing. In 1981, we marry. This time I get brave about commitment and have a wedding with three-dozen friends and his family. The wedding is in Coconut Grove where we live. Allan Berlowitz, a platonic friend, a lawyer, who I have known since Atlantic Beach, comes from New York and gives me away. I buy a ticket for my mother fearful of having no family there while many in-laws-to-be are coming from Massachusetts. She brings The Baby to the wedding. At the reception, as soon as I sit down, my mother smiles and with my in-laws listening, says: So you knew *zat Jeem Flad* has been living in Portugal and you wouldn't tell me; he owes me so much *moan-nay*, you know.

Chapter Twenty

It is 1983. James and I are living in a one-bedroom apartment dominated by books and music in Coconut Grove. I'm working on a novel. James is still drawing daily political cartoons for *The Miami Herald*. I make dinner. Sometimes we bring our plates down to the brick courtyard where we eat amongst palms, tropical plants. In the morning I swim. In the evening I watch as he floats in the pool; he gazes into the distance; I know he is creating. You need to daydream a lot to create. It rests and replenishes the mind. Also, you need a peaceful lifestyle, which we have, in general; the exception is my occasional surrender to the fear that I am not worth loving. I throw occasional you-don't-love-me fits, but he rides out the squalls; storms do pass.

On weekends we browse antique and book stores. We get the Sunday newspapers, go out to brunch and read. Sometimes his parents visit and take us out to lunch.

They have been married to each other for more than thirty years and to no one else. My father-in-law is a lawyer. My mother-in-law is a mother and wife. They are dignified, kind and absolutely loyal to each other, James and his two brothers, also lawyers. My in-laws love sharing life with their sons and their families – during good as well as difficult times. They tend to minimize problems so that little or nothing is a big deal; I hear this is typical of New Englanders. Laughing and relaxing is the desired focus when we are together. They did not stop being parents when their sons arrived at an arbitrary age. They are parents for life – a gradual revelation over the years that I witness with pleasure, relief and increasing curiosity over their consistency in giving. It is obvious that James' own consistency and stability comes from the environment created by these parents. And I need it.

I need his strength when my mother calls and says the cancer has returned and is now in her liver and in her bones though I do not know whether or not to believe her.

I need it when she says she lied to me about John Orr/Van David 19 years ago; I cannot move or think when I hear this.

She uses the stage whisper again, which worries me because it always comes with life-quaking news.

Your real father, she says, is named Farquarson. A Swedish businessman in Saigon, named Farquarson.

By now I have been a newspaper reporter for some dozen years. I automatically use an interviewing device: ask the same question again later in the conversation to see if the answer is the same. I ask her to spell his name. She says it's F-a-r-q-u-a-r-s-o-n. Later, when I ask her to spell it again, it's F-a-r-q-h-u-a-r-s-o-n. Then I ask her what his first name is. She says, I don't know.

Now I know she's lying.

I ask her where he is. She says she doesn't know. Oh, please. I have witnessed her tracking a man down – Dad. She would search for years all over the world.

Why would she lie again like this? She says that if I come to Montreal she will tell me the story. Am furious over her attempt to use this ploy to manipulate me into going to her to commiserate over her cancer, if it has come back, if it has spread. Another your-father-is name, misspelled. Too flimsy to be true. I have the overwhelming feeling that she is trying to send me in a direction that would never lead to my father, if he is alive. I suspect there must be something else, besides her not having been married to him, that she doesn't want me to know. Something – that happened in Saigon. I can't believe that whatever she is hiding is more important than telling me who my real father is – but maybe it is to her. Then I wonder if she has hated me for being born. All these years, with my reporting skills, I had been looking for someone, John Orr/Van David, who probably never existed.

By now I know that if you question Dad, you will get what he wants you to know in carefully chosen words. How I wish I could talk to him – always far away. In Portugal he sleeps in his villa in a windowless vault with butchers' meat locker-type doors, one near the foot of his bed, the other by the head. The doors open only from the inside. That is, there are no handles on the outside of the doors, which are about six inches thick. So no one can get to him there unless he wants them to. He has no address, only a post office box. The way to his villa involves turns onto nameless dirt roads. It would take such a voyage to get to him. There is no other way to reach him but to write.

We have been able to talk about much that fathers and daughters usually don't talk about. But I have never been able to talk to him about my biological father, so fearful have I been to lose Dad as a father completely. Now since his letter saying he is happy as a loner – and basically that he wants to be left alone – I feel I have nothing to lose.

I say: Who the hell is John Orr? And who the hell is Farquarson? I have never written to him or spoken to him like this before. I shouldn't be surprised by his response, though I am, for he reveals that he knew much more about how I came to be than I had ever dreamed. I realize that Dad is too smart to marry just anybody with just anybody's child.

Dad never answers my questions per se. He sends puzzle pieces. He writes that Mom as a young girl in Saigon

met and took up with the British Air Attaché, a wounded veteran of the Burma campaign named Mike Wilton. Wilton installed her with friends at the Cotab House (British American Tobacco Co.). Wilton, though married, took Suzy off on a holiday to Hong Kong and there she met some guy she described to me as a British Intelligence type who had been in a bad motorcycle accident and had burned both legs...and that she says is the man who is your father. Wilton and Suzy returned to Saigon, Wilton's wife made a big scene at the British Embassy, then returned to England to get a divorce.

Suzy found herself pregnant and decided to go home to France…[Then] Back to Indochina she came…Eventually I arranged it so that we got married and I was able to put my name on the birth registry at the time of your birth...

End of page end of a rather gloomy letter. To you and James, all the best. Take care of yourselves and let's all wish well to the Dragon Lady. She was once a charming and lovable person. Love, dad

I have to find out who my father is now. I have had it with my mother's lies. Much of this report had to have come from my mother. What is true and what is not?

Her doctor tells me on the phone that she is going to die. Part of me – the secret of me – could die with her. This is my last chance to find my father, then go to her and ask: Why, why did you do this? I have to, finally, know him, see how I am like or unlike him, for it is a key to understanding me. I'm fed up with being a walking mystery. I'm tired of living mystery.

I must not assume Mike Wilton is my father. I cannot afford to make mistakes if I begin this quest. I'm emotionally frayed and afraid. I'm livid over Mom's casual attitude about who my father is; she's says I'm going to have blonde children; how can it not occur to her that I might want or need something else from him? I cannot ask her now about Mike Wilton because I believe she will again lie. I have to find my real father without her. I ask James: What if I find my father and he doesn't want me? This is the biggest fear. James says: Find him.

Is this why I became a reporter?

I reread Dad's letter about Mike Wilton many times. Then I compose a note, print it three times, put each copy into an envelope and seal each of them. The note reads:

August 5, 1983
Mr. Michael Wilton
Dear Sir:

I realize this may be a rather strange letter to receive, but I assure you it is about a matter of the utmost importance.

If you were wounded in the Burma campaign while serving Britain and if you were in 1951 an Air Attaché with the British Embassy in Saigon, I would be extremely grateful if you would call me, collect, at area code 305...I am sometimes away from the phone between 9 a.m. and 2 p.m. our time. My husband and I will be in Maine between Sept. 24 and October 15 at area code 207...Otherwise, please write and let me know how I may communicate with you confidentially.

Thank you kindly.

Danielle Morin

(I do not use the name, Flood, in case he knows Dad married Mom and Mr. Wilton knows I am his daughter and wants nothing to do with me. I need the chance to ask him the questions I must ask without him knowing, yet, that I am Jim Flood's stepdaughter. So I approach him as Danielle Morin.)

I write: to the British Department of Health and Social Services, in case he is my father, is on public assistance and needs help; then to the government's Personnel Services Department; and then to the British Army, since I'm too excited to make the connection between an Air Attaché and the Royal Air Force. I enclose notes in the envelopes to Wilton and money orders for postage to forward them to him. I request return receipts.

Then I go into emotional limbo. I smoke cigarettes and sit staring at the phone while listening repeatedly to a two-hour tape of "Tubular Bells" that James makes for me on his reel-to-reel. It's question-mark music, mysterious, not sad, not happy, tense, a spiral of sounds that help me to think of nothing but the fact that its composer understood there are times in life like this.

I can't read. I can't sleep. It's a chore to eat. I can't write stories for magazines. I can't jog in the park. I watch the news with James and can't remember it. I burn dinners.

Two weeks later I get a letter from the Ministry of Defence saying my letter has been forwarded to the Royal Air Force. A week after that, the phone rings at 6 a.m.

I fly at it, answering before the second ring. An operator asks if I will accept a collect call.

His voice is mellow, not a baritone, not high pitched and his heavy British accent does not reflect regional characteristics. It is genteel, I think.

Is this Mrs. Morin?

Yes, it is.

This is Mike Wilton.

Thank you very much for calling. I really appreciate it. Thank you very much.

I received your letter from the Ministry of Defence. What is it that you want?

I'm hoping you can help me with something, please. I need some information.

Veddy well, I'll try.

I was born in Saigon, in 1951. You were the Air Attaché in Saigon at the time, were you not?

Yes.

My mother was Suzanne Jullien. Did you know her?

Suzy? Yes, I knew Suzy.

Yes, well, I, I'm trying to find my father, you see. The problem is that she doesn't always tell the truth. So it's been difficult. Would you please try and help me find my father?

I would be happy to try and help you find your father.

Thank you very much. Thank you so much. Please may I write to you? May I have your address?

It's 29 Mariot Court, Wallingford, Oxon.

Is Mariot with one or two t's?

One t.

Oxon?

Oxfordshire.

Oh yes, of course, Oxfordshire. It would be wonderful to meet you. I would love to take you to dinner, or lunch. I could come there, or if you would like, we would love to have you here.

I can't travel. I haven't been able to travel for years. I have no legs.

That, I say automatically, doesn't make any difference to me.

And then I realize, and I know he knows, that between the lines I am saying it doesn't make any difference to me that he has no legs if he is my father.

When did this happen? I ask.

In a crash, he says, in a monotone. In the war, in a monotone.

Which war?

He says, raising his voice a bit: The last war.

I know I cannot go further because there is trauma. I can hear it, feel it. I don't want him to relive it.

Are you all right, Sir?

Yes.

May I ask, please, how old you are?

He says: I'm sixty-six! I cannot tell if this is indignation in his voice or amazement mixed with humor.

I say: Well, I'm almost 32!

I want to say: what do you think this is like for me? or It's not my fault that it took so long to find you, but I don't. I muse over the vision of him in my head: a sixty-six year-old-man in a wheelchair with an accent right out of a Veddy-Veddy movie is considering that he may learn he has a daughter this late in life, if he doesn't know already.

I shall write to you, Sir. Thank you very much for calling.

Goodbye.

Goodbye. Thank you very much. Sir.

Right away I call directory assistance in England and ask for his phone number because the address is not enough of a connection for me. I'm afraid he might slip out of my life, disappear as surely as he has come into it, as if he were a dream you can't remember. I write down the number, amazed that he is listed, this possible father.

Then I feel I have to call him. Being 66, I worry about the stress of remembering the crash. He might be alone. And I need to know that if I phone him at this number, that it will work, that it is not an old phone number in the directory, or that it has been suddenly disconnected; that truly I shall hear his voice again.

Mr. Wilton?

Yes.

This is Danielle Morin.

Yes?

I just, I want to say, I hope I haven't upset you.

No.

Thank you very much. Have a lovely day, please.

Thank you. Goodbye.

Goodbye. Thank you.

I remember another man with no legs. He sat on a wood platform with wheels selling pencils outside Bloomingdales during my high school years. It was the first time I had ever seen an amputee. I was horrified for him that he had to continue making his way in the world selling pencils, accepting as one could see, more money than the pencils cost sometimes. No matter how he lost his legs, I felt it uncivilized that he had to carry on like that, alone, in the cold, some days protected from the rain and snow only by the Bloomingdale's canopy. And so when I receive a letter from the British Department of Health and Social Security saying there is no trace of Mr. Wilton in their records, suggesting I contact the Consular Department of the Foreign and Commonwealth Office, I am grateful that Mr. Wilton does not have to survive as that man did.

I daydream that if he is my father, perhaps one day I can fly to dear England, the land of Veddy-Veddy, where the demeanor in the movies is generally orderly and polite, and throw him over my back and take him for visits to beautiful places like Land's End. I wish I could carry him with his arms wrapped around my neck for long walks by the sea, so he can smell the fresh briny air and feel the softness of the breeze through his hair. Or perhaps I could put him in a sleigh behind a horse that I would be riding and take him through the sand like that. But then I remind myself that I do not know if he is my father and that I do not want, I really do not want, a maybe father or a pretend father. No more borrowed people. I want familiarity with my real father, a closeness and to be able to speak my mind to him, which is my right. For now I cannot have this. I can only write.

There is no other way to get across what I must say to Mr. Wilton. And I shall not knock on his door uninvited. Not possible.

I receive a note from the Ministry of Defence saying that my communication has been "duly forwarded" to Squadron Leader Michael Stanley James Wilton. I wonder what this title means. It sounds important. How many planes are there in a British squadron?

The RAF tells me the rank is equivalent to a major in the U.S. Air Force.

In a letter I outline for Mr. Wilton what has happened with Mom, Dad, Ev, Pat, Michael Lambton and The Baby, a bit about babysitting for a living and working my way through college at the AP, about Columbia School of Journalism, about becoming a reporter, getting my captain's license and James. I tell him of working on two novels at the moment. Am too proud, ashamed, to tell him of my suicide attempts, of Mom's dancing, of my cleaning houses to survive. I quote Dad's letter and ask him to comment on its accuracy. I explain that I had to go to Dad asking for information because my mother has given me three different names for my natural father. I write to Mr. Wilton:

Perhaps I shall never know who he is. Perhaps you are my natural father. Perhaps you know who is.

I would simply like to know him, if possible...

I am very sorry to put all this heavy information to you. I realize it is a lot to take, especially all at one time. I feel so plagued with curiosity about who my father is. And, now, I feel helpless, because if you are not my father and you don't know who is, I don't know where else to look. It is like hauling miles of anchor line and then finding out that you lost your anchor probably before you began.

Thank you so very much for considering all of this. I wish you the best of health. I look forward to hearing from you. Sincerely, Danielle Morin

I enclose about two dozen photographs of myself over the years: as a baby, in college, when I married James, and as a 30-year-old. I send a couple of photos of James, one dressed up as a groom with a white carnation boutonniere so he can see we are not from *dans la rue* (on the street).

I wait. I think. I stare at the soft gold wall-to-wall carpet in the apartment. I count days trying to guess when Mr. Wilton will get the photos.

Then I remember the photograph of, supposedly, John Orr, that my mother had given me. I think: a woman might lie to a child about her father's name, if she didn't want her to find him. But a mother really would not dare to give a child a photo of a man and say this is her father when he is not. That would be inhuman and an insult to a child's intelligence. Perhaps this torn photo is the key. I'm excited by the idea. Perhaps this photo is of Mr. Wilton.

I ring him up again, happy, excited. Also, it's an excuse to talk to him again.

He answers the phone before the second ring with his mellow hello.

I'm glad to hear his voice again. Mr. Wilton? I say. Yes? It's Danielle Morin. Yes. How are you? Very well, Thank you. And you, Sir? Veddy well, Thank you. I was wondering if you received my letter and the photographs. Yes, I did, I wrote you a letter. Oh, Thank you very much. Thank you so much. I' m looking forward to it. So you saw the photographs. Yes.

May I ask, please, do you think I look like you or someone else you knew from Saigon?

I think you look like your mother.

The plunging feeling in my chest. I say: I don't think I look like my mother. I do not look like my mother. I am my father's daughter. My mother hated me all these years.

I feel like crying. I hold on. He is quiet.

He says: I would be glad to accept you as my daughter.

I draw in breath. So simple, like that, he says this. It's a shock. But then I realize he is not saying he is my father or that I am his daughter, though he has seen the photographs. He is simply saying he would be glad to accept me as his daughter. I can't, I can't have this. I need to know. I cannot be a Borrowed Daughter. I need reality.

You're very kind, Sir, I say. It's very lovely of you. But I need to know for sure. Look, Sir, I think I have a possible clue.

What is it? he says.

Well, first, could you please tell me if you have a strong heart? Do you have heart problems?

No, he says, my heart is fine. There is a hint of amusement in his tone.

It may be that I have something that would indicate that you are my father. I have a photograph of a man that my mother said was my father but she said his name was John Orr. I think if you are this man in the photograph, that you may be my father. May I ask you some personal questions please?

Yes.

How tall are you, were you?

I was five-eleven then.

When?

In Saigon.

You mean you had legs when you knew my mother?

Yes, yes. He sounds annoyed, like I'm a dummy.

Because this man in the photo is wearing rather loose pants and I was thinking that maybe it's you with prosthetic legs.

My legs were cut too high for prosthesis.

Oh.

What kind of build do you have?

A bit stocky in the torso.

And hair?

Brown.

Eyes.

Hazel.

I am quiet for a moment. Then I say: The man in this photo is blonde and very slender. And then after a brief hesitation my patience tumbles.

I say: This is becoming so much, so stressful, the not knowing. Mr. Wilton, do you have any photographs of yourself around, please? Please could you send me one or some? I would be happy to return them. It's just, you see, my husband is an artist. I'm afraid all this upheaval is affecting his work, too.

He says: I shall send you a photograph. I shall do it.

Oh, thank you, thank you so much. Have a lovely day.

Thank you. Goodbye.

I feel close to the answer. Am anxious. But I worry. Even if he sends me his photo, I may not be able to tell if he is the same man as the one in the photo my mother gave me. From working in the AP photo library, I saw that people look different over the years. The lighting in black and white photos and ten, twenty pounds in body weight make a big difference. So I send the photo of "John Orr" to Mr. Wilton. Surely he will know if he is the man in that photo.

I ask him to call me collect when he gets it. I wait. I think. I stare at the carpeting. I listen to Beethoven's Emperor Concerto, No. 5 in E-flat major, the *adagio un poco mosso.* It is arms-around-you music. I suppose it's pining music, but it is also music to alleviate fear, to remember God by, because if your father doesn't love you, at least He does.

I get a letter from Mr. Wilton obviously written before he gets the torn photo. He writes as I do in a combination of distinctive tiny script and print on blue-gray paper with a fountain pen and navy ink. Each stroke is slightly crooked, as if made by a quivering hand.

29 Mariot Court
Wallingford
Oxon
5/9/83

Dear Danielle Morin -

Thank you for your letter of 26th August and photos –

As I told you I cannot prove or disprove anything but would like to help you if I can. I do not remember taking Suzy to Hong Kong. It's most unlikely as a) I traveled by RAF plane and (b) I always stayed with my cousin who was a colonel in the British Army there -

Two things about Flood's report -

Suzy was installed in my official residence in Saigon as "housekeeper" She only went to Cotab house when my replacement had arrived – I do not know of John Orr or Farquason – I last saw Suzy at Pont St. Esprit in 1951 or early 1952. She was then pregnant – and wanted money – saying I was the father – the dates coincide but I was not satisfied – she was rather promiscuous -

I do not think anything would be served or even help if you came to the UK – We could not put you up as we only have a one-bedroom flat. My wife is not well and has not been for some time – I think you would cause her embarrassment. If you came with your husband it would be different -

I will write again if I can think of anything else.

Do you wish for the photos back?

Please excuse writing – another accident – wartime which smashed my arm.

Yours sincerely,
Mike Wilton

Right away I call him. How dare he say such a thing. I'm furious.

Mr. Wilton? This is Danielle Morin. I have received your letter. I have to tell you something.

What is it?

My mother may have been promiscuous but she was not unfaithful. Is that clear?

Yes.

I never saw her behave in a promiscuous manner. She was not promiscuous when she was with Jim Flood or anyone she was involved with. She had a couple of affairs but she was not unfaithful. Is that clear?

Yes.

I must go now. I shall write to you.

Thank you veddy much. Good bye.

I hang up.

Dad was too smart; he worked for the American Embassy; the Foreign Service community in Saigon was a small small group of people living in close proximity to one another; everyone would have known who was promiscuous; he would never have married a promiscuous woman. And with Michael Lambton my mother was obsessed. Speaking of which, Michael Lambton, Michael Wilton. I have heard this bit before; Lambton said The Baby wasn't his. Is this the stock upper class English excuse for acknowledging paternity, responsibility? But Mr. Wilton is not denying paternity. He says he wasn't satisfied. Mom was so young, 23, when I was conceived and he was about 33. I wonder about her fanatical love for Michael Lambton. Was it because of Michael Wilton? Did she think Lambton was another Michael Wilton? Was Mr. Wilton her original great love? If he was, I shudder to think of how volcanically angry she might feel toward him now.

And then there is the matter of his wife.

I had been hoping that after all these years he might be alone, only because that would simplify things. But he is not. I must deal with it, her. I expect that if she is the wife he had in Saigon she must be allergic to the thought of me.

I reread Mr. Wilton's letter.

It says, "As I told you I cannot prove or disprove anything..." He never said that on the phone. He did say he wanted to help me.

I have no problem discarding the Hong Kong story because it goes with this sleeping with-a-man-with-burned-legs-from-a-motor-cycle-accident tale – that is completely unbelievable.

"Suzy was installed in my official residence in Saigon as 'housekeeper.'" What does this mean? My mother grew up with servants. She could never be a servant. Look at her photograph. Would you, if you were the lady of a house, hire a woman that beautiful to be your housekeeper? Dad's reaction to this: "No bridge: No, I never heard about the housekeeper bit – Suzy and Wilton. I can hardly imagine Suzy as a housekeeper." Later, a friend explains that in those days, a housekeeper was someone who supervised servants.

Mr. Wilton last saw Suzy in Pont St. Esprit, an hour from Avignon. He went after her. You don't follow someone who is just a former servant on a trip riding at least three planes, a train and a car ride to the south of France from Saigon.

He says if I came to visit I would cause his wife embarrassment. Does this mean he sees a resemblance between us from the photos I have sent him? Does this mean she is indeed the same wife he had when he was involved with my mother? If she is not, is it simply embarrassing that he has had a child out-of-wedlock with another woman long before they married? Perhaps I am an embarrassment because I am illegitimate.

He does not deny that his wife made a big scene at the British Embassy or that she returned to England to get a divorce. Boccardi taught us to assume nothing. I cannot bring up this matter of his wife having made the scene at the Embassy and of her leaving him. I dare not ask even if this wife is the same wife he had in Saigon, for fear of offending him and his wife by probing such a personal matter that is less my business than whether or not we are indeed father and daughter. I must take the most respectful stance, in case she is the same wife he had in Saigon, regardless of what happened there.

"If you came with your husband it would be different –" Why? Is it unacceptable for a woman to travel alone in 1983? Or would James simply somehow legitimize me by having married me?

"Do you wish for the photos back?" Maybe he would like to keep them because he sees I am his daughter, he has never seen me before and perhaps he never will.

There is so much I don't know. I do not know if he knows I am his daughter. I do not know where I stand with him. Boccardi said you know when a story hangs together, when it's true. This story is coming together, but there are still too many holes in it. And I'm overly sensitive to all this: I look for meaning in everything Mr. Wilton says, every word, every pause, every breath. I can't help it and it's exhausting.

I write to Mr. Wilton. I say to his wife, through him, that if he is not my father, that I have tried to be discreet, that I do not wish to shake up her life and that I am terribly sorry if I've caused embarrassment and sorry to bring up old difficult-to-deal-with memories. But I also say to Mr. Wilton that if he is my father, please tell his wife from me that if she has children, they need not know about me, that I do not want to upset a family or anyone. I write:

Please tell her that if she likes, she and I do not ever have to meet. If she wants to see me, or know me in any way, I would never ever knowingly hurt her. Please tell her that I have only respect for her...and I am not a threat...I could be a friend.

Please tell her that I have tried to handle this thing, so far, as gently as I could...I was terrified that you would reject me even if I turned out to be your exact image. Please say that I do not like scenes and I do not like to fight. But that this is one dogfight for my real father, a fight between my shy nonbelligerent nature and my absolutely driven will to learn the truth, that I could not, cannot and will not avoid.

The phone rings at 7 a.m. I hear the long distance shushing sound, a squeak and a hang-up click. I walk fast, pacing the living room. It must be him, I think. I said he should call collect when he gets the torn photo. I think it's a signal that I should call him. Perhaps he cannot call freely now because his wife holds the purse strings, or because she will complain about a high phone bill. So I call him. It's noon in England.

He says right away he is not the man in the torn photograph. I say thank you very much. I ask him how he is. Veddy well thank you. I say: I shall write to you. Thank you veddy much. He says: I sent you my photograph. Thank you so much. Goodbye, he says. Bye Bye, I say.

The mailman nods at me daily as I wait for him to finish stuffing the envelopes and magazines into the boxes. I tell him I am waiting for something from England. On the fateful day, he is kind and hands me the envelope with the British postmark.

I tear it open. There is a photograph inside. No letter. I'm afraid to look at it. I show it to the mailman, knowing it's unusual to do that, but I don't care, because I want the opinion of someone not connected to this situation that feels so surreal; I need to share it to get used to the reality that it's happening.

Is this my father? I say cheerfully.

He looks at the photograph and looks at me. Or your brother, he says.

I still can't look at it, but I am pleased that the mailman hasn't behaved as if this is weird. He must be from New York.

I run upstairs to the apartment. I look at the photograph.

I see him. A pain flashes from my lower abdomen up through my torso. I start crying. I feel lost.

I'm frightened by what just happened in my body when I first saw him. I want to tell James. I call, but he's not at his desk. So I call Gloria, a former editor and friend, who knows I've been looking for my father. I tell her what happened. She says but this is a time to celebrate. It's over, you've found him.

She doesn't understand. How can she, without knowing the years of longing for his presence in my life through so many experiences? – Not knowing him has been too saddening to tell James even. But it's not so much this missing him that shocks me so when I first see him. It's that I recognize him.

How can you recognize someone you've never seen before? It is a wondering that continues. I see that look: he has a look about him that I have seen in photos of myself and in the mirror. Or is it from genetic memory? Is there genetic memory?

After a while, when I feel calmer, I call him, before it's too late to call England – it's five hours later there. I discover I am not calm, still. I burst.

Mr. Wilton?

Yes?

It's Danielle. I have seen your photograph. You are my father. You are my father!

And I have something for you. I have something for you, Michael Wilton.

Yes? What is it?

I have love. I have so much love.

I must go now.

Fine. That's what I wanted you to know. That's all I have to say today, now.

Thank you veddy much. Bye-Bye.

Bye-Bye.

Now what? Bye-bye. What does this mean? Bye thee bye? Goodbye forever? Bye for now? Will someone please tell me why I am analyzing the fact that he said, Bye-bye?

I am so tired. I worry that I've put him through too much.

A while later I call him again. I apologize for being so emotional.

I say: I want you to know that I am glad that you are my father.

Jolly good, he says.

It's just, now that I've found you, I want to tell you what I want: We are neither rich nor poor. This is not about money. I paid for all of my university by myself. I have been on my own since I was fifteen. We are fine financially. I just want a relationship, please.

I understand, he says.

That's all I need.

He is quiet.

I shall write to you again soon.

Thank you veddy much.

I shall take my leave of you now.

I hear a whiff of a chuckle. He says, Where are you going?

Nowhere, just getting off the phone.

I see. Bye bye, then.

Bye bye.

Jolly good. Can you believe he said: Jolly good? Can you believe I said: I shall take my leave of you now?

It's all rather much. I suppose I need to dip into a Veddy-Veddy movie from time to time, to rest from real life.

Later, I understood why he was so uncomfortable when I told him I had love to give him. The RAF told me that at the start of World War II the average Squadron would have 12 aircraft, a number that rose to 24 by the end of the war, and that an average Squadron Leader was then responsible for at least a hundred men under his command. His work during World War II was to go up in the sky, kill with machine guns, drop bombs, then return to base, eat dinner and go to sleep. He would have to be a dispassionate sort, or completely reserved, or both, to do this repeatedly.

Too bad. I, his daughter, had a right to say what I wanted to him, finally, and that felt fine.

Chapter Twenty-One

Something else happened when I saw that photograph. I gained new confidence now that I had a father to communicate with, though it would waver. I reasoned that this was the time to find out if he loved me for who I am. If he didn't want me after that, well, I would deal with that when I had to.

In the photograph he sent to me he is wearing shorts, a beige crew neck sweater, sneakers and is at the helm, steering a wooden sailboat. He looks about my age, maybe older, balding; I'm delighted about this. It makes me understand why my hair is thin, fine and almost absent on my arms, unlike my mother. He has a mustache, like Michael Lambton, and a full lower lip, like mine. He has a cigarette in his right hand. He wears his watch, as I do, on the left wrist. I have never seen anyone else with the same muscle structure as ours, especially pronounced calves, slender shins. My friend, Gloria, laughs when she sees him. She says we have the same scrawny neck. My hands and fingers are like his. I wish I could stroke them. It's nice, isn't it – that he sent a photo of himself on a boat, knowing that I have my captain's license and love the sea?

James and I shake our heads and look at each other, knowing we are part of an infrequent experience. How often does a daughter, conceived in Saigon, separated from her father by 32 years and many thousands of miles of ocean and land, find him?

I'm English, I say for the first time. James smiles. I'm happy to be English. I've loved England, its literature, its history and legends, the mysteries of Stonehenge, the sounds of its accents, the pomp and circumstance of the royal family and the Veddy Veddy movies since I was a little girl. I know it's inaccurate to generalize about any population but the image from the media is that most English are polite, proud, caring, reserved, brave and stoic. I have witnessed in literature and movies a certain British behavior: nonchalance in the face of adversity – it makes me feel mushy inside. I'm proud to have English blood.

Dad writes that he never had any doubts about the matter of my paternal ancestry.

Tex writes that I should have been told about it a long time ago.

I am happy, though I fight sadness over the time lost that could have been spent with my father. And I discover within me an avalanche of anger; I did not know I was capable of it.

What does one do with anger like this? This is a curious emotional education. I now understand how someone could murder, though I could not. Not over something as insignificant as money. But over the confiscation of a parent, of someone you should have been given a chance to love and be loved by for more than three decades, all of your life? When you were looking for him for so much of that time? Wondering about him. Dreaming of embracing him. James says: You don't know what it might have been like growing up with him as your father; you may have had a better life without him. I say: I should have had the choice.

I cannot believe my mother did this. How can a mother give her child the photo of a man who is not her father? She keeps asking me to come to her in Montreal. I am incapable of speaking to her. I am afraid my brain would explode, become shrapnel if I began to tell her what I think of her now. I am in my revulsion released from her. I don't want her love. Let my sisters who never had to be her servant take care of her now in her final months, or year. Let The Baby do it.

Out of me comes a long wind of printed words – enraged, calm, cold, bitter. Meanwhile, my mother tries to speak with me by calling collect from "Mrs. Morin," my mother-in-law's name. James accepts the call. I shake my head. I will not speak to her. The Baby's grandmother hires a lawyer to call me from England. He asks me what I am going to do to help my poverty-stricken cancer-ridden mother. I tell him she has a house and assets and is adept at manipulating most people into doing what she wants. Politely, I tell him to beat it. My hardness shocks me, but I cannot help it. This is self-preservation. I am afraid of what I would do if I saw her now, so wild do I feel. My words in verbose letters are imbalanced. But now that I can be me with my father, I'm beginning to feel like I belong in the world, where so many people feel that having a father is as special as the air we breathe.

Did he know I was his daughter all along? Did he ever try to find me? I don't know. I don't want to know. It doesn't matter. What matters is what happens between us now. What happens now will be forever.

I tell my father that my mother is terminally ill and that I shall never speak to her again because of this deception. I tell him she's a paranoid schizophrenic (without knowing what a paranoid schizophrenic is, because I am shocked by her holding back my father's identity from me for all of my thirty-two years; it has at times crazed me). I ask him why she gave me other men's names and never once mentioned him.

I write:

I even tried to give her the benefit of the doubt and considered that she might have thought that if I ever found you, you would reject me, and she was trying to protect me from such a hurt…[I] suspect she hated you and decided to keep me from you forever. She has still not told me your name, never mentioned this whole (Saigon) scene that I have dredged up, and is apparently ready to take it to her death....

It has occurred to me that this is not the first time that this has happened. A bastard child. You are my father, Jim Flood is my Dad... Is that why there are several names for parents in the English language? Father. Dad. Pa. Pappy?

I tell him about the surrogates in my life. How my friend, Allan Berlowitz, gave me away at our wedding, and that Dad, Aunt Sue, Tex and others have not been enough. I say, "I want my blood."

I tell him I send his wife:

my most respectful regards...If I were in her position, I would be livid, at first. She would be in my position too.

I am not only sympathetic, but empathetic about having caused her embarrassment, and I am sorry, truly sorry about that. Now that I have found you and know you are my father, I am trying to figure out how I am going to explain you to my in-laws. They have a right to know where the potential mother of their grandchildren came from...But I am nervous about telling them about you, because although I may not be so concerned with appearances, I must admit they probably are. I am extremely proud. This is embarrassing to me too...

If Wallingford is a small town, my presence might indeed be an embarrassment. If there are people around who have known what you looked like over the years, they would know immediately that I am your daughter, or closely related...If I were permitted to visit you, I would probably have to try and behave like Greta Garbo. Can't you see me now? I might have to wear a large hat, perhaps with a veil. Aha! And I would have to wear sunglasses, so maybe I could find some like Jackie Onassis wears. I might have to come and go surreptitiously, and I shall, if you ask. My husband and I, who are loathe to be apart from one another anyway, would have to stay in a hotel in another town, perhaps.

We would never have dreamed of staying with you and your wife in a one-bedroom flat. I never asked for that and am sorry for the misunderstanding. I asked to see you, to be with you. I spoke of coming alone for several reasons.

For one, liquid assets would permit both of us coming to England, but right now, it would be a bit of a strain. James has this stringent book deadline with 64 full-color paintings to finish with and can't leave just now. Also, as we discussed this matter, James pointed out that it would be ideal if you and I could have some time alone, at least a number of hours, in the beginning, so that we can share our experiences, become more familiar with one another without distractions. I, or we, would never come without an invitation.

In case we never receive an invitation, I confirm for my father that his not having legs is irrelevant. I tell him about fishing with the late elderly Captain Tom Hamblen, whose legs were paralyzed: "He was so tough on me, it was impossible to feel sorry for him. Not even when his wheelchair had a flat tire and he was humiliated. Understanding, yes; pity, no."

As I write, it feels as if each paragraph is my last chance to show him what we have in common, so wary am I that he will turn me off, like a faucet. "Forgive me, but now I shall presume to know why you are so banged up. You're probably very much like me." I tell him I have sprained both ankles twice, torn the cartilage in my right knee, bruised ribs, and developed such bad tendonitis in my right arm from catching fish, I nearly crippled it.

I have grown much more careful, but not before: 1) *I was hit by a car on my mother's birthday when I was nine (just bruised; she sued the guy and had her teeth capped with the money);* 2) *I was involved in eleven car accidents;* 3) *I found myself twice in a small boat with two or more feet of water in the bilges – one time 102 miles offshore in the Gulf of Mexico…*

It seems odd to me why I am still in one piece, why both of us are still alive, and why I have somehow been permitted to find you without the help of my mother. I know it can all be explained...It just seems rather coincidental, don't you think?

...I am very concerned with your health and with your wife's health. Please say I sincerely hope she is feeling better. And please let me know if there is anything I might help with. For example, I could become (quoth my favorite poem, The Love Song of J. Alfred Prufrock,) *"a pair of ragged claws Scuttling*

across the floors of silent seas." And I shall, if you direct. It's just that I have missed you very much.

When I began looking for you six weeks ago, I knew only that you are Squadron Leader Michael Stanley James Wilton, wounded veteran of the Burma campaign, Saigon air attaché, British, that you were married 33 years ago, and that you were friendly with my mother. I still know hardly anything about you, but I shall put myself on the line now and say I feel as though I have known you somehow, all my life, because you are so much a part of me, those parts, I believe that I love. And so that is why I love you, not in the way I love people I know and see all the time. This is a much stronger love. Finally, I understand what Plato was saying in his Symposium on love, in which he (actually it was Aristophanes) describes a being, or entity, that or who loves itself or himself, and the being fissions, or splits, and the parts float around the world or universe until they come upon each other again, and then there is instant love, the strongest love.

Now, I know this love, and it is involuntary, unwitting, instinctive, automatic, compulsory and driven.

I want so to hear from my father quickly, every day. I offer him a Dictaphone so he doesn't have to write, if his arm bothers him so. I tell him he can call collect anytime. I say I shall settle down soon. In my fear that he will withdraw as he did from the phone when I told him I have love, I give him a practical reason to respond, though I will need the information eventually.

I tell him that because of my mother's breast cancer and because my mother's mother died of cancer, as did her older sister, for years my doctor has given me a mammogram twice a year because of the lack of knowledge about cancer in my father's family. I wish to have less of them. I ask him if his family has a history of cancer. Then I write a note saying, "I am peaceful now. I suppose also I needed your ear. I think of you."

Then I write a long emotional letter to Dad reporting that Mom called me months earlier to say that her friend, the late Bernard Fall, the respected French author of books on the Indochina war, had appeared to her next to the television set. She said he was wearing fatigues and that it was very nice of him to do so at four o'clock in the afternoon instead of at night, when he would have frightened her. When I learn that my mother has accepted an invitation from one of my sisters to come and stay with her and her husband in their house, not far from Tex, I warn Dad, of how mentally ill I believe her to be. I tell him of her visit to me and James before our wedding, that just after I swam pool laps at 6 a.m. she told me she had been raped in Boston by nine Teamsters; she said, "*zee* Teamsters are after me," and that this supposedly occurred when I did not know where she was for years, as if this was an explanation for abandoning me in New York, when all it did was make me hysterical for the brief time I believed her. I send copies of these letters to my father because I want him to know some of what it was like dealing with my mother without him.

Just before James and I go to Maine I call my father, to let him know more letters are coming, an excuse to hear his voice. I ask him if it's all right to call from time to time.

He says: It is rather inconvenient sometimes. It upsets my wife.

Then I shan't call again.

But the letters are fine.

Another long letter is coming.

I shall look for it.

I just called to tell you that, and to say, hello. I'll be thinking of you.

Thank you veddy much. Bye Bye.

Bye Bye.

He might as well have died, so do I fear that I have lost him. Upsets his wife. Why can't she be bigger than the situation? Why can't she open her heart? She doesn't have to be involved. I want a relationship with him, not her.

James says: Remember he's in a wheelchair. You don't know how much he needs her, how dependent upon her he may be with no legs.

In Maine, James takes photos of me sitting near the seawall, by the healing sea. I try to sit in the same position that my father sat in in the photograph he sent, so he can easily see our resemblances. I squint as he does in his photo.

When we return to Coconut Grove, we see his letter on the same pale blue stationery, in the blue fountain pen ink. This time he does not write Dear Danielle Morin:

30th September 1983

Dear Danielle,

Thanks very much for your letters all of them & photographs –

I was particularly glad of your letter of 16th Sept – in which you say you are now peaceful – I am glad.

I much appreciate your anxiety to know who your real father is – you are now convinced –

There is no history of cancer in my family – my father was a country doctor – my mother a Cameron of Locheil I went to public school in Scotland. Thereafter I went to the Spanish Civil War and fought on the Republican side (We lost!)

I flew throughout the last war as a pilot – then flew with the French Air Force in Indo-china & was shot down in Tonkin.

Your husband must be a very understanding man as well as very talented–

I wish you well both of you.

Am sorry about the telephone call

1. I hate the telephone

2. The room was full of people

3. It upsets my wife.

Yours ever,

Mike Wilton

Am returning photos under separate cover. I have seen them & I shall not forget.

The photos come back to Coconut Grove. I wrote that he could keep them. James says his wife made him send them back. My father underlines: I shall not forget. I am not well over this. It is lovely that he signed off: Yours ever, instead of, Sincerely, as in the first letter, but I am afraid of the connotation of the phrase: I shall not forget. Does this mean we may never see each other? That I may never hear from him again?

October 11, 1983

Dear Father...I hope you and your wife will accept my apology for phoning you. I realize it was rude – and that you never offered me your phone number...I wanted to hear your voice again.

I am truly sorry to have upset your wife. I wish there was something I could do. Hold her hand and comfort her. She has nothing to fear from me.

Fear is razor sharp, is it not?

I quote from a poem I found in the New Yorker *magazine in 1977. The poem, which is my second favorite poem, is called* Like Wings *(by Philip Schultz). Quote:*

'Fear is the edge that is the risk that is loving
'It stinks of blood, draws sharks...
'I have read of ancient people
'who held razors to their doctors' throat
'as he operated – as if love could have such balance,
'like wings.'

...Balanced love – perhaps it doesn't exist. Perhaps we can only wish for wings.

I thought it might help you to know what I want:

I want to speak with you once in a while, every few months or so, at your convenience. I will gladly bear the expense.

I want to know that if I mail you a letter you will read it.

I want to meet you, to see you, to be in the same room with you at least once, but preferably once a year or every two years.

If I am to realize that I will never see you, a part or all of me will be devastated and that is no exaggeration.

No matter what you say, or what your wife says, I shall always hope to see you. Further, if you ever find yourself alone, I will be there as soon as you summon me; the same applies to your wife. If you ever need anything – help, money, whatever, – I shall get it for you. As long as you receive my mail, you will always know where I am.

I am not afraid to love.

...I said, I shall not call again. I would like to amend that statement so that it reads: I shall not call again unless you signal me to call, as follows: Ring once or twice. Then hang up...Then ring once or twice again. Hang up. Then ring three or four times or until one of us answers. When one of us answers, hang up. If I am home, I will call you back.

I enclose two most recent photos. I am normally very pale skinned. The tan comes from simply living in the tropics. I burn easily. I do not sit out in the sun – boring.

You may have wondered as you looked at my pictures why my teeth are not exactly like yours...When I was about six...there was some operation done on my teeth. My dentist explains that either my two front teeth were growing in crooked or there was going to be a space between them and so the operation to correct.

Also enclosed is a humble gift (*a small gold heart-shaped locket*) *I wish you would accept.*

Your daughter,

Danielle.

I burn dinner. In the morning I watch the red numbers change on the electric clock radio by the bed, wishing that the next time I open my eyes, it would be time to go to the airport to see my father. In the afternoons, I hear the mailboxes clang open, then clang closed. I run down the stairs to open our box. But there is no letter from England.

I count the days since my father wrote his last letter to me. I count the days since he probably received my last letter. The weeks toll by. I prepare myself for the worst: that I shall never hear from him again. I stop listening to music. I will not go fishing. I stop jogging. I stop praying. I stop eating. Finally, I ask James to check the mailbox when he comes home from work. When he comes in the door, I'm afraid to search his face. Then I do. Then I look away.

Chapter Twenty-Two

On the 18th day after my father would have received my last letter, James says he has to write to him. November 4, 1983. He introduces himself, says we've known each other for four years, tells him my problems are his problems, that my experiences "seem almost unbelievable" but are true, including the sorry state of Mom's mental and physical health and "the way she chooses to treat her daughters."

He describes his more conventional family and writes:

The pain of growing up without a parent or parents is hard for me to understand. It is not unlike watching on the television news the parents of a dead U.S. Marine killed in Beirut. I can only sympathize with their feelings but I am incapable of understanding it. In Danielle's case I do not have to experience her pain in order to feel it. I need only see her cry herself to sleep…or see her totally incapable of concentrating on her work… That, too, is why I write you today…

As Danielle's husband I cannot allow the present state of affairs to continue indefinitely. The uncertainty of whether Danielle ever can see her natural father is torture for her as it would be for anyone under similar circumstances. I appeal to your sense of humanity as well as that of your wife to allow a meeting between yourself, Danielle, myself, and should she wish to be present, Mrs. Wilton. The date and time could be set at your convenience.

I write a letter to go with James':

November 6, 1983

Dear Father,

...Although I was disappointed that you returned the photos, I was glad to hear of your background and am very proud of it. I would like to hear more.

I am not sure that I am peaceful yet, although I am quieter than before I realized you are definitely my father. I wish for peace for all of us. I could not help but notice that you do not acknowledge that I am your daughter, but then, I also noticed you do not say I am not. I cannot help but wonder – am I not good enough?

And does the return of the photos mean I should send you no more?

The photo of you on the boat is framed. Please let me know if it is inconvenient to keep it.

I, too, despise the telephone and refused to have one for a period of five years, until I married James...It has been reassuring sometimes to speak with you as the reality that you exist has been difficult sometimes to believe, to comprehend.

And I have been concerned about how dependent or independent you are in your condition...

I think of you often and hope you are both well...

Faithfully,

Danielle.

Twenty-three days after my father was to have received the letters from James and myself, and 68 days since my father last wrote to me I face what I have known in my heart: James cannot force my father to see me or his wife to let him see me because I will not see him without an invitation. He has to want to see me. I begin to resign myself to continued estrangement. Who could be more expert at that? I realize I have nothing to lose if I call him one last time.

His wife answers the phone. Damn. I did not want to hear her voice. I ask to speak to Mr. Wilton. She sounds weak, as if she might cry when she says, Just a moment please. (Oh, thanks.) He says hello in his mellow voice. I tell him I'm only calling for a minute and that I have been worried that he is ill. He says he has been ill but is getting better. I ask if it's serious. He says it is not. I ask him if he would like to receive any more letters from me.

He says: Yes, I would.

Oh, thank you very much. I shall write to you. I hope you feel better. I shall be thinking of you. Have a lovely day.

Thank you veddy much. Goodbye.

Bye-bye.

I am calling James with the news. Up from the chair, I grab my keys and run down Mary Street, past the bank, down the hill, past the marina to the small park by Biscayne Bay where I jog for almost an hour, glad to feel my heart beating, the breeze and the sun playing light games on the water. Breathless, I walk toward the coral boulders at the water's edge, close my eyes, think of Britain and of him, sitting in his wheelchair. I wish my arms were long enough to reach across the thousands of miles and touch him gently on the shoulder as he wakes from a nap perhaps, so I could say: Did you sleep well? Was it a nice rest?

There are no more angry things to say. Only tenderness is left. Now I have another chance to give him what I had hoped to give him all along: Transportation, perhaps, from his wheelchair world into another that is just for the two of us. I can do this, I think, but I know I must expect no letters in return. I can do this until someone says, Stop.

So I write, send photos. I say I wonder what he does all day, that I would be amused if he watched soap operas on TV. I send James' cartoons. I ask what his birthday is. I send a Christmas gift to him and his wife, and say I hope this does not upset her, that she does not consider it to be too forward; the gift is a record of Beethoven's Piano Concerto No. 5 in B; I tell him it is the *adagio un poco mosso* on side two that causes me to think of him.

My mother has moved all her furniture from Montreal to my sister's house near Pittsburgh. Dad has gone from Portugal to Pittsburgh, a relief. Tex is in her nineties and her heart is not in good shape. I had been worried about my mother bothering Tex. My mother does call her and she does upset her. My mother argues with my sister's husband and returns to Montreal. She sold her house before moving in with my sister. None of us knows where she is now.

Then Tex calls me on December 15 to say a nurse has called her from the Royal Victoria Hospital in Montreal. She says the nurse says my mother will not likely be alive for Christmas. Tex says I should go to her.

I want to kick my suitcase as I pack. Why me? Why doesn't The Baby go? I call The Baby in England. The Baby says: Will try to go to Montreal. The airlines ticket agent asks when I am returning. I say: I don't know; they say my mother is dying; please, why don't you help me out; pick a day. He says how about in a week, on the 23rd? I say, fine. I fly to Montreal. My room is on the 14th floor and has a huge window that frames the big cross on Mount Royal. It glows in the black night, the only lit thing in sight. I say the Our Father and order a glass of red wine. I miss James, but I do not want to share this; he has to work; he's put up with enough of my mother.

I wonder how I shall be when I see her. Some of the anger has dissipated; mistrust remains. Now that she is too sick to harass my father, I can tell her I have found him. How is she going to explain her lies now? She might say she was afraid I would copy her, assuming that children automatically do what their parents did. Me, get pregnant out of wedlock? Oh, sure.

Her private room in the terminal ward is across from the nurse's station. Is this the death watch room? Or the room for patients who have sufficiently alienated most or all members of their families, where they might be less lonely as they lay dying because they can hear the nurses murmuring just beyond the door that is ajar?

I push the door open. She sees me. Shock on her face. I step, defiant, my shoulders back, chin high, around the foot of the bed to her left side. My long camel-colored coat whips around my legs when I stop. Am in dramatic mode, wary of her eliciting sympathy, her manipulations. She stares at me with fear in her eyes. But there is nothing to be afraid of once I take in the sight of her.

In that instant all anger leaves. She must weigh 80 pounds. She is bald and frail. For the first time in my life she seems helpless. Yet she is beautiful. She looks 17.

Whoa, whoa, whoa, she says.

I say, I'm never going to leave you again. OK, OK.

Wha, whoa, whoa, she says.

Understand? Everything is fine. Everything is going to be fine.

The expression on her face is more relaxed, though she seems curious. Wha, wha, wha, she says.

Grandma called. A nurse from here called her. I'm going to talk to the nurse. I'll be right back.

I go up to the nurse sitting at the station. Excuse me, please, would you be so kind? I want to know why my mother is making these noises. Why isn't she speaking? The nurse says Mom can't talk anymore. It's part of the progression of the cancer. I look at her. She looks at me. I go back in the room, trying to get used to this development.

Whao, wow, whoa. She sounds like an animal. She, beautiful animal. She watches me with her large brown eyes.

I stare back. Then I realize I can say what I want to her. She can only make these noises. She can't try to boss or manipulate me. She can't lie anymore.

But then see I will never get the answer to Why. Why she didn't tell me who my father was all these years. What happened in Saigon? It's useless to ask. She's too frail to write anything.

I put down my bag and take off my dark hat, gloves, scarf, coat. I stand beside the bed, close to her and look her in the eyes.

I say: I wouldn't speak to you all these months because I was so mad at you.

She watches me. Her eyebrows knit. Creases line her forehead.

I found Mike Wilton.

Her eyes widen. She looks afraid of me again.

He has no legs.

Her eyes crunch closed. The corners of her mouth turn down. Her chin puckers in grief.

I forgive you. I forgive you for lying to me all these years.

Her face muscles relax. She blinks.

So now you're going to rest. O.K.? Just relax. I have to make a phone call. I'll be back. Everything's going to be fine.

I feel better. The anger is gone. I want a cigarette. But I have to know just one more thing, now, before it's too late. Perhaps she can nod or shake her head.

I say, Do you hate me?

She says: I *wuv* you.

The people who work in the ward of the dying in the Royal Victoria Hospital are kind. They let me use the telephone, in a room down the hall where I can speak in private, to call long distance. I transfer the charges. They say nothing when I bring a bottle of wine and sip at a glass every few hours over the days. They let me smoke in a little lounge, though there is a man in his thirties on a gurney in the hallway waiting for a room where he can die of lung cancer. His mother who speaks only French cries unabashedly on my shoulder from time to time over the days. I am more at ease with the French woman with the English accent who reads to her dying British husband who acts cheerio throughout my stay. So I try to behave in a cheerio, purposeful manner too. It feels more orderly what with the raw feelings, and the question of when.

I call Patricia near Pittsburgh and say Mom would love to see her. She and her husband start the drive to Montreal. I call Ev but she can't come from California. This doesn't feel alright, but I don't know what to do so I tell her I'll call her back. I call Dad who is visiting Tex in Pittsburgh. He wants to know everything that is happening. He tells me to call back, sometimes twice a day. He always answers after one ring, notable because

Tex's house has three stories. There's one phone, in her study by the kitchen. He must be staying close by it because I don't think he could get to it by one ring if he were in the living room or the library. I note: this is such a coincidence that the only period of time in the last dozen years that I have been able to easily reach Dad by phone coincides with Mom dying and he couldn't have known before his long trip from overseas that this was going to happen just now.

Since there is no introductory tour of the terminal ward one discovers things. I find a bizarre-looking but practical old fashioned coin-operated phone booth phone, without the booth, on wheels down the hall. I roll it into Mom's room, hook it up and call Ev. I say: Mom can't talk, but she can hear, so say what you have to say to her in case you can't do it tomorrow. I hold the phone to Mom's ear for about seven, eight minutes. I don't know when Ev is finished, so I put it to my ear at one point and I hear her say: "What you did with your life..." Then I put it back to Mom's ear. I'm glad when the call is done. It was one of those things that needed to happen – some kind of peace may have been achieved.

There is a tape machine by the bed. I find some tapes not far from the nurse's station. I choose James Galway's *Songs of the Seashore* and Chopin's *Nocturnes*. Out of the corner of my eye I see a man go into Mom's room. I follow. She is alert, looks perturbed as she glances back and forth between our faces. He stands with his coat on, speaks to her gently, says "Good girl," when he sees she is passing urine into the catheter bag by the side of the bed. Who's this? Such familiarity between them. She purported she was alone in the world. But in the back of my mind I knew she never was.

His name is John Mortimer. Says he is Welsh. He says they've been close friends for eleven years. I think he's a year or two younger than me, maybe 30. (She's 56.) He looks like a gigantic cherub, with curly blonde hair and a baby face, very tall, well-built. He says that when she returned from Pittsburgh he helped her find a nursing home. He couldn't take care of her at his apartment. She needed too much; he had to work. He works in computers. I play the Galway. The expression on her face softens. It's lilting flute music. After a while Mortimer goes home.

She slips in and out of a coma. The next day when I put on the Chopin, she flutters her eyelids. She doesn't want it. I put on Galway again. A mist of a smile is in her lips. So Galway it is, over and over. I take breaks from the bedside and smoke. I call Dad. Pat arrives with her husband. They pray the rosary out loud, right then and there.

I'm restless, must do something. People give flowers at funerals when the person who should most enjoy them is dead. I have to find flowers....

Pat helps me put them in water. We use the wastebasket when we run out of vases. The nurses stop, startled, and look about when they come in to take our mother's temperature. The room is a garden – cut roses, carnations, lilies, and potted plants, all kinds. The French lady with the English accent passes by and says, good. I give her some flowers for her husband. Outside, there's snow and ice on the street. But you can smell Mom's room from down the hall.

It's Monday. No Baby from England. Mom starts breathing fast, too fast. I don't understand. I get the nurse. I'm scared she's going to die that minute. I guess I appear nervous because the two nurses who came seem about to ask me to leave. But after a few minutes Mom breathes normally. Pat and her husband go back and forth between Mom's room and the chapel. They call a priest. Mom becomes conscious. A last Confession is coming. She should have privacy but I'm afraid to leave. The priest talks to her in French like she is a little girl. He tells her all is forgiven. She makes *ainh ainh* sounds. She looks into his eyes like she is going to cry, then looks away, but the priest puts his face in her line of vision and repeats that all is forgiven. Then you can see she believes him. He blesses her. She is peaceful. Mortimer comes. He says I need to go out to eat. I won't leave. At about 10 o'clock I tell Pat and her husband to go to the hotel and get some sleep. They go. I smoke. I sip wine. All other visitors have left the ward.

I am smoking in the little lounge at 1 a.m. when I hear someone call my name. A voice says: Danielle. The tone is so even, I cannot tell if it is a male or female voice. I go out into the dimmed hallway but there's no one around. Down the long hall, I see the nurses with their medication cart. I go to them and ask if they called me. They say, No, look at each other and at me, like something is wrong with me. I'm exhausted. Never mind, I say.

Either I am hallucinating or it's some sign that I must go to my mother's bedside again. I need to cool it with the smoking and the wine.

I watch her. I believe that people in comas can hear what is going on. I put her long fingers in the palm of my hand. It is the first time I see her nails without polish. Later, Mom gasps, opens her eyes and raises her head perhaps an inch, then drops it back on the pillow. She stares at the space at the foot of the bed, then her gaze fans to either side of it. She looks afraid, as if there are people in the room who should not be there, but I see no one. I say:

Mommy, it's going to be beautiful. Don't be afraid. It's going to be beautiful.

I think: Where did that come from? She closes her eyes again.

I am shaken. I go smoke again. I'm afraid. The hallway is dim. Am afraid I was hallucinating when I heard someone call my name. Am afraid of going out of my mind. But then, if you do, perhaps you don't know it.

I make myself go back to her bedside. Her feet are cold. I rub them. I put my coat on them. I put on Galway music again. I sit in the chair facing her and sandwich her cool left hand in mine, to keep it warm, to try and keep the circulation flowing in it.

Then: A hand on my shoulder. I wake up. A voice says:

Your mother has passed away.

I turn. It's a nurse. I turn back, look at the hand in mine. It is much cooler than mine. Inert. I pull my hands away from it slowly, then put it on her chest.

I look at her body. She's not in it anymore. Her spirit is not in it any more. In that instant I know it's somewhere else, in the air, perhaps. That spirit was too strong to disintegrate. It has to be somewhere. It is somewhere. It's just not in that body.

The jaw has dropped open, making the head gruesome. The nurse fetches a small rolled towel, tucks it beneath the chin, wedging the mouth closed. It looks less macabre.

The nurse asks if I want tea or coffee. I don't know. She brings me coffee anyway.

Mortimer gives me the name of Mom's attorney. I call to ask if there is any arrangement for funeral expenses in her will; I do not wish to impose financially upon my husband any further than I have. The lawyer's response is: "The child in England is the sole heir." The lawyer did not know Ev, Pat and I existed. Doesn't matter. Mortimer says Mom had four bank accounts and he has a locked box of jewelry and its key, which Mom has instructed that he give to The Baby.

The Baby, who is 18, arrives later in the day; Michael Lambton's mother, the Honorable Monica D. Lambton, 69, daughter of the third Viscount Hampden, also arrives, wearing mink. They arrange for the cremation, the funeral, the limousine and the Mass attended by about thirty people at Marie Reine du Monde Cathedral.

At the hotel room I call Western Union. I compose a message for my father. I gasp at the cost to send fifty words. The Western Union operator says run the words together without spaces so they can only charge you for one word. I send him this:

Motherdiedpeacefully4:30amDec20herhandinmineinRoyalVictoriaHospital MontreallearnedIlovedherwaswithherlastfivedaysofinandoutofcomacouldn'tsp eaktoldherIfoundyouhereyesgrewwidetoldheryouraccidentfacecringedsaidIforg aveshesmiledsufferingoverSemperDanielle

The Mass and funeral feel filtered by an invisible screen slightly out of focus. I feel like I'm in a dream. I cannot remember my last sleep. Am dying to sleep. The limousine moves by banks of deep snow that fell in silence as she was dying.

Mortimer drives me to the airport. Am too tired to think, and yet he puts a music tape on in the car. He says, It reminds me of her, eh?

I expect something soothing. But no. It's called *Mama*, and it isn't motherly.

It's rhythmic boom-boom music with tribal clapping. A keyboard synthesizer makes other worldly sounds – weird, beautiful, tense, sexy. I'm startled. It's a group called Genesis. Phil Collins is singing: "I can't see you, mama, but I know you're always there; ooh to touch and to feel you, mama; oh I just can't keep away…so say you'll help me, mama, cause it's getting so hard..." Collins laughs devilishly. I can see my mother laughing. She thought wicked was funny. Men, obsessed by sex, were funny. I remember she said: Laugh at *zee* pain.

I wonder on the plane ride home whether or not her death will make a difference to my father's wife – if it will help me get to see him. I have a new life now without the threat of Mom's interference. I wonder how long I can go on writing to him, expecting no answer. It's better than not having my father in my life at all.

It's Christmas Eve. James is at the airport to get me. Back at the condo he hands me a small envelope. Inside there is a modest card, sold in aid of The World Wildlife Fund. On the face of the card is a drawing, *Three Shepherds.* My father uses brown ink this time:

Danielle & James
With all good wishes for Christmas and the New Year.
Love from Mike.

The card was posted before he got my telegram. Even after all my letters of turmoil, he wrote: *love.* You see? There is a Santa Claus.

Chapter Twenty-Three

Death buries trivia. I stop writing Dear Father in favor of Dear Mike. I tell him of hanging around in a full-length Stewart plaid skirt, listening to the Royal Scots Dragoon guards playing bagpipes. I do not know how the Scottish grieve, but this is soothing. I tell him what a lovely lady Mrs. Lambton was, having handled the limousines and funeral. Our letters cross in the mail. His says:

Wallingford
30/12/83

Dear Danielle -

Thank you for your Telecom bearing sad tidings – So sorry for you about Suzy -

Thanks also for record and flowers (received Xmas Eve) -

Have not a record player – nor do I want one – will play it on someone else's -

Also thanks for letters -

And James's – will answer in due course – I am afraid it is an effort to write -...

Yours sincerely

Mike

It is an effort for him to write. Does this mean it's painful to write? Does he have other pain? Sitting sores? Phantom pains – pain in the legs that are not there? And, maybe worse, depression? Does he become sometimes, as I did, speechless? And what of his wife? Does she love him? Does she have to bathe him? Is she resentful of it? I close my eyes. I tell myself to be careful. Don't write too often; don't be intrusive. Have faith. Still, am fearful of saying anything his wife can criticize, or of a letter arriving that says, Stop, No more, Don't bother us.

I write every two weeks – about the new video recording device that tapes something on the telly while it's turned off; of the cleaning duo, Thelma and Dolly, and the loud boogie music they played before they left the hot iron on the carpet; of running a charter fishing boat trip during which our French anglers persisted in unhooking many fish, though we did end up with 46 mackerel. I describe James' new book of humorous paintings of birds to be published by William Morrow: the Razorbill has a razor for a bill; the Sandwich Tern peeps from between pieces of bread. I send feature stories I wrote for New York newspapers, magazines. I say it's fun to be married to someone who laughs at the news. But I am not always so blithe.

The Baby's grandmother had written me two lovely letters. Then we receive one she wrote before meeting me at Mom's funeral. She says she, my mother and The Baby feel that The Baby's well-being would not be furthered by "a greater degree of contact" with me or Pat. She says The Baby can contact me after finishing university, if the Baby desires.

I tell Mike about this, and that James and I are stunned. I love The Baby. Now I am cut off and I don't know why. I tell Mike about Mortimer. Mortimer who says that my mother complained many times of the thousands of dollars she was constantly sending me, when in fact she sent me $30 in the last 17 years. She also accused these people of being "after" her for her money: me, James, Mortimer, her neighbors and Patricia and her husband, who invited her to come and spend her last months in their home.

Mike writes:

Wallingford

1/3/84

Dear Danielle -

I am sorry about the delay in replying to your letters – idleness breeds – re (the Baby) I think it is a diabolical liberty – No wonder you and James were upset. I should pay no attention.

Did James ever get the appointment he wanted -

Am returning the clippings herewith

You are a clever girl.

My writing is getting terrible

Yours

Mike

His handwriting appears more shaky. But he called me clever.

I prance about the apartment, barefoot in my tee shirt and jogging shorts like a parade majorette. I go jogging. When James comes home I can't stop smiling.

See? My father is not heartless. "A diabolical liberty"– precious language. It hadn't occurred to me to ignore Mrs. Lambton, so I shall. Because my English father said so (and he's almost as old as The Baby's grandmother), so his words carry as much weight, if not more, because he was a squadron leader, which beats being a rich widow. So there. And he went right on with the matter of James' wanting to be syndicated. Carry on. He took me by the hand and led. Like a father would. You think that's nothing? It's not nothing to me.

But he says nothing of our repeated plans for a trip to England, to Paris to see my uncles and to Portugal to see Dad.

I begin sleepwalking again. I tell Mike of having climbed over a fence in my sleep and of putting our hibachi seven feet out on the horizontal wooden trellis in front of our building and how James keeps his guitar against the front door now so he can hear me if I go out there asleep again. I tell him of being nervous when we go to see my in-laws in their new Florida home as I'm afraid I shall do or say something wrong (because actually I do not know what to make of family get-togethers, what one says, etc.) The flame trees on our street bloom.

He writes in black ink this time.

Wallingford

July 26

Dear Danielle,

Thank you for all your letters, the Buddha and cartoon reprints also the original one.

Nervousness is a sign of lack of self-confidence. You should tell yourself you are as good as the next person – if not better!

Sorry James has not heard re syndication yet – I hope he will -

My writing is getting worse

Yours sincerely

Mike

He thinks I am as good as the next person – if not better. I shall never forget this day, I think, as I gaze at the scarlet blossoms out the window. Life shimmers. I tell him:

...I am, perhaps for the first time in my life, entering…a hopefully long-lasting period during which I may become more secure…It is almost as if I had been conditioned, in the past, to expect that people I love will reject or abandon me and when I received your letter I am aware that I nearly marveled that you have not moved away or in any way dropped the emotional guillotine...In September I will have been married for three years to a very steady young man. I thought to myself: Why hasn't that been enough to make you quiet, secure? I don't know. I suppose I see him as unique...And now you are still there, and writing to me even though I can see it takes a great effort on your part...I am a very lucky person.

But he says nothing of our planned trip to Europe.

I send Mike and his wife a picture book of New England for Christmas and order roses to arrive on Christmas Eve – because no matter how his wife feels about me, how can anyone complain about that?

Just before Christmas we receive a sparky red Christmas card with MERRY CHRISTMAS in gold on its cover. Inside on one side it says:

Many thanks for letters and cartoons.

So glad James got the syndication he wanted. Am keeping the book until Christmas Day.

See you in the spring, maybe.

Mike

On the other side, it says, again in his distinct tiny writing:

Danielle & James

With all good wishes for Christmas and the New Year

love from

Mike & Dora

See you in the spring, maybe. Love from Mike & Dora. There are degrees to happiness. After writing to him for a year and a half, this one is deep and calming. Some days I feel like a little girl again. On Christmas Day James and I have a picnic at the beach on Key Biscayne. I build an elaborate sand castle. A passerby, I tell Mike, says it looked very professional.

In his next letter Mike sends regards to James. I write excitedly of our itinerary and of our new macrobiotic diet. Jim Flood, I say, has sent directions to his villa in the Algarve; must take three nameless roads to get there; I have learned that *A onde e a casa do senhor Americano* means: Where is the house of the American? Two weeks before I am to leave for Portugal, and Paris, where I shall meet Uncle Dany for the first time, and London where I shall rendezvous with James at the Diplomat Hotel in Belgravia, Mike's letter arrives:

Wallingford

10/3/85

Dear Danielle -

Thank you for your letters and 2 lots of cartoons – also your itinerary –

We hope to see you & James while you are over here – no doubt you will ring us from the Diplomat – when you arrive – we are not vegetarians but carnivores – good meat – so you will have to take what is on offer!!

Yours ever

Mike

I close my eyes in relief. James can't keep up with me as I race over the cobblestones to Mike's flat in Wallingford.

I shall never forget the first sight of him. He is almost a silhouette. From the doorway of the tiny drawing room I see the back of his head and shoulders above the wheelchair. The vision is framed by light coming in a large picture window about ten feet in front of him. The room is otherwise dim.

I step, in my brown leather flat ballet shoes, to his left side. I face him in his dark green crew neck sweater and gray boxer shorts. It looks as if part of a nostril has been shot off.

I ignore this as he touches his left cheek with his index finger. "You should," he says, "give me a kiss." I do, with pleasure. Then I step back and smile at him. He smiles back, lips closed, and like me two small puckers – hints of dimples – appear beneath the corners of his lips. In this moment there is no one but us.

He looks at me, then out the window, then back at me again. He bounces slightly in his wheelchair. He has a characteristic hunched way of sitting, leaning on his forearms that rest on the arms of his wheelchair. There is something impish in his smile, his stance. I say: We brought you some flowers. (Freesias; fragrant.)

He nods. Looks out the window with the little smile and bounces slightly again. Then he looks back at me in my beige corduroy suit and white blouse with its small white-on-white embroidered collar buttoned to the neck, the pearls my mother-in-law gave me.

I don't know where James and Dora are. Down the hall by the door, still,

I suppose. I can hear their voices. When she opened the door and first saw me, she rolled her eyes at the ceiling. James saw it, says she did that because of the strong resemblance between me and Mike. Go ahead then, she'd said, and I scooted in. I think she and James lingered in the hall so Mike and I could have a first moment alone, that moment that is forever.

He and I spend a great part of the time looking out the window that overlooks a small patch of grass, a sidewalk and the brick wall of the flats across the way as we talk. Throughout the four-hour visit, especially when Dora is in the little kitchen preparing lunch, I catch him, when I glance at him, staring at me. When this happens he quickly looks away, out the window, and bounces again, as if readjusting himself in his seat and the corners of his lips go up. Purposely sometimes, I look out the window so he can continue to look at me without my obviously noticing.

I give the flowers to Dora when she comes into the drawing room with James. He is wearing the gray pinstripe suit and yellow tie he wore for our wedding. Dora is tall for a woman, has huge brown lovely eyes and like Mike wears casual clothes. I am glad she wears a happy pinkish lavender sweater with the gray skirt. Is it a sign that she is in a good mood? Oh, why am I so nervous, and why do I have to look for meaning in every little thing? Because, from time to time, there is meaning in little things.

Mike asks about our hotel. It's within walking distance of Harrods; not fancy; our room is large with high ceilings and there's a charming elevator that's like a cage. I tell of getting a bottle of wine after we got settled there, but when I asked for a corkscrew at the front desk, the girl there with a Cockney accent said there was none. When I asked how one opens a bottle of wine she said, we generally push the cork inside it. We all laugh and Dora says we should sit as she arranges the flowers.

Though we are now slightly less tense, everything feels magnified: The cream porcelain vase holding the freesias is indelible in my brain and seems huge for some reason, though it's only about 14 inches tall; Mike's small ears that are like mine; he missed a spot shaving to the left of his mustache; how the sleeves of his sweater are pushed up to the elbow like mine often are; the Cameron ring he wears on his pinkie finger; the seams in the skin sewn together at the ends of what is left of his legs; the hair on the sides and back of his head that has been dyed dark brown. I think: Is he a little vain; is he trying to look younger? I see that it is fine in texture like mine; it's been left a tiny bit long in the back and a little curl mingles with his sweater collar; how modern, I think, of its slightly long length. His complexion is a bit ruddy like mine. When he smiles widely I see the space between his two front teeth that I was supposed to have, except for the operation to prevent it that I had as a child.

Dora is giving us some white wine for which we are grateful as I don't know what I expected of this first time together but I am aware I am in shock; I feel vaguely as I do after too much espresso; overly alert but also a little stupid, as if there is a little delay in brain function. James is quiet, somewhat stunned as one might see from his unusually straight posture. I keep catching Mike peeking at me. He asks how my trip was to Paris and Portugal. I say it was fun, that my aunt in Paris took me and my cousin to the ballet of *Romeo and Julliet* at the opera house; that I dug a garden for Dad and the English lady he has been living with as she's elderly and he's not so well but that one needs a jackhammer in that part of the Algarve; every time I put a shovel in the ground I hit rock. Need dynamite, Mike says. I smile at his terseness. Dora goes into the kitchen and he says softly: This is the most I've spoken to anyone in years.

For years I have thought of that sentence. I was afraid to ask why.

The subject of Portugal reminds me: I bought Dora a silver and diamante ring there. I give it to her in a little box. She's pleased. I am relieved. I say it's a friendship ring. She thanks me. She goes down the hall and comes back with two packages. We open them. I have told them in letters how much we love books and here we are with one for James on how to be a cartoonist – this is Mike's sense of humor – and one for me called *The Young Visitors* by Daisy Ashford, first published in 1919. Miss Ashford was 9 years old when she wrote it. Privately I think if this Ashford kid can write a book when she's 9 then I should be able to at 33. But then also perhaps that is what Mike is telling me.

Mike lights a cigarette. I ask if we can smoke, then say perhaps we shouldn't; it's not good for them. Mike and Dora give me a look that says: You're out of your mind, or aren't you a bit cheeky to indicate what we should or should not do? Dora offers me a Silk Cut, non-menthol and says, these are better for you. She offers one to James. We both take one. But I feel so wired I could have smoked two. We light up.

What is the soft watercolor on the wall over there? It's of the facade of an old white house with green vines climbing over the gate at its side. Dora says it's of the house they lived in abroad. Until not long ago, they lived for seven years in Spain and seven years in France. I say, why? She says, because we wanted to; we like France and Spain and we wanted to. My mind blurs a moment thinking of them living in France or Spain. I wish I could have lived with them there. I wonder which country they were living in when I was in college. Then I think: you made your way through college; got scholarships. Fool: Nothing can remove this source of self-esteem. I hear Dora's voice again.

It's beautifully toned, deep at times without being masculine and high pitched sometimes in an operatic way without being shrill. She has a heavy accent and naturally says ray-lay instead of really. I say I think it's a beautiful accent; ask if it's a type of London. She says she was born in British Guiana; her father worked there.

She chatters, as I do in my letters as if expecting no response, which helps to move things along, though I am startled sometimes by the information she proffers, because even though this is our first meeting, some of what she says is not something I would say to anyone at any time. I sit straight up when she says: I know I have a big nose but I'm not Jewish; I'm Roman Catholic. Right away I say I'm a Roman Catholic, too, glad to have something in common, amazed by her forthrightness and discomforted by her association between Judaism and big noses, but the last thing I want is to argue. I ask if she has a profession. She says she was a photographer's assistant when she met Mike and that she's older than he is, actually. I'm 72, she says, which makes her almost five years older than Mike. Mike has a cousin, she says, who doesn't live so far away and Mike's only sister Rosemary lived in Spain and died recently. I say, I'm so sorry. She says: He is the heir, gesturing gracefully with a smoking cigarette toward Mike. She says: Rosemary was widowed and had no children. There isn't anything left in his trust fund, she says; it was used up when his mother was dying as she needed a night nurse and a day nurse; she had pneumonia; it cost quite a lot actually, a day nurse and a night nurse; we're used to nurses; Mike has nurses who come every day and hoist him out of bed and bathe him.

I am embarrassed by the announcement about his impending inheritance and the trust fund I did not know about, but am glad to hear that someone helps take care of him; it's a lot to absorb at once. Since she said that Mike's sister had no children, I ask if they have any children. Dora rambles: We didn't want children, so we never had any children, we don't like children.

Mike says: Except when they're grown.

Dora gives him an irritated look. He turns his expressionless gaze from the brick wall out the window up to her face. I think: please; we only want pleasantness. Dora asks him if he would like to go to the loo. He says, yes, please. I wonder if this question was placed to remind him that he needs her.

She wheels him down the hall. Later, she wheels him back. She asks if he wants another drink. He says, yes, please. She pours him more wine.

He turns to me and says he used to have an adopted child, through a magazine advertisement. I think of the giant hungry brown eyes of half-naked children in dozens of magazine ads I've seen. Then my gaze rests on the current issue of *Harper's* on the chair by Mike. Those ads ran in *Harper's* or *The Atlantic*, or both. He says: I stopped sending the money because I didn't think the child was getting it. James says he has heard of scams with such adoptions. I wonder if Mike was thinking of me when he adopted the child, then I discard the thought. We have something precious, this minute, in these hours, all I have ever wanted in my life.

Dora says she has a sister and a brother-in-law in Wales, beautiful countryside, and nieces; they're grown. They do come to visit us from time to time, she says.

We move to the small table. When I rang him from the Diplomat Hotel after we arrived, Mike had said: We will give you lunch. I was amused over this form of invitation. Now he says: Everything that's good to eat in the

U.K. is imported. I smile. It's sweet that he's trying to make us laugh. Dora serves asparagus in vinaigrette. James uses his knife to cut it. Mike and Dora and I stop eating for a moment when we see this. I whisper to James to use his fingers. (In the U.S. one uses a fork; in France and the U.K. one uses the fingers to pick up asparagus.) Dora then serves cottage pie - ground beef with onions between mashed potatoes topped with melted cheddar - and it's tasty, though it is swimming in meat fat, which makes it tastier, but I worry about their cholesterol. She's put cinnamon in it which Mom never used in shepherd's pie. I say I thought this was shepherd's pie. She says that's with lamb; cottage pie is with beef. Dora brings a large chunk of Stilton cheese and a bowl of fruit. Mike says that when he used to go to his gentlemen's clubs they served a large wheel of Stilton. He says a hole was carved out of the middle of it and filled with Port. He says the Port seeps into the cheese and it's quite good.

I announce we are going to Scotland the next day to see The Baby. Mike looks at me quizzically since I had complained a year earlier of the upsetting letter from Mrs. Lambton saying not to contact the Baby again. I explain that I told The Baby, through Mrs. Lambton's lawyer - our only avenue for communicating with The Baby - that we were coming to the U.K. The Baby invited us to visit. The Baby goes to the University of Edinburgh. I look at Mike and say, must let bygones be. He shrugs. I say we're going to take the train there and return by train the following day. Dora says, that is something of a trip.

It's Tuesday. Dora asks if we would like to come back and have a drink on Friday afternoon after Scotland. I say, Yes, thank you very much. We are excited about the trip to Scotland as we've never been there but I am more excited about having been invited to return; this is Dora's prerogative, etiquette-wise. It's a relief.

I help to clear the table. We smoke. Dora serves Courvoisier from a large bottle. We smoke some more. Dora asks if we would like coffee. No, thank you. More than anything I want to feel less startled. And we must heed the bus departure for London.

Dora had put our coats in the bedroom down the hall. She says to James: you must see the paintings in the hallway.

Mike and I are alone again finally. He stares out the window at the brick wall. His hands are clasped in front of him, shoulders hunched.

So, I say, looking out the window, we'll see you Friday.

He lets out two sounds, like hiccups. Immediately, I think to pat him on the back, so I get up to do so and out of him comes an unearthly wail.

Oh, shock. I crouch in front of him and look up into his face, his eyes wild wide, his facial muscles drawn, taut.

Oh, no, oh, no, I say.

He sobs, draws in breath. I'm sorry, he says, for all those years.

Oh, no, I say, oh, no.

I do not want this. I did not come here for remorse.

I say, Don't cry, oh, no. I wipe tears spilling from the edges of his eyes, wipe my hands on my skirt. Please, I say, you're so beautiful. I grasp his shoulders and kiss his face repeatedly from the right cheek to the left as he says: I am?

I draw back to look at him. He blinks. We are eye to eye.

I say: You are to me.

Now I am half standing and kissing him on the forehead, then I draw back and straighten up. I take him in. He blinks and looks relieved.

I say: We have so many good times to have together.

He looks out the window again.

And we'll be back on Friday. I'll be back. Maybe I can come back in six months or so. We have each other now. We have each other forever now.

I look to my left. I thought I saw a box of tissues. There it is. I pull a tissue out of it and hand it to him. We'll be right back on Friday.

He nods.

Okay? So everything is fine. He says nothing. Dora is at the entrance of the hallway holding my coat. I give him a last quick kiss on the cheek. I am putting my cheeks to each side of her cheeks, saying, thank you so much and see you Friday. When I get outside, I go to the patch of grass in front of the window and wave at Mike. Because of the sun, I can't see him, but I know he can see me.

James and I are silent for a while as we walk up the cobblestone alley to the market square bus stop. After a few minutes he says: What happened?

I don't know; he just freaked. Did she say anything?

He says: She pretended nothing was happening; we both did.

On the bus to London he loosens his tie and says: The four of us finished that big bottle of Courvoisier and I'm completely sober.

Me, too.

All the way back to London I see Mike's face when he wailed. His expression was so wild, I don't understand. It seemed full of terror or horror. For years after that I am afraid that is how he felt just before his plane crash. Or maybe it was the accumulation of everything; grief that he couldn't walk and be free to come see me, or anyone; or the fear that after this trip to England we might never see each other again – I don't know why I felt he thought that; that was a feeling I ignored after it grazed me like a knife. There was fear here, in this scene. I could smell it. Something to do with Dora? Was she in any way punishing him for my existence? Was this wail and apology as close as he was going to get to recognizing me as his daughter? If so, fine. It's our time together now that matters. And I would see him again. Nothing could stop me from seeing him again.

Chapter Twenty-Four

I can't stop smiling all the way to Scotland and back. I am aglow. Nothing can dim me. I got to see my father. He loves me. I know it. He knows how much I love him. All my life I can remember how soft his hair was at the back of his head when I touched it as I kissed him, how it is fine like mine. Now, always I shall know the sweetness of his body smell from when I was comforting him. I recognize that smell; he smells like me. We are in love with each other, my father and I, and it is a beautiful thing, natural. James, because he loves me, is only happy for me. Because love cannot be measured, he understands it doesn't take away from the love I have for him, my husband. It only adds to it because there is more of me now to give, because of this love. I am becoming whole.

You can see it in the photos James took of me on the train to Edinburgh and back. With my hair combed back off my face, like Mike's, accenting the look in my eyes: I know a love now that I've never known before.

Ed-in-burr-rah! The Baby teaches us to pronounce it correctly. I show off when we get back to Mike and Dora on Friday. Courvoisier, I say, in a perfect French accent, though I am wary of mentioning much else that is French, because it would not be tactful to bring up my mother.

I am unable to bring up several matters as we visit again. I can't ask when Mike's legs were removed, or about the crash in Tonkin. I am not able to know if he was taken prisoner, or how he was treated by the North Vietnamese; how he got out of there alive. I can't. I don't want him to relive it. But I do want him to remember my mother.

I want to know what happened in Saigon but I cannot ask because of

Dora's presence. Where did he meet my mother? How long did they date? Why did he follow her to her family's home in the South of France? Even when Dora is in the kitchen, I am afraid. She keeps popping back into the drawing room. How can I ask? I know from Dad that Mike was married when he was involved with Mom in Saigon, that his wife made a big scene at the British consulate and returned to England to get a divorce. I cannot ask if Dora was married to him when he was in Saigon, or how long she has been married to Mike, for fear of controversy. And so I have to assume she is the wife he had when he was in Saigon, in order to give her the benefit of the doubt, in case she is now indeed behaving in an extremely modern and heroic manner by receiving his child by adultery during their marriage.

The visit is a sort of minuet. I move close, he moves back. He moves close, he moves back. He moves close, Dora moves him back, or so it seems.

I notice the tiny framed oil painting, perhaps three inches long, an oval, of a woman in Victorian garb, hanging by a ribbon to my left and when I ask Mike who she is he says, Cousin.

That is how much I am to know.

Mike hands me a tiny package clumsily wrapped in decorative paper. He watches as I open it. A pin. It's beautiful. Gold and enamel depicting a green wreath surrounding a serpent coiled around a staff, topped with a crown and a blue ribbon on the bottom that says: *In arduis fidelis*. Mike says: It was my father's Royal Medical Corps pin; he was commander of a royal hospital in Cairo.

A country doctor who was commander of a royal hospital. I run my thumb over the pin, unhook the latch behind it and put it on my blouse. Thank you very much. He can see I am moved. I tell him I love it. I do not tell him how important it makes me feel. Then Dora says: You can get those anywhere, in all kinds of used jewelry shops in London. They're quite common. Anywhere.

I think: you cannot get the pin my father gave me anywhere.

Why is she saying this? And why is she asking if my brown tweed suit from Edinburgh is a Harris tweed? She says if it is Harris tweed, it should have a big label inside the jacket. (It does.) Does she need to know if we can afford the real thing? Or if I have the taste to choose one? What will make this woman happy? That I should disappear? I am not going to disappear. I feel like I am walking in heavy traffic. She leaves for the kitchen to get cheese and fruit.

I can ask Mike what his parents' names were. He says his father was Stanley James Wilton and his mother Norah Marjorie Henderson. Dora comes back. I can't ask how a Henderson can be a Cameron of Locheil as he had said she was in a letter; I am afraid to ask too many questions as I do not want to seem too nosy, too excited, too elated, too delighted, too nervous, too wary, though I am.

Mike says the Cameron war cry is: "Sons of the hounds, come here and get flesh." He says they used to say it during fox hunts. He smiles wickedly as my eyes grow wide. Hearing anything about our family makes me feel more a part of it. I am touching my new pin to make sure it hasn't fallen off. Dora is rambling again, about York ham, about Egyptian cotton sheets. And then she is gone into the kitchen for something. I take my camera out of my leather satchel and look through it at Mike. I focus the lens, feeling more at ease as he has spoken of our family and I say, may I?

He says: No, we're very private people.

I feel red, my ears hot. I quickly aim to the left of him and take a picture of the freesias in the cream vase. I put the cap on the lens. He knows I'm upset. I say: it was just for me. He says: the best pictures are in the mind. He touches the side of his temple. I nod as I hurry to put the camera away before Dora comes back. I think: Does he not want anyone to know I've been here? What is it? Why can't I have just one more picture of him? I only have one. And then I remember his nose. It really is messed up, though I'm used to its sight by now. I feel like an inconsiderate fool.

I excuse myself to the loo. I need to calm down. I have a time in there. I look at Mike's little black comb. I want to take the strands of his hair out of it and put them in my pocket, but I don't: I am so afraid of doing anything else wrong now so that we're not invited to return. I notice the black Chanel for Men atomizer. Am glad she buys that for him. I see the special shower and the special extra wheelchair for taking a shower in it. What was I thinking? I was only going to take a picture of his head. Oh dear. Am I ever going to see him again after this?

Back in the little drawing room, I catch Mike peeking at me, then looking quickly out the window again, knowing I caught him. I think he's having fun seeing himself in me. He readjusts himself in his chair with his slight bouncing. I feel the camera thing is over – good.

The light outside the big window is fading. We have to catch that bus to London. This time Dora stays with us while we say, goodbye. I wonder if she scolded him for his wail the last time. He doesn't look at me unless I crouch in front of him and look into his hazel eyes, which I do. I say, I'll write. And he says, thank you veddy much. I say, I'll be thinking of you and I'll be right back, in six months. Softly, I love him.

I kiss him on the cheeks and press my cheeks lightly against Dora's and thank her, looking her straight in the eye, because none of this could have happened if she hadn't allowed it. And then we are gone, exhausted from the excitement, the worry about all going smoothly. I know she must be so tired too. He said she had not gone to bed until 4 a.m.

Again, Mike and I do not have enough time alone for me to ask him about my mother.

I order thank-you roses for them and a York ham from York. I send James' newly published bird book and a couple of inoffensive American classics. I write of how I'm happier than I've ever been and that James is happier because I am. I tell them of a dream I had: In it Dora is conducting a choir of half a dozen neighborhood children singing lovely songs with no words; the picture window in their flat overlooks the side of a mountain, huge, blue, grey and close, as if it were across the street. I am too shy to tell them that also in the vivid dream Mike has legs and is standing before me. He's wearing a blue blazer.

He says: I love you as much as anyone can love anyone.

The dream seems so real. And I believe him.

Mike writes:

Wallingford

Dear Danielle & James,

Thank you for your letter the roses & ham – most kind but quite unnecessary – Have shown James book to several friends – all very impressed & found it brilliant – you must get it published over here

Frankly I do not think any purpose would be served by your coming in the fall – I shall not be available – perhaps next year when you both come

Yours sincerely

Mike

I am sick with fear. He uses black fountain pen ink to write this letter, except for "when you both come," which has been added in blue.

Coconut Grove
May 27, 1985

Dear Mike and Dora:

Thank you for your letter.

Sorry if I made you uncomfortable with my now discarded plans to visit Wallingford alone. I get caught up with enthusiasm sometimes; I forgot the situation. I will not forget again.

I am afraid I might also again inconvenience you with the phone and so I shall not call. Besides I do not like the phone either.

Thank you also for your compliments on James' book.

James' syndication is holding. He lost 3 small clients but gained 2 medium-size bigger papers which more than made up for it.

Must go now. Much to do. Take care.

Semper,

Danielle

I listen for the mailboxes to clang open, clang shut. I wait to hear the mailman go through the iron gate, then I go down, open the mailbox. I crave the sight of the Queen on a stamp, but she does not appear.

Twenty-five days later I paint a small watercolor of flowers and send it to Mike and Dora. I can't write. I am disabled. What can I say? What do I do? Is this it, God? Is that all I am to see of him? Eventually I remember he wrote: perhaps next year when you both come. So there is hope. What is the problem with my coming alone? It's hard for James to get away from his commitment to do five cartoons a week for all the newspapers that subscribe to his work.

Finally, on Saturday night, June 22, I call. Dora answers.

He's had a stroke, she says in her operatic voice.

I am able to say: How is he? She says: He's not well; he's in hospital. Am so sorry. I shall pray for him, for you both. Quickly, I get off the phone, before she can say something that hurts more than this.

Forever, I can hear her saying: He's had a stroke, had a stroke. Stroke, stroke, stroke. I'm terrified he might die.

I want to be by his side, smile at him as he wakes up. Read to him, play music for him, feed him. But then what would the nurses say? Who's this? This woman, who is the age the daughter of a man his age would be, who speaks with an American accent. Is this his daughter? They would see, of course, because of how much we look alike. We're very private people, he'd said. What if Dora's nieces came? They would know right away. Mustn't cause any embarrassment, especially for Dora. Mustn't do anything to upset him, or her. I fear she would make him pay if I upset her. Did I upset her by saying I would be back in six months? Did she make him pay?

My body is stone. I am trapped inside it. When I think of the idea of trying to see him, it feels impossible to move. Squadron leader's daughter. Illegitimate daughter. Walking embarrassment. Evidence of betrayal, infidelity, unkindness, ugliness, ruthlessness, selfishness. Be invisible, non-existent. Disappear, you; you, who have no right. To what? To walk into a hospital and say, Please may I see my father? To ask, Is he being given all the care he needs? To say, I want to sleep on a cot beside him. Do I have any rights? I don't know. I am so consumed with emotions I cannot think. Rights. The word comes with connotations of conflict. Forget it. He needs peace and quiet now. Knowing he is getting better is all that matters. I do not need to sit on a throne of recognition, though I wouldn't mind.

I want more than anything to escape this pain but music seems a trite option. What can I do? Nothing else to do but move forward, to give whatever might be accepted. May I offer concern for Dora's welfare too? Anything to cause alleviation of this feeling, of this incomparable dread, fear.

On Monday I call Dora. I ask how he's doing. Still in hospital. How she's doing? Is she eating well? Anything I can do?

Thank you veddy much. She is much less abrupt, nice actually, on the phone this time.

May I write? Yes, you may write.

The gate opens. I write. Of the refreshing early morning rain that came the other day and cooled the day to come, of setting aside my novel to freelance for a Fort Lauderdale magazine, of seeking an editing or writing job because the novel takes so long. Of looking for a house, of finding one, of negotiations. And did you know how many people have completely recovered from strokes? Did you know the oldest woman in Florida is 113 and recovered from four strokes?

A month later a typed letter comes. The Queen is on the stamp.

29 Mariot Court,
Goldsmiths Lane,
Wallingford.
Oxon. OX10 OXD
25 July, 1985

Dear Danielle,

Thank you for your letters and moral support.

I am glad about the Editorship and hope it comes to fruition.

I am now back home, although not completely recovered from my stroke.

We hope to see you both next year – meanwhile all the best.

Yours

X

He cannot sign his name, but I recognize the slightly crooked quality of the X from his shaky hand. Later, he tells me this letter was typed by the secretary of a friend.

He wants to see me again.

Chapter Twenty-Five

I barrage Mike and Dora every two weeks for eight months with images – of fifty rose bushes I grow in the garden of our new 1923 house, of exotic palms, crimson bougainvillea, fragrant gardenia – and cheerful chatter during short phone calls because Mike's diction is still often unintelligible. I go on, telling of a frost scare, of the garden looking like it's full of ghosts because so many palms and bushes had to be covered with sheets, of the fire in our fireplace, of nothing substantial really, but I keep talking, sending photos, letters and flowers as if they will keep him alive.

When we see him in March, almost on his birthday, not knowing it was his birthday, it is evident a part of him has died. His arm hangs limp, the hand frozen turned inward at the wrist, but he jokes about it, saying, Wrong arm; he is right-handed, like me. He tells me not to wrinkle my forehead so, and then when I relax it, he jokes that it's too late; the deep creases are there, like his.

It's a short visit with a *Salade Nicoise* lunch. He gets tired easily, especially after the wine Dora pours. He looks older, markedly pale. She lights his cigarettes for him now. We see that he will not be able to write again. There will be no more letters unless she writes them.

He is even more dependent upon her now, for everything. She wheels him to the loo. They are there for a while. She wheels him back.

I wonder how she gets him, with no legs and one arm, into bed but I do not ask. I'm wary. I almost wasn't going to be able to see him again because I said last time I wanted to come back in six months.

We're staying much closer than before – no more London hotel. This time we are in Henley-on-Thames, a magical place, I think, full of history. It has been home to rowing regattas for some hundred and fifty years.

Mike says something but it comes out garbled, from the stroke, though he is working with a speech therapist. He's frustrated, embarrassed. Dora translates: He says you should go to a good restaurant called The Little Angel. We say we went to a pub across the road from the hotel called The Angel. But he says, No. The Little Angel. We nod. He says, with difficulty, we should go to Oxford, not so far away. He says, You should see it. This we understand, but some of his words come out so garbled I see that it will be impossible to ask about my mother, in case Dora has to translate. Even without going to that subject, we are embarrassed for him when he cannot speak clearly. Still we carry on.

I tell him we're staying at The Red Lion Hotel, right on the river, overlooking the Henley Bridge. He says, I know it well. He says he's stayed there many times. I am so struck by this coincidence as I ramble. The young men rowing early in the morning on the Thames. They're not wearing shirts. It's so cold; how do they do it? They concentrate as they row. They do not look up at the excited young woman jogging on the bank, trying to keep up with them. I wonder who lives in those beautiful mansions on hills bordering the river, with bright green lawns rolling down almost to the water's edge. We find swans living by the river. They're quite contrary, which is incongruous, I think, with their beauty. Or maybe not. Such a coincidence – the hotel.

There are so many places we could have chosen to stay in. Windsor and Windsor Castle are not so far away either. But without knowing Mike had been there I chose The Red Lion, as if blind-folded and putting a pin to the map

I wonder, as we sit smoking by the window in our room overlooking the Leander Club across the river, if Mike sat here taking in the same view, if he went to any of the parties there. It's claims to be the oldest rowing club in the world and while we are there a party sends music floating across the water until 4 a.m. I wish I could have belonged to it. I wish I could have rowed. I wonder if Mike ate game pie in the pub downstairs. Or if he walked as we have along the Henley Reach, the straight stretch of river outside The Red Lion where the rowers race.

From Florida I write, saying thank you for the house gift money; I bought a little crystal vase with it in Henley and a lavender-colored rose bush at home. I tell them we found The Little Angel – James was raving about the baked brie covered with spinach and a crust, *Moules mariniere*, venison with shallots and red wine sauce, pancakes in whiskey crème. And, I say, I found a special place on our last day there. It's down the Henley Reach from The Red Lion, past the mallards and swans, the bleak but beautiful countryside. In the middle of the Thames we saw an island with a small white house on it. On top of the house is a kind of gazebo with white columns. A craggy bending willow tree, still winter bare, graces the front of the house. I wonder what it's about, who lives there, I'm drawn to it. I didn't want to leave it.

Almost two decades later I learn that my grandfather lived for some time in Maidenhead, a little more than 5 miles from Henley-on-Thames. He was a surgeon and took all his undergraduate and medical degrees at Oxford, graduating in the class of 1904. He was a member of the Trinity College rowing crew of 1891.

I write to Mike and Dora for almost a year, usually once a month, then call a few days later because, except for a Christmas card, Dora does not write. I have to know how he is. In January I learn we could save about $700 in airfare to London if I dial the Virgin Atlantic Airlines promotion number non-stop on certain days starting at 8 a.m.; it's like winning the lottery when my call goes through. I am jumping up and down, calling Mike and writing letters about our arrival. I have visions of our room at The Red Lion, of swans, game pie and Mr. Ractliff – that's Charles Ractliff whose family owns The Red Lion – who runs it and is nice to us, in his vested suit and puts us in a room on the water.

I write to Mike and Dora before we arrive:

We are hoping you will allow us to make you our guests at The Little Angel. We know it is difficult for you to travel but if it is possible we think you might be very comfortable there. There is a private dining room available. The Bailey Room. It has a private entrance from the outside. We would so love to treat you to moules mariniere and whatever else. I remember Dora loves moules mariniere. They said they could serve us dinner at noon or 1 p.m. or whatever hour you prefer to eat.

As I dial his number from The Red Lion, I can see his dim wheelchair silhouette.

I say, Hi, Hi, Hi, we made it; we're here. How are you?

Mike says, in his mellow voice, veddy well thank you. Can you come on Thursday?

Yes, thank you. (I am disappointed that we have to wait a day and a half, but am grateful nevertheless for the invitation.)

We will give you lunch. Come at eleven.

I say: We can't wait to see you. They gave us our favorite room overlooking the water here at The Red Lion. Did you ask Dora about going to The Little Angel? We could arrange for a car to come and get you. Or we could come and get you, whatever you prefer. We'd have so much fun. It would be a break from cooking for Dora. Do you think we could do it? What do you say?

Silence. Then I hear a knock, like someone's dropped or put down the phone.

Mike?

I realize that perhaps I've been talking to myself. Perhaps he's dropped the phone.

Mike?

I hear Dora's voice, loud, clear in the room. She says: A pest; she's just a pest. A pest. A pest. She just wants to inherit.

Then silence. Then mumbling, I can't tell who. Then silence. I feel I should get off the phone. Is this an accident? Or not? Was I meant to hear this? Do I want to hear any more? No. I do not. But I am riveted. Is this the truth? How she really feels about me? But there's only silence now. I hang up.

I wish I could go to sleep and wake up and find that this had never happened, that Dora never said this.

After I tell him what happened, James is angry. You told them, he says, a long time ago that we don't need or want money. He fumes, smokes cigarettes out the window overlooking the Leander Club. He says he doesn't want to go see them on Thursday.

I almost don't want to go on Thursday either. But it was Dora, not Mike, who did this. I cannot let Mike down. I cannot come this far and not see him. If we went back without seeing him, it would affect him. I know it would. We have to go. James is explosively silent. I have never seen him so angry. And I?

It would be so easy to slip down into the black hole, become mute, tread in that mind's place where speech and thought are pointless, but that would be a luxury. It's a luxury that only those who have no one can afford. And I have a dear husband and a precious father.

The next morning I think: We'll go to The Little Angel tonight. James will calm down. I jog on the Leander Club side of the Thames, fighting jet lag, ignoring the mud, grateful for the dampness softening the cold air in my lungs as I pant, craving that sight.

That little white house topped by the gazebo with columns on the island in the river. After a few minutes I can make it out in the distance amidst trees that are stark, dark, bare, except for some evergreens on one side of it. It comes into sharper focus. I see its pale green dome. It's much sturdier than a gazebo. Then I see the weathervane on top of the dome. Whimsical, formal, like Mike.

It seems empty. It seemed empty the last time we saw it. I could live there, in spirit. It could be mine. I could haunt it. One day when I'm dead I shall haunt it if I can. But, I think, why do I have to wait? It could be my place, my island in the U.K. What harm is there in daydreaming that your soul occupies a pure white sacred-looking structure, austere, safe, cushioned by soft grass and the arms of a willow tree, barricaded by water? You can pretend it's yours and that your spirit is protected there. Doesn't have to be the conventional spirit of a dead person, a ghost like the kind in books and Veddy-Veddy movies. It could just be my invisible spirit, with my love for Mike, in there, always. And no one can touch it, ever, on that island.

Then I think: What if something happens to the house? Doesn't matter; I'll still be in that space.

I kiss James awake. We go down to breakfast. We see in the hotel lobby many tiny paintings of pretty English gardens. Soft colors. Gentle. We study them, then go in to eat.

I don't know what's the matter with me. I'm famished. I eat a full English breakfast of eggs, sausage, bacon, grilled tomatoes, bread, jam. I'm still hungry. But I stop eating. My clothes are getting tight. What shall I wear to see Mike if my clothes are too tight? I think Charles Ractliff at the front desk notices my corduroy suit is tight, but maybe it's my imagination.

We ask him about the artist who did the little paintings. His wife. Ah, Christine Ractliff. They're so lovely. Oh, just wanted to ask about that unique little white house, with columns on top, on the island down the Thames. Saw it when I went jogging. Do you know it?

It's called Temple Island.

I see.

Later, I learn it was built in 1771; it's designs were discovered in Pompeii. Am touched by the coincidence that I love to fish and this elegant spiritual place was built as a fishing lodge for a mansion on the Henley Reach. Well, the owners don't have to know how important it is to me – what it guards and that it's really mine now, in my head.

It's so easy to slip into an imaginary Veddy-Veddy movie when you're in England. Must make a reservation at The Little Angel. Must find a flower shop and send some freesias ahead of us to Mike and Dora. Set the tone for lunch the next day. Ignore what she's done. Oh, James, let's go walk in the village. Let's pop into St. Mary's. Let's have some scones and clotted cream. Let's go down to Temple Island again. Feed the swans. Nasty swans.

We come back in the late afternoon with a bottle of claret. Mr. Ractliff helps us get it opened (without pushing the cork inside it). He joins us in the little sitting area. We enjoy again the tiny paintings by his wife. I say James does cartoons and paintings. Could we meet her for a cup of tea? Going to see my father in Wallingford tomorrow. Can't wait. Jolly good.

Oh, Veddy-Veddy.

When Dora opens the door, James, still insulted, passes by her quickly and goes into the drawing room. I look her straight in her eyes. She looks down.

I know she knows I heard what she said when the phone was off the hook. I think it was intentional that I was to have heard it. But I am Danielle Flood, Mike Wilton's daughter, Jim Flood's stepdaughter. I have no time for this. It's beneath me.

How are you? I say.

Veddy well, thank you. Please come in.

Thank you.

I see him from the entrance to the drawing room, the shadow of his head and shoulders above the wheelchair framed by the light coming in the big window. It's a consuming sight: a wave moves over me, then ebbs, leaving me full of tenderness.

His face has more color in it than last time. I kiss him hello. I smell so much Chanel for Men I can't smell him. We smile. Our impish puckers appear. He's wearing Stewart plaid boxer shorts this time – the red rather festive above his stumps – and a dark blue crew neck sweater. I dust the dandruff off his shoulder, enjoying the feeling that I have the right to do so. I ask him how he is. Veddy well, thank you.

I have to tell you, I say, about this magic place I found called Temple Island. It's down the river from The Red Lion.

He says: I know it well.

You know it? I stare. My mind is blank with surprise.

He says: I used to go there.

Why?

Just to go there.

How did you get there?

By boat.

It's another short visit. He still gets easily tired. His diction is more clear than the year before. Dora is off to get prawns ready for lunch. He gazes at me and asks if I've put on weight. I say, I think I might be pregnant. The corners of his lips turn up and he bounces in his chair a bit. I can tell, in his reserved way he is pleased. I say, looking out the window too, that if I am, we would like the baby's middle name to be Wilton. Would he like that? He nods. Crows feet appear by his eyes. Then I notice two peach-colored roses blooming in the tiny garden before us. In January, and everywhere there are patches of snow melting.

Dora gives Mike an eight-ounce glass of Scotch and asks us if we would like some. No thanks. A little wine? With lunch, thank you. I wonder, looking at Mike's large glass what happens when someone consumes that much Scotch at one sitting, especially when one's body weight is so much less than normal. But I say nothing; not my affair. Dora is sipping rosé. Offering Silk Cuts. I don't want to smoke.

Dora says she's commissioned a bust of Mike. I wish so much that I could have it, or that I could have another made for me, but I say nothing, again wary, wanting only a peaceful visit. What has Mike been doing? Watching *Falcon Crest* (the American night-time soap opera with outlandish characters), he says. The puckers appear beneath the corners of his lips though Mike is trying to keep a straight face. Dora leaves to serve lunch. I consider: the squadron-leader-fighter-pilot watching *Falcon Crest.* I ask him what he's been reading.

He thrusts a newspaper magazine at me, as if it were some secret cache. You may have that, he says. The puckers appear. The cover story is on the

Windsor jewels to be auctioned off by Sotheby's in April. I think: Are you giving me the Windsor jewels? (How lovely.) (I especially like the leopard pin.) I ask: How do you feel about the late Wallis Simpson (the American divorcée, for whom the king of England abdicated)?

Foreigner, he says. I smile.

Dora asks Mike if he would like to go to the loo. Yes, please. She wheels him down the hall, then wheels him to the table for lunch. After lunch she brings him another 8-ounce glass of Scotch. When I see this, the cheer from all of our having pulled off the afternoon without unpleasantness leaves me. The oily-looking gold liquid says: It's over. How could anyone be conscious after drinking a second big glass of that? Or even a first one? Dora says: Mike has to have his nap soon. Yes, of course, I think. But I know this glass is too much. I can say nothing. Do I have a right to say anything? Would you dare to say anything after hearing what I heard on the phone? I am afraid of anything that could cause him to become upset or unavailable to see me again. Now, after this phone thing, I know she has hassled him about me. It was clear last time that he had lost the use of his arm and will always need her to go to the loo. And so, when I see a drop of blood stream from the seam of one of his stumps and I want to find a gauze pad or a tissue for him, and I see she sees that I see it, I look away. I really want that drop of blood on a handkerchief or tissue so I might put it in my jewelry box or missal, like some people do with a loved one's lock of hair, but I do nothing. Am afraid. Dora asks if we would like to come for a drink the next day, but I say there won't be enough time. Packing. Gatwick. I do not say that I don't feel well, that James and I are exhausted from pretending that nothing unusual happened on the phone. Pretending, for us, for her, especially for Mike.

I put on my new full-length navy trench coat and stand before Mike. I tilt my head to one side, smile at him in my white beret, extend my arms away from my torso a bit, palms toward him like a little girl. Sometimes he makes me feel 7 years old. I'm 35. So what? It's fun. This is how I should have felt then, at 7: relaxed, wanted, safe. I ask: Should I tie the belt in a knot or buckle it? Tie it, he says.

The taxi is here. Mike is sullen, still, looking at the floor. I think commiserating will do neither of us any good and might irritate Dora. I kiss him, then step back and twirl in my trench coat tied at the waist. My cheeks against Dora's. James is shaking Dora's hand. Outside the big window I step rompishly by the roses blooming in winter and tilt my head to the side again, feeling somehow like a marionette I don't know why. Then I frame my smiling face with my hands, palms facing him and pose. I wave cheerfully, refusing to let him see me feel as I really do. But when I get to the curb by the taxi, the tears fall, cold as they touch my skin. Every time we see him I am afraid it is to be the last.

The only things that solace the absence of his presence are the sound of bagpipes, the memory of his glad demeanor, his efforts to make us laugh and the thought of Temple Island. Christine Ractcliff's English garden paintings soothe me, too.

We meet her before we leave. I give her a fistful of flowers. She agrees to paint Temple Island for me. She frames it in silver-painted wood and sends it to me. Whenever I miss Mike and I look at it, I am reminded of what's in there, safe; it will outlive me.

As soon as we get back to Florida, I learn that I am pregnant. Soon thereafter I lose a twin.

I write. I call. James calls Mike to tell him his healthy granddaughter has been born.

I call Mike every other Saturday night. He doesn't seem to mind. Dora is pleasant when she answers. It's always afternoon in Florida when I do. I'm facing the dark green hedge outside the window as I dial from the dining room, the sun sparkling off the smooth leaves. It's charming when you phone the U.K. When you call in the States there's a ring, a pause, a ring and so on. When you call the U.K., it ring-rings, pauses, ring-rings. It sounds old-fashioned, somehow. One afternoon it ring-rings twenty times.

Well, I know he and Dora aren't out dancing.

I hang up and call again, in case I dialed wrong. It ring-rings twenty times again. I call information. When I get the second hospital and ask for Michael Stanley James Wilton, the nurse says: Is this his daughter?

Yes.

Would you please tell me his date of birth?

March 23, 1917.

I'm very sorry to inform you, but he died almost a week ago, on April 25th.

This time, it is I who cries out. Maybe he can hear me wherever he is. In the sky? Over the sea? Invisible beside me? Where? Where do squadron leaders go when they die? To the clouds? British reserve. I don't care. Now I know how he felt when he wailed the first time we left him in Wallingford. He didn't care then who heard. Sometimes in life it's all so much, you do not care who hears. I don't care now.

Then I remember the nurse on the phone. I say: I'm so sorry, I...

She says: Please, is someone with you? Are you alone?

No, I say, my husband is here. It's all right. He's here. I'm so sorry. Thank you very much.

Mike was able to see photographs of his granddaughter, to hear that she was beginning to crawl and that mobiles of the sun, the moon and the planets hung from the ceiling of her room. When I told Mike the doctor said she was going to be born on October 4, and I forgot to say that that was the due date, he said, amused: The doctor knows when she's going to be born? I was pleased the baby had his attention. The Christmas present and card he and Dora sent her was a surprise. I bought a little gold heart with it. His granddaughter wears it.

Chapter Twenty-Six

Dad died, almost a year after Mike, in the vault-like room in which he slept in his villa in Portugal. He was only 65. The official *Report of the Death of an American Citizen Abroad* said he'd had a stroke. He had been drinking a great deal, quietly, all day, every day. I saw it when I visited him. I asked him if he was happy. He said he was content, in the French sense of the word. He had been listening repeatedly for several years to the movie soundtrack of *Ryan's Daughter*, the World War I movie about a young married Irish woman who is attacked by a village mob after she has an affair with a young British officer, who kills himself.

As I left him in the Algarve and the antiquated train was pulling out of the station, I ran to the steps at the end of the car and leaned out over the platform. Dad was still there by the tracks. He waved at me again. There was deep sadness in his face. Never had I seen him allow himself to show that and I knew that that was the last time I would see him. He knew it, too. Staying on the train then took great effort.

He will always be my Dad. Mike will always be my father. After all and forever, I had two.

Chapter Twenty-Seven

When time allows me to become accustomed to the idea that I can see Mike and Dad in settings all over the world whenever I want and I'm sure plenty of time has passed for Dora to inherit, I think of her alone, nearing 80. I feel sorry for her. I think Mike would want me to transcend the effect of her behavior and cheer her from afar, so I call.

Oh, hello. She sounds glad to hear from me. Right away she proffers that she couldn't get the phone number for *The Miami Herald* to tell James that Mike had died. Mike had had another stroke. Something about his ashes having been sprinkled in a little garden at the crematorium.

I send books, cards, flowers at Christmas. She sends cards, writes of her siblings' deaths. I try to console her. After a couple of years, I say I would love one more photo of Mike, perhaps in uniform. She doesn't respond. Once, on the phone, I gather the energy to ask what had happened to Mike's legs. She says something about veins or arteries collapsing. She says, They had to keep cutting. Then she changes the subject. I freeze, realizing she doesn't care if I understand. I don't bother to bring up Saigon.

One Christmas she says I sent her a card that is a reproduction of a print hanging in their bedroom – *The Boulevard de Clichy Under Snow* by Norbert Goeneutte. She notes I was never in their bedroom. True, I say. I don't tell her this sort of thing has happened before, but I am hesitant about attributing meaning to coincidence; but I wonder.

During another phone call she thanks me profusely for flowers and books but says don't send more, postage is expensive. I feel she wants to be on her own. So I stop sending. She stops sending.

Dora died almost 12 years after Mike, in 2000, at age 87. I was surprised when I later learned she was not the wife Mike had when I was conceived in Saigon. I thought back to all the visits – the anxiety from her. About what?

Mike had two wives before Dora.

Chapter Twenty-Eight

For most of my life – especially during the years when I did not know who my father was – I wished to learn that I had come from some constant love, that lasted more than half a century or more, a marriage, legitimacy in a neat box with a bow. But when I found my new sister, Mike's other daughter, I was released from that desire.

Locating her, Ariel Josephine Wilton, in Australia, born in England nine years before me, was a surprise because Dora had said she and Mike didn't have children. She and Mike had let me think Dora was his only wife.

I immediately went from thinking I was Mike's only child to learning I was his younger daughter, which made me feel less special, for a little while. I wondered, as I flew from Miami to British Columbia to meet Ariel at her mother's deathbed, what kind of relationship Ariel had had with Mike. Did Mike go to her graduations? Did he give her away at her wedding? I told myself I mustn't be jealous of whatever time Ariel had had with Mike.

But her mother, a debutante who had been presented to the Queen, divorced him in 1945 after a brief marriage when Ariel was three. Joan Kinloch, formerly Wilton, said she wanted to see me at her deathbed and when she did, she said loudly in the hospital to me, her current husband and several of her grown children that Mike was a drunk and a womanizer. She said he didn't want the child she was carrying and she elaborated, a lot. When I heard this, I wanted to flee, remembering he was a very young man when he married her after knowing her three weeks. Also, I was upset that Ariel was hearing this.

But Ariel behaved as if she'd heard it before.

She said she never tried to find Mike, though she grew up and was educated in England. He never knew she married a French vice-consul, that she'd had four of Mike's grandchildren, that she was divorced and later obtained an undergraduate degree in communications (like me). He didn't know she'd lost a daughter – who looked like me – in a bad riding accident at age 15. And Ariel didn't know about his plane crashes. I was the one to tell her he lost his legs and of his strokes. She didn't know he had died.

He couldn't have found her as I did through a blip about her half-sister on the Internet. Why didn't she try and find him?

"Lazy, I guess," she said.

I don't believe it. I said: "How about emotionally reticent?" She did not look at me. I said: "Emotionally careful?"

She said: "Love the world without trusting."

I said: "You could have found him, through the RAF. You knew he was in the RAF."

She said: "Love the world without trusting."

I remember that Mike had a friend's secretary write to me after his first stroke, that he saw to it that his older, third wife was provided for after he died, that in his wheelchair he adopted a child in a magazine, that there were times his squadron needed food during the war and he went off and got it, somehow, and that the flying log writer said it was much appreciated. I told Ariel that I believe he would have loved her. She stared at me, silent.

I was still in shock when I left Ariel in British Columbia, but as the plane gained altitude, I began to see all I had been through in a new perspective. I was out of some clouds for the first time. Looking down upon them, I no longer wanted what I didn't have. I would never trade the time I had with Mike for Ariel's legal connections to him – her mother's marriage to him, her having his surname.

Mike and me. We had the light coming in that window, lunches together, Stilton cheese, the sound of our voices, the sight of our letters, the smell of flowers and of each other, the feel of our skin, our hair, laughter, a sharing, of knowing looks, books, bagpipes, Beethoven and images of Windsor jewels, of fear, mystery, grief, strength, tenderness, the Thames, The Red Lion, swans, nasty swans, dreams of each other and Temple Island.

My gratitude for these gave me strength, then, when I would have to face final questions about Mike, Mom, and Dad in Saigon. I almost would be forced to do so. And then, when I looked back at how my life with them had played out, I wondered how much of it had been my doing, and how much of it had been part of some greater design.

Epilogue

It is as if the love story of Mom and Mike and Dad was restless, tossing in time, wouldn't leave me alone.

It had been fourteen years since Mom had died, ten years since Mike and nine since Dad. I was settled, quiet, chauffeuring the kids to violin and tennis lessons, making school lunches to the sound of lawnmowers, leaf blowers. James survived a few more of my you-don't-love-me-enough scenes, but he does. I was working on a novel and looking for missing socks when the letter that would change my life came. It eventually made me know more of who I am.

It was from Aunt Sue, Jim Flood's sister, retired, taking college courses in Pittsburgh. She enclosed a copy of two paragraphs from *The Life of Graham Greene Volume Two* by Norman Sherry, appointed by the late English author as his authorized biographer. There are many dozens of books about Greene who traveled over the globe for three decades gathering material for his 26 novels and other fiction. These paragraphs concerned the source of characters in Greene's novel, *The Quiet American*, set in Saigon while Mom and Dad and Mike were there. In the paragraphs, Sherry, compares Dad to Alden Pyle, *The Quiet American* character:

There is no evidence in his journals that during his numerous visits to Vietnam Greene met anyone remotely like Pyle, though he met most of the Americans in Saigon – in 1951 there were very few of them. He built Pyle's character up from a number of diverse elements.

When Greene first went to Saigon he heard of a British air attaché who was living with a Vietnamese girl in Saigon, made her pregnant and then was called back home. Hearsay has it that the attaché went home to his wife and children and paid his pregnant girlfriend 300 dollars before leaving. There is a passage in the novel where Pyle becomes angry over Fowler's 'dirty cracks' and asks: 'What can you offer her?...A couple of hundred dollars when you leave for England, or will you pass her on with the furniture?' (2) A young American then working in the American aid mission called Jim Flood decided (with a Pyle-like sense of injustice) that the air attaché's offer was not enough; the Vietnamese girl needed protection, so he married her in Saigon. Tom Peck in the consular passport department was Flood's best man at the wedding. Ambassador Donald Heath came to the reception for Flood (a junior member of his staff) and his bride. The story of Jim Flood's marriage was the gossip of the rue Catinat and Greene had heard it.

---

(2) The Quiet American: by Graham Greene, Penguin edition, 1974, p.78.

Aunt Sue wrote:

The young American who worked for the U.S. government in Saigon in 1951 named Jim Flood – who else could this be but your Dad and my brother, Jim Flood?

The pregnant 'Vietnamese girl' whom he married – wouldn't this be your mother? (Never mind that your mother was really Eurasian. That's a detail that could have been unknown to the author or even Graham Greene himself.)

The 'British air attaché who was responsible for her pregnancy – who else but Mike Wilton, the man whom you yourself concluded is your natural father?

In all important details, the account fits. It would be too much of a coincidence for it not to fit the actual persons and events.

I can't get over the fact that I simply stumbled on this nugget of our family history, and your history, hidden away…in Carnegie Library. (Underlining is hers.)

Later, she wrote to me: *Norman Sherry surmises that Pyle was sort of patterned after your Dad…*

We Americans are not all fools bumpkins and boors. Yes, Pyle is brave, but he is a fool nevertheless...Is Jim Flood, Pyle? Of course not...[but]...the similarity between Jim Flood's narrative and The Quiet American *is amazing... I found the fact that he was even mentioned in Sherry's book, and in very specific terms, to be astounding.*

Not to me. Jim Flood was a very quiet man. He was not one to proffer information, not even to his sister, not even to me about my real father, never about his work and rarely about himself.

I'm distracted by certain words in Sherry's (or Greene's) account: "girlfriend" - My mother was just a girlfriend? "300 dollars" - How would Sherry or Greene know that? Such an unlikely thing for Mike or my mother to tell anyone, if it was true, though it was noted by an American Legation employee who was there and knew them all that that was a great deal of money at the time. And, "paid" - Why would Sherry or Greene use such a word? Prostitutes are paid. Why not "gave?"

I wonder where I can hide from this. How can I make it disappear? How dare Sherry or Greene use such a word.

I feel slapped.

I can't make Sherry's words disappear. They're there, in the second volume of three, totaling 2,251 pages, examining the life of the controversial Greene, who though a Roman Catholic and a moralist, slept in apparent nonchalance with many dozens of prostitutes and with a number of married mistresses while he himself was married.

The Sherry paragraphs scare me, make me wonder what kind of liaison I had come from. Had it been a meaningless affair? Is a person less significant if he is born of a casual conception? Was I? Am I? Am I tainted? It shouldn't matter. But it does, to me.

And, did what happened in Saigon shape my parents, all three of them? Did the fact that they lived on death's threshold much of the time as young people guide their choices later as they forsook their children?

Some questions about what happened between my parents in Saigon may never be answered. But I would learn enough about them during the many years of journalistic investigation I would undertake for this book to satisfy me, though some of the experience felt quite unfamiliar.

It was strange because I am a part of the story, and a reason for much trouble in it, though I was so young I don't remember it. I was trained – like many journalists – to keep myself out of whatever story I was covering and so it felt odd sometimes to write this entire memoir. It has been startling to establish a reporter-source relationship with someone who was close to my parents and to sometimes feel close to him and then to learn after many years of interviewing him that he was an undercover CIA officer for some forty years, including in Saigon. This happened twice, actually, though I found myself feeling close to only one source who turned out to be a CIA officer. And then it happened a third time – another source, another vice consul, was revealed as working under cover for the CIA in Saigon; this one only just knew my parents then and there; they weren't good friends.

It was touching but also startling to receive from a CIA officer photos of myself, thirteen months old, learning to walk during my first Christmas in Saigon, 1952, with his daughter, also a toddler, with her fingers in her mouth, in front of an American Legation Christmas tree.

And I was taken aback to find six photos of a bombing aftermath in downtown Saigon, complete with dead children, in Dad's family photo album in Pittsburgh. Most are heretofore unpublished. They were of the real two-car bombing that inspired the single-car bombing that Greene featured in *The Quiet American*. We were there in Saigon during that double bombing. There's a small photo of me and my mother on the cover of this book, taken when I was 2 months old, within two or three days of the January 9, 1952, two-car bombing. We appear to be within about a city block of the opera house – in front of which one car bomb exploded Another of Dad's photos showed car pieces a block away from Saigon's city hall, the *hotel de ville*, where the other bomb went off. Clearly my mother and I could have been fatal victims.

The Quiet American is called a murder mystery, a political novel and a love story. It's about a young American government official in Saigon who falls in love with and proposes marriage to and takes the Vietnamese mistress away from an older British man, whose wife is in England and who has been called back home by his employer.

Tom Peck and other legation officers in Saigon during Greene's early visits – when he gathered material for *The Quiet American* – say there was no one at the U.S. Legation/Embassy except Jim Flood who had fallen in love with and asked to marry a woman who was all or part Vietnamese, who had been living with an older British man, whose wife was in England and who had been called back home by his employer.

"That was certainly a unique situation," said Peck, who as the American Legation consular officer had to concern himself with nuptial matters as part of his job. "There were no other Americans that matched that description."

Peck said that while he was in Saigon, December, 1950 to the spring of 1953, the period during which Greene visited Saigon most frequently, there was only one other legation officer besides Jim Flood who was married in Saigon and he married an American girl.

There were some 40 officers including economic aid types at the U.S. Legation in early 1951 and four officers at the British Consulate, not including Mike. Considering how small the Anglo community in Saigon was, how many times Greene went there, and how Greene made it a habit to seek out attractive women and proposition them – even if they were married – it would be surprising if he didn't know Mike, Dad and Mom, especially since my mother was very tall, beautiful and stood out in a crowd.

Meanwhile over the years, when scholars probed as to whether or not Greene modeled his characters after real people, he insisted, "I do not take people straight from real life in my novels…There has once or twice been a little straight reporting in my novels. There was some in *The Quiet American*, but no real people. Real people would wreck the design. The characters in my novels are an amalgam of bits of real people; one takes the isolated traits from many; they are fused by the heat of the unconscious. Real people are too limiting."

It's not normal to find so much information about your parents' private lives, and your own, in a fat book of literary history – a controversial one at that, because Norman Sherry was criticized by Greene's family in England and others for various reasons. Readers can decide for themselves whether or not my parents inspired some of what went on in Greene's novel, a novel that was popular and taught in colleges in the United States and elsewhere off and on for more than half a century, while I was looking for my natural father for a good chunk of that time – 30 years.

I asked Sherry to confirm that Greene himself told him he knew the story about my parents. I also asked why he used the word "paid." I asked if that was his word or Greene's. Sherry wrote to me in an email: "I have nothing to add for my sources of information than have already been quoted in Volume II." He did not answer the question of "paid."

There are certain inaccuracies in Sherry's, or Greene's, account:

Jim Flood was not, as Sherry reported, in the economic aid mission. He worked for the USIS But *Quiet American* Pyle was with the economic aid mission. Did Greene, Pyle's creator, make this mistake as he told Sherry about Dad?

Mike, though often referred to as the air attaché in Saigon – he first responded to me in our first phone conversation as such – was the air liaison officer, also a diplomatic post. There was no air attaché post while he was there. His replacement, Wing Commander Nick Simmons, was the first Royal Air Force attaché in Saigon.

Also, Mike was married at the time to Agnes Margaret Wilton; they had no children. Further, Sherry's, or Greene's, account in the two paragraphs quoted above from Greene's authorized biography is incomplete.

Here is the true love story behind the novel.

Mom

As I browse through the Jullien family portraits taken in a Hanoi photo studio before oil-painted backdrops of dramatic cloudy skies, I am reminded that my mother was once a child – slender, about six years old, wearing white anklets and dark leather strapped flat dress shoes, looking uncomfortable in a vested suit with pleated skirt that, like her coiffure, matched that of her older sister. This escapes me most of the time, probably because I never saw a photo of her as a child until I went to France to gather documentation for this memoir, in the wake of 9/11 when I was almost 50.

I would get from my youngest uncle, Guy Jullien, many of these family photos and most of the family history of when it was in French Indochina. In many of the photos my mother and her siblings are posed, dressed in elaborate matching clothes – even in matching sailor suits; in one studio photo, my grandfather is in a tuxedo. But there is a less formal black and white picture of my mother when she is about ten, about 1937, in a sleeveless short summer jumpsuit, wearing a ribbon in her hair, tied in a bow. She is standing beside a concrete gatepost, the post much bigger than she is, attached to the concrete wall surrounding the family home in Thanh Hoa, southeast of Hanoi. It says: look at me, a happy, pretty, little girl who aims to please with a ribbon in my hair. A little girl with hope and affection – the simple message in another snapshot of the beautiful young French army specialist she was, petting a dog in Saigon, perhaps a little out of uniform in her stylish espadrilles. The latter photo must have been taken shortly after she arrived because her hair is shoulder length and Saigon was hot and humid and so, the Anglo women who were there told me, they kept their hair short or pinned up.

Until I saw these photos I wondered if what she had said was true, about all the servants, the privileged life style she had in Tonkin, north French Indochina. And there was her attitude: that she was entitled to call someone from another room to bring her tea, that she was owed somehow all the comforts of life, that she was superior. Where did that come from? There was a whiff of that in my two older uncles.

But then the photographs spoke, embellishing descriptions by Uncle Guy. I began to understand as I studied the one of my grandfather's first big house on the river at Kim Lu, upriver from the *Golfe du Tonkin*. After his military service to France in China, Aymond Jullien worked as a civil servant overseeing the construction of a substantial bridge and of the Vietnam-Yunnan railroad line; as a result he was bestowed a title by the Emperor Bao Dai, by "Imperial Order of the Dragon of Annam," according to the elaborately-decorated certificate documenting that he had been made a chevalier – a knight. After meeting and falling in love with my grandmother, Marie-Jeanne Jarno, he was able to have this huge house constructed for his 1924 bride, though it was rustic living, without plumbing or electricity and in the bush. There was danger; a panther coming to drink fresh water close to the house at night; another that had to be shot by my grandfather at the request of a nearby village, because it was attacking and eating its supply of fowl; there is a photo of that cat, what we would call a leopard. The photo doesn't show the time Marie-Jeanne had to escape with four small children through the brush and jungle up the mountain behind their open-air thatched roof house when during a long storm the river waters rose so that it was flooded. She had to leave Grandfather Aymond at the house with some servants to try and save their belongings. And the photos don't show that there were times when it was difficult to get enough food to feed the seven of them, even later, when my grandfather's salary increased as an inspector general for alcohol (manufactured by the government) for Northern Annam. In this capacity he rode most days in a Citroën 11 Légère, a big black car driven and cared for by a chauffeur. (In one amusing photo, it is brimming with children.) Many times, food appeared on the table in the Jullien house because Aymond went out with his three German shorthaired pointers – Bristou, Patol and Cuet – and shot it: wild cattle, big game boar, partridges, snipes, quail, woodcock, and pheasant. Or some got there because my grandmother had two large vegetable gardens, tended by gardeners, though most of their many servants worked part time, so they would also have time for their own families; this was my grandmother's preference.

When Aymond took the inspector general position, he had a house built for the family in Thanh Hoa with a view to spending time with his family at the beach in Samson, fifteen minutes away by car. This house in town was made of concrete and would have electricity, a refrigerator, fans, switch-on lights and a fireplace in every room.The children would go to school half-boarding (all day) in Thanh Hoa or full-time boarding in Hanoi. In addition to all, Aymond would manage to provide for his five children a real German wheel: two metal circles about five feet in diameter connected by horizontal bars so they could practice acrobatics, a relatively new invention in the early 20th century patented in Germany. For himself and friends, he was also able to import some barrels of wine.

My mother and her family had had a life in Vietnam, created and earned by her parents, full of the memories of the struggles and triumphs it took to achieve that world. What a shock it was for her, for all of them, to suddenly lose everything and to live daily in fear for their lives for so many of her teen years, which is what happened during the Japanese occupation of French Indochina. What happened to the Jullien family after that made it part of the classic story of mass migration all over the world – part of the vast story of displacement in the wake of wars.

When she was thirteen, in 1940, the Japanese invaded the French border forts between *Indochine* and China, two hundred miles from where she lived, and killed some eight hundred Frenchmen in two days of fighting. For a while, when she and her sister were in boarding school in Hanoi, in a district of large French villas, the Japanese allowed the French administration to stay in place as a kind of puppet government. But then, on March 9, 1945, when she was 17, the Japanese struck nearby French garrisons, beheading the French governor and a French general, jailing hundreds of French civilians and soldiers who surrendered in Hanoi, massacring French soldiers elsewhere who resisted.

My grandfather, anticipating trouble, moved the family from Thanh Hoa to the beach resort of Sam Son, on the *Golfe du Tonkin*. They shared a friend's villa with a British couple that the Japanese jailed as spies. They saw the Japanese take away the couple, and the couple's children after the soldiers said the couple had died of an opium overdose in prison. There were interrogations. One day the Japanese came and took away all six of my grandfather's rifles, described by my Uncle Alban, as of high quality and accuracy. In reaction, Alban wrote, that he had never seen Aymond as upset as he was from that. Of course he was not given a receipt.

Then the Japanese told the Julliens to put all their belongings into two big trucks, which they did. The Japanese said the belongings would be returned to them at a certain nearby hotel. This did not happen. My grandfather wrote to his brother and his wife in France that he and his family had "lost everything, absolutely everything."

They were ordered to take a bus to Hanoi where they were confined to a French ghetto. They stayed in the two-room house of a French officer who had been jailed or killed and received as French nationals a subsistence enough for, usually, a piece of bread, a banana and two cups of coffee a day.

When she was 18, my mother often woke up to see dead bodies on the patch of grass between the house and the street. This happened daily to the Julliens and others, including the mayor of Hanoi at the time, because of a famine that killed two of the ten million North Vietnamese. The famine was caused by the Japanese stockpiling rice for themselves and their forcing the planting of industrial crops instead of rice. My mother saw people digging in garbage and cooking grass and rats in the street to eat.

Still in her 18th year, she saw Hiroshima as a "fortunate event," as Uncle Guy put it. But then in the resulting power vacuum, Vietnamese Communists announced their seizure of control from the balcony of the Hanoi opera house, of classic French design, where my mother had her secondary school graduation dance.

A few months later, in February, 1946, Aymond decided to take his family home to the safety of *Mas de la Prade*, the ancestral house in St. Paulet de Caisson, near Pont St. Esprit in the south of France. His brother,

Daniel, who had no children, lived with his wife, Marie Eugenie, in the limestone farmhouse there, with the first of three floors measuring more than 3,600 square feet, built circa 1700.

More than three hundred years later the hands of two medium-sized men reaching around the *Platane* (plane) tree trunks in front of the house cannot touch. The ceiling in the attached stone barn is raftered with mulberry tree trunks. I could stand in the kitchen fireplace. The property, called *La Prade*, was the largest vineyard in the area at one time. It had been in the Jullien family since long before the time of Napoleon. It stands in an area where the light is gold because, locals say, there is gold in the soil. It's within walking distance of the St. Paulet cemetery where generations of Julliens are buried.

Aymond had been away from *La Prade* for 52 years. From Vietnam his wife, Marie-Jeanne, wrote to the family there for more than twenty years. Now, he told his children, that they had lost everything, at least *Mas de la Prade* would provide sanctuary until they could recuperate. It became a source of relief as they fled from French Indochina.

The family took a small boat followed by gunshots down Hanoi's Red River. In March, 1946, they sailed for France on the steamship, *L'Eridan II*, also transporting wounded soldiers, that sailed through the Suez Canal and arrived finally in Toulon.

My mother's older sister, Nicole, stayed in Hanoi to be with her fiancé, an officer in the French Surete. Later, a letter arrived in France: he had been assassinated, shot in the back on the street by Vietnamese terrorists who escaped on bicycles.

My mother was 19, her brothers were 18, 16, and 14. Her mother, Marie-Jeanne, was 51. Her father, Aymond, was 73. All were exhausted from the long journey from French Indochina. They had not been able to sleep in beds of their own for many weeks and sometimes in no bed at all. When they thought, finally, they could rest, after arriving in the train station in Pont St. Esprit, their ethnic make-up was examined.

It didn't matter that Marie-Jeanne's father was French from Brittany, that she was attractive and educated. She was a metisse – a woman of mixed blood – and she had brought with her a brood of metis – each one-quarter

Vietnamese. Aymond's brother, my great uncle Daniel, allowed them to stay in a small house at *La Prade*, said to have been the caretaker's house, within sight of the main house. They stayed three weeks. Guy said *we really felt we had to get out* because his mother looked Vietnamese.

The Jullien family then lived for about a year in the ruins of a small house without electricity, water or heat near a landing field that had been abandoned by the Germans in Pujaut. Guy said he fetched water from a kilometer away on a bicycle with no air chamber. My mother watched her brothers cut down a telegraph pole to fuel fires for cooking and heat.

Aymond and Marie-Jeanne returned to *La Prade* in St. Paulet de Caisson and eventually were allowed to again stay in the smaller house on the property. World War II was over, but France was struggling to dig itself out of the stripped and bombed-out devastation that resulted from the German occupation. Eventually, Uncle Daniel joined the army, Alban joined the air force and Guy joined the navy. My mother later told Dad that her father wanted her to marry a farmer. So she joined the army.

She risked her life for years living in a war zone rather than to stay in St. Paulet de Caisson in the South of France surrounded by grapes in all directions and by hate because she and her mother were part Asian. Her youngest brother, Guy, repeated to me that she didn't want a career in the military. So when she volunteered to return to French Indochina, to live and work in Saigon in wartime, clearly she had to be hoping to find love.

In the army, at first, when she joined in February, 1947, she was a telephone switchboard operator in Toulon, France's large port and military installation on the Mediterranean. In late 1947, she arrived in Saigon with a specialist rank equivalent of sergeant. She was 20.

My mother told me none of this. Not even about joining the army – that was a surprise. Ironically, she, her siblings and cousins later inherited the huge house, *Mas de la Prade* – the ancestral home where she and her family were denied shelter – along with the surrounding vineyards and the smaller house on the property. But that did not happen for many years. She didn't tell me about that either.

Saigon

Four months after Mom arrived in Saigon, two American women, State Department staffers, were murdered on the outskirts of the city, off the back road to Ton Son Nhut Airport – their brains blown out at close range. Somehow they had lost their shoes when their burned bodies were recovered in a jeep by the French military, and one of them, the head of USIS in Saigon was still wearing her diamond ring. My mother had to have heard of that; it was reported in a Saigon newspaper, but not publicly explained. A week earlier some 150 French and Vietnamese were killed in an armed convoy between Saigon and Dalat, to the northeast of the city.

Danger and death in what had been called for many decades the *Paris of the Orient* was constant and continuous when my parents were there. It's difficult to say whether or not it was more or less dangerous inside Saigon city limits. Travel by car outside the city, even to the airport, usually necessitated an armed escort. This induced, the British information officer said, "a real sensation of claustrophobia." And the persistent around-the-clock feeling that turning a street corner could end your life.

Mom abhorred bloody violence and yet she stayed for years in a time and place where the French were spying regularly on the Americans while accepting U.S. Navy bearcat fighter planes by day and painting them with their own insignia at night; they were used to fight in the North and in the countryside the often seemingly invisible communist Vietminh and other Vietnamese who hated their French colonists of almost a hundred years. The French and Vietnamese wounded and amputees were sent to Saigon where U.S. Central Intelligence Agency officers were recruiting Vietnamese spies to train in Saipan. Some Vietnamese were pitted against Vietnamese, for some also hated the Vietminh; some were suspicious and resentful of the American, British and other foreign presences there; some hated all the intruders.

Vietnamese children tossed grenades over high wire fences that did little to protect diners in outdoor cafes; a grenade would roll down the aisle in a movie theatre; more than a dozen Foreign Service Officers and or their wives said an average of five grenades a day exploding in Saigon was normal in those days. The French editor of Saigon's second largest daily was killed when assassins tossed two grenades in his car as he drove home for lunch. The manager of the British American Tobacco Company factory had been murdered. One had to get used to the feeling that went with not knowing what would happen next. At night one could watch, from the rooftop bar of the Majestic Hotel by the *Riviere de Saigon*, tracers and the flashes from exploding mortar rounds on the other side of it. The Indian consul was shot at while leaving a dinner party. The blonde pregnant wife of one American attaché was threatened by a Vietnamese man with a grenade while shopping for a cradle in Cholon, Saigon's Chinatown. Two French priests were murdered in western Cochinchine when their convoy was attacked; they were stabbed to death and their crosses taken as trophies.

Mike

Mike was born in Ide, Devon. He began boarding school when he was nine at Hurst Court, in Sussex, and went on to attend the prestigious Merchiston Castle School in Edinburgh. He spent summers at his Scottish mother's house in Dinard in Brittany, played tennis, squash and golf and became so fluent he could interpret French and Spanish by the time he joined the RAF at age 21, in 1938 when flying was also very young. He preferred the attraction of danger rather than study at university, though his mother, an heiress, could have afforded the education. His father, a surgeon, was a scholarship student; his half-sister by his father's first wife, also wealthy, like their father also graduated from Oxford.

In September, 1940, he married Joan Bainbridge Landon in York, England, the granddaughter of a knight and the daughter of a colonel. On her deathbed she illustrated how much Mike had in common with *The Quiet American* character – Fowler – and Greene, himself. Joan said he boasted of having his first sexual encounter with a girl while on holiday in France when they were both 14, reminiscent of the line where Fowler says of Phuong, "I'd rather ruin her and sleep with her than, than…look after her damned interests." Joan ranted about Mike's repeated adultery. Fowler's wife in a letter to him wrote: "You pick up women like your coat picks up dust."

Mike was hospitalized at age 26 in July, 1943, after crashing in a *Harvard Mark III* on takeoff at Haripur airfield, India. He crashed two months later in a *Hurricane IIC*, beyond his unit's capacity to repair, on take-off at Risalpur. In between these crashes he flew a *Harvard FE 489* under the bridge at Attock, within sight of the Hindu Kush, and though he managed to get the plane back to base after having gotten tangled in some of the bridge wires, he was court-martialed and lost rank.

During World War II, as a flight lieutenant posted to No. 28 Squadron or later as commander of No. 4 and No. 60 Squadrons, he fought in the long battle for Imphal, an Allied military base on a plain some 700 meters high in northeastern India and thus repeatedly watched his fellow pilots bail out and sometimes disappear. He saw their planes catch fire and or spin to the ground or crash land at up to 240 miles per hour. He knew his could have been one of them. Like Greene, and Fowler, the older British correspondent in *The Quiet American* who lives with his Vietnamese mistress, Mike took risks, as if he had a death wish.

He continued almost daily during certain months in 1944 to lead bombing/strafing raids around Imphal over closely bedded steep mountains and hills near the Burma border. In October, 1944, his squadron dropped 103 tons, 780 pounds of bombs on the Japanese. In his report, he wrote, *we are pleased with the month's work.* The following month his squadron dropped 151 tons of bombs on Japanese targets. A ground troop commander told his squadron its air support was *magnificent…First three strikes November 3rd were masterpieces.*

Ironically, a couple of weeks later my bomber-fighter-pilot-squadron-leader father had to stop flying for the rest of World War II when his Jeep hit a bullock cart that was spread across a road with no lights at night and he broke his leg. Maybe that saved his life. He was highly decorated with the

1939/45 Star, the Aircrew Europe Star, the Burma Star, the Defence Medal and the 1939/45 War Medal.

In October, 1947, he married, in London, Agnes Margaret Harris, a divorcee and a daughter of Cyril Edwin Mitchinson Joad, the English philosopher, broadcasting personality and author of more than 75 books.

In January, 1949, he was posted to Saigon as air liaison officer for Indochina. In his 1949 air liaison officer's report for the year, Mike wrote that terrorism continued in the area to be everyday occurrences and that the road to the airfield was closed at nights except to armed convoys; a strict curfew had been imposed on the town.

Mom and Mike

Mike was 31 when he arrived in Saigon. Mom was 21 and had been promoted to secretary and typist. Six months later she was promoted to sergeant chief grade.

By then she was used to the sight of the lightly-clothed drivers of *pousse-pousses* – hooded seats mounted in front of tricycles – bathing in the open street when it rained, the frequent power outages, the skinny white cows on the local golf course, the squatting old Vietnamese women chewing betel nut and spitting out the red-brown juice that speckled sidewalks, the smell of *nuoc mam* – sauce made of fermented fish–, the muddy *Riviere de Saigon*, and at parties the French perfume, Chanel No. 5 and Je Reviens by Worth. While at the Zoological Garden, large languid turtles occasionally surfaced in a slimy green lily-pad-laden pond and dragon-shaped carvings adorned staircase handrails, it would take three weeks for a snake to digest a duck; meanwhile, elsewhere a small child could be seen eating a banana peel off the street.

Servants chased, with palm frond brooms, the rats that fed off Kapok mattresses. Air conditioning was rare. Hot water was not a given. Most houses had glass-free windows without screens through which bats and birds zoomed and flies and mosquitoes meandered. Mosquito nets over beds were a necessity and often served as hammocks for lizards of various sizes. Flying cockroaches, enormous praying mantises and spiders the size of a small woman's palm were sometime surprises. The temperature was mostly in the 90's, Fahrenheit. Minister Heath's wife said you could bathe four times a day and always be perspiring, beads of perspiration over the lips and forehead was normal like clothes wet in the back and around the waist; the smell of mold was frequent, even from beds; it was hopeless to try and dry towels during the rainy season, when "the heavens open[ed] and it pour[ed]," so that the wood shutters needed to be closed. Life centered around the fan. The violence continued. Who would want to stay in such a place if they didn't have to?

Ten months after Mike arrived, in October, 1949 my mother re-enlisted.

In March, 1950, after the U.S. aircraft carrier *Boxer* sent out forty-two planes on a flight over central Vietnam and two U.S. destroyers docked at Saigon, between three and four thousand demonstrators, including students and workers carrying Ho Chi Minh's Communist flag, rioted in Saigon for hours, injuring some 80 persons, burning down the central marketplace, overturning fifteen buses, tearing down U.S., French and Vietnamese flags, shouting anti-U.S. slogans and hurling bricks and bottles at police.

In April, 1950, Chief Sergeant Suzy Jullien, whose brother repeated that she did not want a career in the army, re-enlisted again.

Around this time she and Mike were seen by Charlotte Loris, a gregarious American Legation secretary, who later smoked opium with Graham Greene and years later became a high ranking US Foreign Service Officer. She said Mike and Mom "were riding around in a jeep with a bunch of balloons; he was driving...She was so happy. She had what you call *joi de vivre*."

A high French police official was slain. The under secretary to the governor of Central Vietnam and a councilor of the French Union were assassinated. The French publisher of *Saigon Presse* was shot in the head as he backed his car out of his driveway in the fourth attempt on his life in two years. The next day 84 guerillas attacked a police patrol in Saigon's gambling and night club hub of Cholon; then eleven were wounded when grenades were thrown outside a crowded gambling casino. Police uncovered a plot to kill Minister Heath.

A week later, in September, 1950, Mom took a month's leave without pay from the army. There is no mention of Mike taking a leave in his service record at this time. Was this when she and Mike began living together?

At the end of Mom's month-long leave, in October, 1950, she left the army but was granted permission to stay in Saigon. She was decorated with the *Medaille commemorative de la campagne d'Indochine* and the *Medaille coloniale agrafe Extreme-Orient*.

Charlotte Loris said Mike and Mom "lived in one of those big French villas…very expensive…they had big rooms and overhead fans." I read to her from Mike's letter in which he called Mom his "housekeeper." Loris said immediately, loudly and emphatically: "She was his *mistress*."

My throat muscles tightened. I said: What's the difference between being a mistress and having an affair? Loris said being a mistress was a long-term thing, that an affair lasted a couple of weeks. She said there was nothing wrong with being a mistress.

But there was and is something wrong with that in the Jullien family. The studio photos of my mother's Holy Communion and again for her Confirmation – she, veiled in lace, in a beautiful white lace-trimmed dress, her white gloved hands palm to palm – say her parents did not want her to sleep with a man out of wedlock under any circumstances, ever.

I was shaken for a while after talking to Loris. Finally I looked in the dictionary: it said a mistress is "a woman who has sexual intercourse with and, often, is supported by a man for a more or less extended period of time without being married to him."

And then what? That's it? They go their ways? This didn't sound right.

My mother left her job in the army that came with meals, a place to live, and a paycheck. She wouldn't have left the army if she thought there was no future in her new situation. Why would anyone leave their job to be supported by someone temporarily? In the middle of a terrorism-ridden war? Is the answer in *The Quiet American*?

Fowler, the older British correspondent, misleads his mistress and lies to Pyle about his wife's willingness to give him a divorce. Did Mike lead Mom on? Did he tell her he was trying to get a divorce? Or did he try to force his wife to accept that his mistress was living with him in their official residence when she came down from England?

At least I know my mother wasn't a mistress by profession. She had to have been much in love. She had to have trusted Mike, at least for a time, like Phuong, Fowler's mistress in *The Quiet American*.

Phuong had been a taxi dancer before living with Fowler. My mother bore little resemblance to Phuong, except that she spoke almost no English though she was an Anglophile, she was beautiful and she went from living with her married older British lover, who had been called back home, to the arms of a young, single American at the U.S. Legation in Saigon, a young American who had proposed marriage to her. Fowler in the novel describes Phuong as "wonderfully ignorant," someone who would have had to ask who Hitler was. My mother was educated and aware of world developments. Greene gave Phuong no surname, no history except that her father was a mandarin in Hue. Her belongings were transported in a box when she changed residences. My mother traveled with trunks, suitcases. Phuong relied on others, including her older sister, who promoted her. Mom also had an older sister, but was more sophisticated than Phuong, more feisty and independent. Phuong lived with Fowler in a room over the busy *rue Catinat*.

Mom lived with Mike in his official residence at 57, *rue Edouard Audouit*, on the airport side of town. The late Margaret Simmons was the wife of Mike's replacement who took over the residence when Mike had to leave. She said the first floor had a large room, that there were four or five bedrooms upstairs and a big tile roof. "There was a kind of ghetto with servants' quarters in the back; we had a garden, a very nice garden; and there was a guard at the gate." There was a monastery in the area. She said she heard the bells. She said Mom and Mike's three or four servants went with the house – Mom would have been good at directing servants, having grown up with them; and she knew how to delegate work.

Mrs. Simmons said the Foreign Office informed her and her husband, Nick, that Mike and Mom were living together and had been "for quite a long time." She said, "His wife came down and didn't like it there and went back."

The Wife

"...didn't like it there..." Dad said Mike's wife made a big scene at the British Consulate, which is reminiscent of the scene in *The Quiet American*, when Fowler makes a commotion at the American Legation after Pyle has taken the Vietnamese girl to live with him – the girl having learned that Fowler has lied to her about being able to get married.

As with as many details as possible for this book, I had to have it from a second source that Mike's second wife, Agnes Margaret Wilton, had gone to Saigon at some point. It was not unusual for him to leave his wife in England while he took a post overseas; he'd done it before. But his wife encountering a gorgeous woman ostensibly running his household would show me how wildly arrogant Mike was: such as when he let his first wife, Joan, see lipstick that was not hers on his barracks pillowcase when she was pregnant; or how stubborn he was about not wanting to give up living with my mother or how much he wanted a divorce out of Agnes.

I braced myself as I dialed, in 2002, Mrs. Wilton's London number. If she had made such a scene at the British Consulate, she wasn't going to be wimpy with me. And she wasn't. I told her I was a writer in Florida, working on a memoir supplemented with reportage, and that I was Mike's daughter, born in Saigon.

Immediately, she said: "Who was your mother?"

She did not question whether or not I was his daughter or if he had had a child born in Saigon. She had to ask who my mother was.

I said: "Suzanne Jullien. Did you know her?"

"Yes, I knew her," she said, "And I don't want to talk to you." She hung up.

Her divorce from Mike came through on my mother's 1956 birthday, May 1.

Mom and Mike

Mike knew his tour would be up at the earliest in January, 1951. How could my mother not know that he could be posted elsewhere at some point after that? She had been in the military. She had seen for some three years in Saigon the military and diplomatic personnel come and go. She knew the normal Foreign Service tour was two years. She wouldn't have left her position in the army if she had thought there was no hope of continuing her relationship with Mike or of marrying him. When do you think he told her he would be leaving? Before or after Christmas, 1950? What kind of Christmas was that?

By February, 1951, she knew he wasn't staying. She may not have known if he was going to continue their relationship, but she knew he was leaving because Margaret and Nick Simmons, the RAF wing commander, Mike's replacement, had arrived and were to take over the official residence. Mom was 23, Mike was 33.

In the novel, Fowler has been called back to England by his newspaper. He writes the lie to Pyle that Fowler's wife has agreed to divorce him. Then he lays back and thinks of his mistress: "'At least she won't leave me now before I go…'" He ruminates: "The thoughts of the coming April, of leaving Indo-China, of the hazy future without Phuong…"

Is it a coincidence that Mike finally left Saigon on April 7, 1951?

Margaret, Nick, Mom, Mike, Michelle, Arthur and Graham

Margaret Simmons was pregnant with twins and had a toddler of 16 months with her when she arrived in Saigon. She had obligations and a lot of work ahead of her. Despite the violence, there was a strong social scene in the foreign community in Saigon in those years. There was no theatre or symphony to speak of in this time before television, cell phones and computers. (There were landlines, radios and gramophones.) The cinema was not popular once grenades started rolling down theatre aisles. At Saigon's racetrack, the *Cercle Hippique*, it was chic to be seen at the competitive shows of horses, cars and Paris fashions; elegant silver cups were awarded there as prizes. Aside from casino gambling, drinking in bars to the dramatic tunes of Edith Piaf, the soft romantic music of British bandleader Victor Sylvester and the human violin, Tino Rossi – France's Frank Sinatra – or smoking opium, there were literally hundreds of cocktail and dinner parties given each year, sometimes every night, at least four a week in the early1950's – many that the diplomatic community members couldn't get out of, or had to give. The parties were sometimes attended by Cambodian Prince Norodom Sihanouk, the Prince and Princess Savang of Laos and the Emperor Bao Dai. But Margaret was more concerned about finding a doctor. She needed to know where to buy things in town for her children, for herself and her husband, Nick, and for entertaining. She said my mother took her around. Margaret said: "I must say, she couldn't have been kinder to me."

My mother was kind to Margaret even though she had to move out of the official residence, even though she knew Mike was leaving. Where was she to live? What would she do for work?

Since relatively few Saigon residents at the time, early 1951, spoke English, Anglos and other foreigners who were fluent in it tended to gravitate towards one another, Margaret's life-long friend, who she met in Saigon,

Michelle Breen, said. Michelle spoke English though she was French, from Biarritz. She was married to Arthur Breen, half Irish and half Chinese, from Hong Kong; he was a British citizen. She said he made his fortune in Saigon between 1946 and 1962 as the agent for a large French insurance company and so they always had big houses and entertained a great deal. The Breens were friends with Mike. Arthur had been an undercover member of the Special Operations Executive, the espionage-oriented British World War II organization against Axis powers that aided local resistance fighters, and had been dropped behind enemy lines in Burma when Mike flew there during the war. And the Breens were friends of Graham Greene.

I told Michelle that Mike had written that my mother had been his "housekeeper" – the quotes were his. Michelle said, "That was his way of saying that she was his other wife. He was living with her." Margaret said that before leaving for Saigon, the Foreign Office informed her and her husband that Mom was living with Mike though it "wasn't allowed" as he was in a diplomatic post. So, she said, she and Nick at first thought the situation would be "a bit difficult."

"But we didn't find it difficult at all. [Mike] was very discreet…and he introduced us." She said it wouldn't have been appropriate for Mom and Mike to entertain the rest of the Foreign Service community but that he took her out. Margaret said "Mike was quite taken with [your mother]…[But] he was in a diplomatic post. If he didn't love her, he would have kept her quiet somewhere where you wouldn't see her. If he didn't love her, he wouldn't have introduced her to us. He wouldn't have taken her out with us."

Michelle remembers Mike bringing Mom to Michelle's 29th birthday party on February 13, 1951. "She was there, I remember, a very beautiful woman." He also brought the Simmonses to meet the Breens that night, about a week after Graham Greene had left Saigon for the first time.

Michelle said the British diplomatic wives were not very pleasant to Margaret because she was always with my mother. "It was because they

[Mike and Suzy] were not married. You don't know how high-minded the diplomatic service is…She was Eurasian. And you know certain English women or American women in those days, looking down their noses to anybody Eurasian…It's terrible."

As a Eurasian of Vietnamese blood, Mom was considered Vietnamese by Anglos and French, just as President Obama is considered to be an African American because his father was an African American.

Mom and Mike went to this party around the time I was conceived, for I was born November 12, 1951. What was my mother thinking as she socialized with Mike's replacement and his wife? How could she have had a good time, knowing that Mike was leaving? Nick's appointment was effective February 16th. What had Mike said to Mom so that his leaving Saigon would not seem to interrupt their relationship?

It had to have been shortly after that party that my mother went to stay with Mike's friends at COTAB house, a residence for the British American Tobacco Company employees. I don't know exactly when she discovered she was pregnant with me. It was not happy news. Mike's first wife told me on her deathbed he did not behave in a welcoming manner when he heard that she was pregnant.

Margaret and Michelle said my mother went to see Arthur. "Your mother," Michelle said, "being Eurasian and my husband being Eurasian himself – I suppose she thought it was easier to confide in him." The word came to Margaret. Arthur told her husband, Nick, that Suzy had been to see him in tears and that she was pregnant with Mike's baby. Margaret said, "I think Mike probably really loved Suzy but he already had a wife...He had to go back, you see, to England…Life was very on a knife's edge...In war time there are lots of romances and that's how things happen."

Michelle Breen proffered twice that Arthur was discreet, that he would never have told Graham Greene about Mom and Mike when Greene stayed with her and Arthur in their house on the *rue Champagne*, or the one on the *rue Pellerin*. Though Greene often stayed at the *Hotel Continentale* during his trips to Saigon in the following years, Michelle says he stayed with them usually on weekends. She said, "You had to have a lot of whiskey to have

Graham Greene as a houseguest." She said Arthur and Greene talked about Greene's *Quiet American* novel frequently and until late into the night. She said Greene sent them a signed copy after it was first published in 1955.

Mom and Dad and Mike

Dad said he met Mom at the COTAB house. He was a little over six foot, slightly taller than Mike, and had pale skin, very short straight dark hair, parted just off center, and light blue-grey eyes which my mother loved. He had been away from home, Pittsburgh, for nine years.

As a teenager, he'd set up his own short wave radio and learned the Morse code. At 18 he joined the army, then studied at Georgia Tech, served in the Philippines - partly as an engineer –, worked as a foreign editor for the Associated Press in Singapore, then covered politics in China for the AP until shortly before Mao Tse Tung took over. He then studied languages in Pittsburgh and at Georgetown University, where he was studying Tsarist Russia, Geopolitics and the history of the Far East when he was assigned by the State Department to go to Saigon. He had, as Fowler describes Pyle in the novel, "an unmistakably young and unused face" and "With his gangly legs...and his wide campus gaze he seemed incapable of harm," though that description could have been used to describe a number of men who worked at the American Legation, a number of whom were tall and in their twenties. Dad was 27, had a sense of humor and great equanimity, or more, sangfroid, which appealed to a young pregnant woman with no permanent residence after having given up her job in the military and a place to live when she moved in with Mike. And Dad, like Mike, spoke excellent French, having received a top rating from the State Department in the language.

I don't know exactly when Mom left Saigon to go to her mother in the South of France. There was a period when Mom and Dad dated each other exclusively. It is likely that it was during this period that Mom and Dad smoked opium together in one of Saigon's 40 dens. (Neither of them was normally oriented towards taking drugs. Opium was part of the Saigon nightlife; Graham Greene smoked a great deal of it in Vietnam and took at least three American Legation members along for the experience.) They spent enough time with each other for Dad to be smitten by her before she left. And enough time for Mike to have noticed them together.

It had to have been March or in the first week in April, 1951, that Dad saw Mike at the *Cercle Sportif Saigonnais*, the swimming and tennis club, after having met Mom. Years later, I asked him if he spoke to Mike when he saw him by the pool. When Dad said, "No," I asked, "Why?" He looked at me as if I were out of my mind and said, "Because he was the paramour."

That is how, in real life, gentlemen behave in that kind of situation. In the novel, *Quiet American* Pyle, risks his life to follow Fowler into the war zone to tell him he's fallen in love with Fowler's mistress, saying, "I can call you Tom, can't I? I feel in a way this has brought us together. Loving the same woman, I mean." And, in the novel, Pyle actually asks Fowler to help him propose marriage to Fowler's girl (because Pyle's French is so bad; but he's taking lessons).

I don't know if Dad proposed to Mom before or after she returned to France, to her mother, who was being allowed to live in the smaller house at *La Prade*. That was an emotional reunion – Mom's father had died while she was away in Saigon. Then she had to tell her steely-haired strict mother that she was unmarried and bringing the unborn child of a married man beneath her roof. If I had done the same, my mother would have killed me or thrown me out. Dad wrote: "Her mother wouldn't have her in village, evidently she considered her a shame on the family." At least Mom was there long enough to see Mike again.

Mike left Saigon April 7, 1951 and arrived in the U.K. on the 28th. He then took disembarkation leave until May 17th. Sometime between leaving Saigon and the end of his leave Mike went to see my mother in Pont St. Esprit, about 4 kilometers from *Mas de la Prade*.

If he followed her straight from Saigon, he had to fly to Calcutta to Karachi to Beirut to Marseilles during a 33-hour trip, if there were no delays; then he had to get from Marseilles to Pont St. Esprit, northwest of

Avignon, which even in the early 21st Century is not a quick trip, and requires much driving and or a train ride.

Even in 2001 St. Paulet de Caisson was so small a town a stranger was immediately noticed; Mike's visit was fifty years earlier; there were even fewer people there then. He said he and Mom stayed in a small hotel. That would have been noticed. If my great aunt Marie Eugenie in the big limestone house at *La Prade* had heard of this, it is likely she would make trouble for my grandmother living on her property.

In the hotel, Mom and Mike argued. She asked him for money – how else was she to survive with a newborn? He accused her of promiscuity. Mike then went to England where he was posted on July 28, 1951 as adjutant of the RAF base at Hucknall.

Dad didn't know that Mike had taken the long journey to go see Suzy in France. He told me she returned to Saigon six months pregnant, which would have been around mid-August. She had to have hoped that she was returning to love and security when she, big with me, took the 33-hour trip – if there were no delays – back to Saigon. He wrote: "I was much enamoured of Suzy at the time , but I would have lost my job if I had been caught living with her, so I had to hide her out in a crummy little hotel out in Cholon (Saigon's Chinatown)."

Dad's first request for permission to marry Mom was turned down. His boss, Donald Heath, then still a minister, knew that Mom had been living with Mike and was disapproving of the marriage. Dad's friend, Tom Peck, a vice consul, said Dad supported Mom, and me, from then on. Dad said he signed the birth register as my father and paid the five thousand piastre medical bill for my birth in November. (Fowler notes in the novel, "Pyle believed in being involved.") Dad said Mom's 13-hour labor was accompanied by screams of "*Je vais me jete par la fenetre*!" (I'm going to throw myself out the window.) He was there, taking care of her, at the Clinique St. Paul, where Tom's Peck's daughter, Barbara, was born on September 24th, and where the Simmonses' twins were born, as was the Breen's son, Michael, and Vice-consul Charlie Baker's son, Reid, and other legation babies. "All the people we went with," Tom said, "thought Jim was noble to step forward and we all knew you weren't his child." Charlotte Loris said she brought a present for me to the *Clinique* from a French shop on the *rue Catinat*. She said Dad repeated to her about Mom: "I love her and I'm going to marry her."

Dad would ask for permission to marry my mother again.

Greene

Greene first arrived in Saigon about two weeks after Dad did on January 9, 1951. Both Dad and Greene were then staying in the *Hotel Continentale*, Dad, for a lengthy period because of a housing shortage for State Department employees. In his diary, Greene mentions "Jim" in a room close to his.

Dad's good friend, Charlie Baker, a vice-consul at the legation who was also working under cover for the CIA at the time, said that Dad would have been "a natural" to have known Greene. "Jim was one of the best informed in Saigon. He always had his ear close to the ground." He said that as a public affairs assistant, then as the legation's information officer, part of Dad's job was to keep the press and foreign correspondents informed, and Greene initially was working as a foreign correspondent when he went to Saigon. "Jim was easy to meet," Baker said. "Jim was very much at home with an international crowd and had a flair for getting to know foreigners and making them comfortable."

Greene returned to Saigon two weeks before I was born in the fall of 1951, then went back and forth many times between Saigon and Phnom Penh, Hanoi, Haiphong, Macau, Phat Diem, Hong Kong, Kuala Lumpur and Singapore for more than three months. Though he despised Americans perhaps as much as he favored Communists, it was during these months that he spent more time with Americans in Saigon than he had in early 1951.

He picnicked twice with correspondent Seymour Topping– who as Dad had, worked for the AP– and Topping's wife; drank with other reporters;

smoked opium with Charlotte Loris, vice consul John Getz and his wife, Libby; and took the Getzes to a brothel. He "lunched with an American information officer." He also met Mrs. Getz for a drink as he had the wife of the British information officer, Dermot Swan, a year before.

It was during this period in late 1951 through early February, 1952, that Greene's visa was delayed. Per the U.S. attorney general's edict - due to Greene's membership in the Communist Party - Greene's U.S. visa was ultimately shortened from a year to one month by Dad's friend, Tom Peck, vice consul for consular affairs. Peck said Greene was "visibly angry" when he shortened the visa issued February 6, 1952 in Greene's room at the *Hotel Continentale.*

Scott Cohen, in his 80's when interviewed, said he met Greene in Saigon while sharing office space with Dad in an old movie theatre in the *Galerie de l'Eden*, also called the *Passage Eden*, one of those winding alleys off the *rue Catinat*, and across the street from the *Continentale.* Cohen was director of the Foreign Broadcast Information Service, an overt activity of the CIA that monitored and translated into English, with four Vietnamese translators, the radio broadcasts of some 10-15 Vietnamese factions. He said Dad was an editor for USIS and that he and another editor were overseeing the translations by some 30 Vietnamese of documents for use by the legation. Cohen said the building shook when the first of the two car bombs exploded on January 9, 1952.

The Bombings, Dad, and Greene

This was the most destructive bombing in the history of the city at the time and there would be no bombing of that magnitude for 12 years, in 1964. Greene modeled the car bombing he created in *The Quiet American* on these real car bombings that killed at least 12 persons, including two children, and injured 25. Charlotte Loris said there were body parts in the trees.

In the novel Fowler indicates that Pyle is working undercover and that he is responsible for at least 50 deaths connected to the car bombing.

In a subsequent nonfiction work, Greene insisted that Americans working in Saigon at the time fomented the real life bombings. (See Notes.)

I wondered about Dad and two undercover CIA officers buying photos of the bombing from *L'Atelier CINE Photo*, a shop just around the corner from the blast in front of the opera house. Dad wrote on the back of one of these photos that showed a Vietnamese woman in *ao dai* sitting on the ground with a dead child a few feet from her. His words written in light pencil, are blocked by the torn glued black paper of the album. What is visible is this: "This is __ who __ killed+ The 2 women I spoke of."

I had to know if what Greene was saying in his nonfiction work was true – about Americans working in Saigon having been connected with the bombings. Much as Dad is a part of me, I didn't know a great deal about him. By the time he retired he spoke French, a little Portugese, Mandarin, Cantonese, Japanese, Korean, Tagalog and English. I knew that he was a zealous anti-communist who had worked in many communism-threatened places Vietnam, Thailand (a suspected hub of Vietminh assassins in the early 1950's), Taiwan, Korea, Laos. But this proves nothing. Even Pat, his youngest daughter who lived with him longer than anyone described him as "an enigma." I asked Aunt Sue if she thought Dad could kill anyone. Her response: "A scary thought."

I asked her to describe him. She wrote: "In my sporadic contacts with him I found him charming, good natured, an intelligent and interesting conversationalist. He showed this charm and affability with all other people. But one trait puzzled me, and hurt me too: he could easily put aside all relationships, simply walk away from them, without any feelings of regret, as if he had never known those people, those places, those experiences which you would think would have created a bond. The only ones who felt the loss and yearnings were those he left behind – most especially his mother, and later his children."

The CIA refused to say whether or not Dad had ever had a relationship with it. Tom Peck said he didn't know if Dad worked for the CIA later, but that he was not with the agency in Saigon. But whether or not Dad or anyone else worked for the CIA in Saigon appears to be irrelevant as far as the January 9, 1952 bombings are concerned, as the facts show.

The British minister's daughter and many American Legation wives (See Notes) including one with a two-year-old and a new mother, were shopping in close vicinity – sometimes a short stone's throw – of the car bomb that went off in front of the Saigon opera house, and across the *rue Catinat* from some American Legation offices; the idea that Americans were responsible for the January 9, 1952 bombings, as Greene charged in his non-fiction book, is not credible.

Mom and Dad

Dad asked Donald Heath, again, if he could have permission to marry Suzy Jullien, whom he was trying to keep safe, along with me, from this violence. This was denied a second time.

I know this much about Dad. He was, like Mom and Mike, stubborn. I shall never forget the night in Washington that he let the air out of the tires of the car parked in the space he rented. Like Pyle, he did have a certain sense of justice or injustice. He had to have been furious that Heath was running his love life, his family life. His response was to manage the problem quietly, as with the tires, hissing in the night.

He made love to Suzy Jullien and she became pregnant with his child. I do not believe this was an accident. It happened around February 23, 1952, three months after I was born, six weeks after the bombings. Three days later, Dad requested a transfer out of Saigon. This was refused, delayed or ignored.

It's amusing that Greene has Fowler wonder, in *The Quiet American* novel, if Pyle, 32, is a virgin. This is amongst several Pyle qualities that make the character different from Dad and many of the legation and CIA officers in Saigon at the time for it was a source of amusement amongst them that so many had children there. One CIA officer working undercover as vice-consul for political affairs in Saigon during this period and over his career, Paul Springer, joked that his seven children were his cover.

Dad was finally given permission to marry Mom when she was five months pregnant. He did so amidst the persistent violence in the area: a few days before the Saigon marriage, at *Cap St. Jacques*, a nearby beach resort where French and Americans often frolicked, some 20 persons – most were French including 10 children – were killed and some 20 were wounded in a grenade and sub-machine gun massacre; the week before, 38 Vietnamese children were killed when grenades were tossed into a Vung-Liem school. Mom wore a white sharkskin suit to her July 25, 1952 wedding at Saigon's city hall, in front of which one of the two January 9, 1952 car bombings had taken place. Dad wore a white suit and white bucks. Tom Peck and the American Embassy's personnel officer, Thelma Jenssen, were consular witnesses. The mayor of Saigon presided. Ambassador Heath and his wife gave the wedding reception with 24 guests in his official residence on the *rue Mayer*.

Mrs. Heath said, "It was all very informal and pleasant. Our cook made a cake which he assured me would be white – and when I went out to see it ten minutes before it began it was beautiful and elaborately decorated with yellow frosting and covered with nuts. I made a terrible scene – everyone was scared, I guess – whereupon he assured me he'd 'fix' it – and so it turned up all covered with white of egg and sugar (uncooked) done in elaborate lacings."

It's interesting that Greene – whose authorized biographer says Greene first heard of Mom living with Mike in January or February, 1951 – knew that Dad was finally able to marry my mother because it took about seventeen months for that drama about permissions to wed a foreigner to play out.

Mike, Mom and Dad

In October, 1952, Mike left the RAF nine days after his father died and two years short of retirement. He would inherit from his father's estate. I was almost a year old then. Mike then flew with the French Air Force and was shot down in Tonkin, North Vietnam.

He went back to *Indochine*. Was he looking for me? For Mom? Were we still there when he came back? I wish I had been able to ask him, but I didn't want him to relive the crash. Anyway, Mom, Ev and I had been assimilated into the American Embassy community.

In March, 1953, Dad was transferred to Japan where he became director of the USIS Cultural Affairs Center in Fukuoka. His boss said Mom was a great hit at the party USIS gave there for Joe DiMaggio and Marilyn Monroe. Greene's records show that after his period of many meetings with American Legation officers over his U.S. visa he left Saigon on February 9, 1952 and didn't return to Vietnam until late December, 1953. In March, 1954, during the Battle of Dien Bien Phu, Dad was transferred from Fukuoka to Bangkok, where my sister, Pat, was born and where Charlie Baker was doing another CIA tour. He and his wife, Nancy, gave Mom and Dad a send-off party when Dad was transferred to Washington. In Washington, Mom and Dad married again in the Cathedral of St. Matthew. She wore a tiara and a full-length white satin wedding gown.

She looked like a princess.

And then our family blew up.

My younger sisters live quietly with their own families. Two are grandmothers. The Baby in England has three lovely children and a stable loving spouse. Ariel, living happily with a partner in Australia, and I usually greet each other every Christmas. Each of my uncles' three daughters in France thrive, having been raised and educated in normal ways. I have friends, formerly borrowed people, for decades now. Tom Peck, like some other Saigon Foreign Service/CIA officers, has been married more than 60 years and has great grandchildren – which goes to show that long happy marriages are perhaps not so rare and that war has nothing to do with the life of all loves; it's heartening. I will always wonder why people like Mike and Mom and Dad had such trouble sustaining relationships, though there is a line in *The Quiet American* that describes what happened with Mike and Graham Greene: Fowler says: "One starts promiscuous and ends like one's grandfather, faithful to one woman." Is that a matter of practicality?

I found a huge white tiger as I sifted through the world of my parents' love. He was in *The New York Times*, in a Chinese proverb quoted in an editorial about Vietnam that ran when Mom was with Mike in Saigon. It said: *He who rides a tiger is afraid to dismount.* I knew right away he was mine. I had climbed on his back long ago.

The tiger is the danger in fear. He is shame. He is a man who would betray his lover and wives, a beautiful woman who would betray her noble young husband, a mother who would betray her children, a father who would do same, letting them smolder in wreckage. He is the fear of love, or of not being loved or loved enough. He is the snake that falls on your shoulder from a tree on the *rue Catinat*, the fragrant smell of Saigon flowers, of sex, sweat, overbearing heat, lies, mistrust, cruelty, selfishness, carelessness, kindness and forgiveness. He is my parents and who I am – born in the Vietnamese *Year of the Cat* in a complicated tangle, of love in a bed of violence. He is what I come from – like everyone: what is true. After years of lies, truth is an under-appreciated beauty. I found the truth of me because of who I am, the eye of the beholder.

I dismount the tiger – as he sleeps – and slip away, after decades of estrangement, into the feast of affection from my newfound cousins, aunts and uncles in France, from my sisters and Aunt Sue, from The Baby in England who calls me darling and means it, from my lovely children and husband who put up with all of this, from friends and even from the dog, who opened her eyes when softly I called her just before she died. But I still look for home in my house – a reflex.

It growls at me.

I see it behind these windows that are my eyes – most of the time.

Notes

This is a work of non-fiction. No person or situation is a composite. The names of the persons I worked for as a mother's helper or babysitter have been changed to protect their privacy, except for the Rosen family in Atlantic Beach, NY; Marge and Lester Rosen are deceased and I feel they wouldn't have minded being written about in such terms. Everyone else's name is real.

I revere accuracy. I was taught as a journalist not to trust memory. I wrote most of this book from memory, then supplemented and confirmed whatever I could with reportage. I found my memory has served me well. I cannot confirm that each word of some conversations were uttered. I wrote them as I remembered them. The book on memory that I read when I was nine said that you can remember anything you want; it affected me. I then began memorizing portions of my life, especially those with emotion attached to them. I understand this is not unusual.

I confirmed and supplemented information in this memoir by consulting hundreds of U.S. Department of State and British government declassified documents. These include cables between the U.S. Legation/Embassy in Saigon and the U.S. Secretary of State; documents of the French *Surete* (Security) and certain French autopsy reports; Royal Air Force and French Army Records; many hundreds of unpublished letters including: those sent home to America from French Indochina by Louise Heath, wife of the first Ambassador to Vietnam; those sent by my maternal grandmother, Marie-Jeanne Jullien, nee Jarno, from French Indochina to her in-laws in the South of France between 1924 and 1954; the letters of my grandfather, Aymond Jullien, 1945-46; every letter written to and from my father; and most letters to and from my stepfather, his mother, his sister, my sisters, my mother and The Baby. I also examined other French and British public and family records; copies of the passports and the actual letters and "diaries" of Graham Greene (I put diaries in quotes because many have pages torn out or are torn out pages, dates changed in different inks). I also researched out-of-print British government and U.S. State Department publications, particularly those showing where American Foreign Service Officers were posted and when, in the late 1940's and 1950's overseas. I studied books on French Indochina, articles, official records of birth, death, divorce and university transcripts. Much information came from personal interviews with elderly British and American Foreign Service Officers and others who were living in Saigon while my parents lived there, and some came from what I could get out of Jim Flood's personnel file through the Freedom of Information Act and from my biological father's Royal Air Force service record. Other sources are cited below.

Prologue

2 **Greene knew much more:** from Norman Sherry's *The Life of Graham Greene Volume Two*: *1939-1955*, p. 413.

2 **Greene first arrived:** Details of Greene's visits to Indochina come from *The Graham Greene Papers*, Diary – Vietnam, in the Special Collections Division, Lauinger Library, Georgetown University However, many pages of the "diary" are sometimes torn chunks of pages, pages pulled from a previously bound book, some dates are added in different ink; Sherry notes his *The Life of Graham Greene Volume Two* that Greene once rewrote a version of his day in another "diary;" I agree with Sherry that the Vietnam diaries seem to have been "doctored." I tried when possible to confirm dates in his passports kept at the John J. Burns Library, Boston College. See also the chronology in *The Viking Critical Library The Quiet American*, *Graham Greene*, Text and Criticism, John Clark Pratt, ed., Penguin Books, 1996.

3 **Since the late 1800s:** from Stanley Karnow's *Vietnam A History*.

3 **Vietnamese communist-instigated:** from numerous interviews with Foreign Service Officers working there and *The New York Times.*

3 **the 100th U.S. shipload of military:** *The New York Times,* January 29, 1952.

3 **suicide-bomber double assassination outside:** *The New York Times,* August 1, 1951. This classic terrorist act was also cited in a 2003 study: *A Tangled Web of Southeast Asian Islamic Terrorism: The Jemaah Islamiyah Terrorist Network* by U.S. Army Captain Wayne Turnbull.

3 **his authorized biographer says Greene:** *The Life of Graham Greene Volume Two,* p. 413.

3 **Greene insisted came from his "unconscious:"** *The New York Times Magazine* interview with V.S. Pritchett, February 26, 1978 and Graham Greene's *Ways of Escape.*

Chapter One

5 **Marilyn Monroe carrying me:** Dad lost his slides of Marilyn Monroe. His USIS colleague, Cliff Forster, said in a 2005 interview that he assigned Dad in 1954 to fetch Monroe and Joe DiMaggio at the airport so that DiMaggio and Lefty O'Doul could demonstrate baseball techniques to the Nishi-Tetsu Lions at the USIS Fukuoka cultural center Dad directed.

8 **Formosa, she says:** All references to Jim Flood's postings and positions were confirmed by the US Department of State, Office of Human Resources, 44 personnel documents, Jan. 9, 1951 through June 28, 1974.

Chapter Two

16 **grandfather left France:** These details of the Jullien family life in Indochina not attributed to my mother came from interviews with my uncles the late Guy, Alban and the late Daniel Jullien; many details were confirmed by photos.

18 **Ev and I suspect:** The CIA refused, even after a lengthy appeal, to reveal whether or not Dad had had any relationship with it.

18 **some people retired from the CIA:** From interviews, including a 2002 email from retired Foreign Service Officer Harry Kendall, of the Institute of East Asian Studies, University of California, Berkeley. He wrote: USIA "was quite firm about not allowing CIA to use USIS as a cover for its agents…"

19 ***The Jing Affair*** by D.J. Spencer, Funk & Wagnalls, 1965.

19 **Dad wrote me a letter:** July 24, 1983 letter from Jim Flood, Algarve, Portugal.

Chapter Three

23 ***Jamais* cut the salad:** Emily Post, in *Etiquette*: *The Blue Book of Social Usage* Funk & Wagnalls, 1960, explains that before stainless steel, vinegar caused steel knives to turn black and so it was not acceptable to cut salads with a knife, unless it was silver. When stainless steel utensils became common and such knives acceptable to use with salad, Mom did not change her mind about this.

Chapter Four

33 ***Dao Tien* means peach from heaven:** Confirmed by University of Wisconsin Vietnamese instructor ThuyAnh T Nguyen.

33 **She insists her real last name:** In her "novel," "Blaze Starr: My Life as Told to Huey Perry," full of facts I know to be true, her real name is said to be Fannie Belle Fleming.

However, in an AP story published in the *The Post*, Frederick, Maryland, May 4, 1962, her real name was reported as Belle Glorioso.

38 **Not so long after:** Ibid and my mother told me about it.

Chapter Five

44 ***The Borrowers*:** From *The Borrowers* by Mary Norton.

49 **He is the cousin of Lord:** Michael Charles Lambton is also descended from the Duke of Buccleugh, the Duke of Abercorn, the 3rd Viscount Hampden, and the 2nd Earl Durham, according to *Debrett's Peerage and Baronetage* and *The Peerage.com*.

57 ***Hero of Trafalgar*:** A.B.C. Whipple's *Hero of Trafalgar: The Story of Lord Nelson*.

Chapter Six

64 **"By the shore…":** From *Song of Hiawatha* by Henry Wadsworth Longfellow.

Chapter Seven

68 **He's in *The Times*:** July 23, 1963, p. 5. This was a heavy day of testimony for Keeler during the Profumo Affair, during which it was revealed that Keeler slept with Michael and others. Michael was not named in *The Times* index, July-August, 1963, but he was in the July 23, 2963 story. He lost his job in publishing as a result of the scandal.

68 **she was engaged, Miss Keeler:** From *The Daily Telegraph, July 23, 1963 and July 30, 1963 and The Daily Mail, July 23, 1963.*

69 **he is rich:** *The Times*, July 23, 1963, p. 5.

69 **"she had had intercourse with Mr. Profumo…":** *The Daily Telegraph*, July 23, 1963.

Chapter Eight

76 **I wonder when he was engaged:** Keeler describes her relationship of more than two years with Michael in eight sections of her autobiographical book, *The Truth at Last My Story* published in 2001, but does not make it clear when it ended. Michael is also described as her boyfriend in *An Affair of State The Profumo Case and The Framing of Stephen Ward* by Phillip Knightley and Caroline Kennedy, published in 1987.

Chapter Nine

89 **We are not encouraged:** This, some spellings and the confirmation of many details of our time at St. Mary's came from Dublin solicitor Elizabeth G. Mullan; memories were embellished with photos and historical details about this Dublin order of nuns, the school, and its chapel by the late Dominican Sisters Terence O'Keefe and Fanchea Foley, St. Mary's, Dublin.

89 **Antonio Ciseri's:** Sister O'Keefe identified Ciseri's painting and the Van Dyck with stories and photos from *Immaculata*, the school magazine, 1964.

91 **sprinkled with holy water:** Sister O'Keefe reminded me of the details of the Salve Procession in a letter of November 9, 2003.

Chapter Ten

100 **she changed her name legally:** She is named as the mother of Michael Charles Lambton's child in *Debrett's Peerage and Baronetage 2003* as Suzanne Clara Flood.

103 ***Crying in the Chapel*:** These titles are of various songs by popular 60s groups.

Chapter Eleven

124 **A phone call to Paris:** From the New York City phone book, 1968-69.

Chapter Fifteen

160 **lost the lawsuit:** Confirmed by District of Columbia Superior Court documents. The reason, a court clerk told me, is that the judge considered a stepfather to be as responsible for a child as the child's biological father, regardless of whether or not the child was living with him or the mother.

161 **they are described:** From Jacqueline Susann's *Valley of the Dolls.*

Chapter Eighteen

183 **when her father shot an elephant:** I believed this until I was in my 50's and interviewed my mother's brothers in France who said their father never killed an elephant; my uncle, Guy Jullien, said his father had a friend who killed a rogue elephant that attacked villages.

184 **I swallow the pills:** It was not public knowledge in 1972 that consumption of certain anti-depressants, including Elavil, increase the risk of suicidal thought and behavior in children, adolescents and

adults younger than 25. The Food and Drug Administration has ordered drug makers to label this warning on antidepressants; from *The New York Times*, May 3, 2007.

184 **of barefoot children:** From *The Wayfarer* by Padraic Pearse, Irish hero.

185 ***And I have gone upon my way*:** Ibid.

Chapter Twenty

197 **met and took up with:** July 24, 1983 letter from Jim Flood, Algarve, Portugal.

Chapter Twenty-One

219 ***The Love Song of J. Alfred Prufrock*:** By T.S. Eliot.

220 **describes a being:** My interpretation from Plato's *The Symposium*.

222 **"my mother a Cameron of Locheil...":** Cameron of Locheil is the chief and the family of the chief of the Clan Cameron, said be one of the oldest of the Scottish clans. I could not document the connection, though my father wore his mother's family ring and recognized the Cameron of Locheil plaid of a skirt I wore during one of our meetings.

222 **"public school in Scotland...":** The same as private school in the United States.

222 **"then flew with the French Air Force in Indo-China..."** The French Air Force says it has no record of Mike Wilton flying with it, although other government sources said this was a "sensitive" matter and that the FAF did use freelance pilots and would not admit this publicly.

Chapter Twenty-Two

237 **"I can't see you, mama…":** From "Mama" by Genesis.

Chapter Twenty-Three

240 **the Razorbill has:** From *Jim Morin's Field Guide to Birds.*

Chapter Twenty-Five

266 **it was built in 1771:** From the Henley Royal Regatta website section on Temple Island.

Chapter Twenty-Seven

276 **Mike had two wives:** from Mike Wilton's service record, Royal Air Force, Innsworth, Gloucester, England. All references to his postings also come from his service record.

Chapter Twenty-Eight

277 Ariel is now Ariel Marguin.

278 **"Love the world without trusting.":** From Gilbert Keith Chesterton's quotation: "Love the world without trusting it."

Epilogue

281 **copy of two paragraphs from:** *The Life of Graham Greene Volume Two: 1939-1955*, Greene's authorized biography, by Norman Sherry, pp. 412-413.

282 **Tom Peck in the consular passport department:** Tom Peck stipulated in a March 17, 2010 phone interview and March 12, 2010 email, that he was a consular witness rather than best man, though he was Flood's friend.

282 ***The Quiet American*:** by Graham Greene, Penguin edition, 1974, p.78.

282 ***The young American*:** October 23, 1997 letter from Sue Flood, Pittsburgh, PA.

282 ***Norman Sherry surmises*:** March 3, 2002 and January 28, 2008 letters from Sue Flood to the author.

283 ***…Is Jim Flood, Pyle?*:** A number of candidates for Pyle models have been proposed by Greene biographers and others, though none asked to marry or married a woman who was all or part Vietnamese who had been living with an older British man whose wife was in England and who had been called back home by his employer except Jim Flood. The most famous of these candidates for decades was Col. Ed Lansdale, a CIA operative. However Greene biographer Michael Shelden and authorized biographer Norman Sherry discard Lansdale because he only came to Vietnam and met Greene in 1954 two years after Greene began writing *The Quiet American*. See Shelden's *Graham Greene The Enemy Within* and Chapter 28, Volume II of Sherry's trilogy, *The Life of Graham Greene*.

284 **This happened twice, actually:** one of these was Charles Jewel Baker, Jim Flood's friend, whose *Washington Post* obituary, August 4, 2005, stated he served CIA tours in Vietnam, Thailand, Laos and Morocco and retired in 1973 as branch chief of the North Africa desk at CIA headquarters. The State department's Biographic Register, 1957, states he served in Saigon between April, 1950 and July, 1954. His cover was a vice-consul for security.

284 **another vice consul, was revealed:** This was former vice-consul, the late Paul Springer.

285 **"That was certainly a unique situation…":** Phone interview with Thomas B. Peck, Jr. May, 2005. Working under cover for the CIA, he served as a vice-consul in Saigon from December, 1950 until the spring of 1953, then returned in 1962 and left in 1966.

285 **some 40 officers:** from a May 22, 2005 email from Tom Peck, confirmed by Department of State's *Foreign Service List*, 1951.

285 **there was only one other legation officer:** this was W. Wendell Blancke, who came down to Saigon for his wedding from Hanoi, where he was consul. From a March 17, 2010 interview with Tom Peck. Louise Heath, wife of minister, then Ambassador Heath, wrote in her letters home that there were only two other legation or embassy weddings besides the Blancke and Flood weddings outside the time Peck handled consular affairs and during the time the Heaths were in Saigon; they were the wedding of CIA officer Paul and Mary Jean Springer in December, 1950 and the wedding of an Embassy Marine guard in July, 1953.

285 **and four officers at the British Consulate:** From the Foreign Office List of 1951, provided by the Foreign & Commonwealth Office, FCO Services, Information Management Group, London, England, February 1, 2002.

286 **he insisted, "I do not take people…":** *The New York Times Magazine* interview with V.S. Pritchett, February 26, 1978.

286 **"I have nothing to add…":** May 27, 2005 email from Norman Sherry to the author.

286 **Mike, though often referred:** from the service record of Royal Air Force Squadron Leader Michael Stanley James Wilton, which is also the source of the dates of all his arrivals and departures in Saigon, some details of his war activities, his education and sports activities.

287 **There was no air attaché post:** information in this paragraph comes from a July 10, 2002 letter from Margaret Simmons of Warwickshire,

England, to the author and a December 4, 2007 email from Ministry of Defence Air Historical Branch (RAF), Middlesex, England.

287 **Also, Mike was married:** From their October 3, 1947 marriage certificate and British divorce records.

287 **they had no children:** confirmed by British divorce records.

288 **descriptions by Uncle Guy:** Unless attributed elsewhere, details not from photographs about the Jullien family's lifestyle in North Vietnam, their war travails and escape from Indochina come from many interviews with my mother's youngest brother, Guy Jullien, of Cuers, France, translated by Danielle Ferre-Culas of Alliance Francaise. In his 70's when interviewed, his memory was so sharp, he remembered Mom and Dad's address in Saigon after they were married. It's accuracy was confirmed by the address in my mother's French Union passport.

288 **as a result he was bestowed a title:** from Alban Jullien's history of the Jullien family in French Indochina, *Typhon sur les Filaos*, Editions Amalthee, Nantes Cedex, 2011.

288 **a panther coming to drink fresh water:** Ibid.

288 **The time Marie-Jeanne had to escape:** from the letters to her in-laws in France by my grandmother, Marie-Jeanne Jullien, nee Jarno, 1924-54.

288 **it was difficult to get enough food:** Ibid. and from *Typhon sur les Filaos*

289 **inspector general for alcohol:** *Typhon sur les Filaos.*

289 **many servants worked part time:** Ibid.

289 **he had a house built for the family:** Ibid.

289 **the Japanese invaded the French border forts:** From Bernard B. Fall's *Street Without Joy, Indochina at War, 1946-54.*

290 **the Japanese allowed the French administration:** From Karnow's *Vietnam, A History.*

290 **"lost everything, absolutely everything."** From the letters of Aymond Jullien to his family in St. Paulet de Caisson, France, 1945-46.

290 **the mayor of Hanoi:** The famine general history comes from *Vietnam, A History.*

290 **Vietnamese Communists announced:** Ibid.

291 **the first of three floors:** From its owner in 2007, architect Ruth-Schneider-Girards.

291 **the largest vineyard:** From a map in the public records, city hall, St. Paulet de Caisson, France.

291 **It had been in the Jullien family:** public records, city hall, St. Paulet de Caisson.

292 **So she joined the army:** All facts about Suzanne Clara Jullien's army service came from the *Direction du Service National Bureau Central D'Archives Administratives Militaires Division Archives Individuelles, Pau, Cedex, France.*

293 **two American women:** These were Lydia Ruth James, 30, and Jeanne R. Skewes, 32. Their bodies were found in their USIS jeep. Mrs. Skewes, divorced, was then acting USIS chief at the consulate where Miss James deciphered coded messages. The French *Surete* said the women told their servants, when they left their home in northwest Saigon at about 6:00 p.m., to make dinner and seat their friends, – two reporters, one from the Associated Press, the other from United Press, and a vice consul – invited to arrive at 7:15 p.m. A report from the *Surete* stated it did not believe the bullet holes in the jeep coincided with those in the bodies. So it appears it was some work to put their bodies back in the jeep, tear the American flag off the front of the jeep, pour their jerry can of gasoline over it and set it afire in a field off the bamboo thicket lined road in the area between northeast

Saigon and Tan-Son-Nhut airport. The *Surete* blamed a local band of five Viet Minh. Declassified communiqués between the U.S. consulate and the Secretary of State include these details and reports of the women not hearing or ignoring a challenge from French military watchtower personnel along the back road to the airport. There was a report of two or three bursts of machine gun fire, a scream, single shots fired later, then smoke rising from the jeep; also the spare wheel was missing from the jeep, but this was returned by the French military who in separate explanations said they had interrupted thieves or had removed the wheel to prevent it from burning. A State Department memorandum stated that prostitutes frequenting the military watch tower said its soldiers were confined there for several days after the shooting, then transferred to another sector; the watch tower or barricade from which the shots were fired was shortly thereafter pulled down. The State Department would neither provide hearses for the womens' funeral nor a headstone for Mrs. Skewes, who was buried in Saigon's European cemetery. It is bewildering that these women took the risk of a drive without protection when less than a week earlier some 150 French and Vietnamese were killed in an armed convoy of some 560 persons midway between Saigon and Dalat, to its northeast. But then James and Skewes were much closer to town. Details of these womens' deaths come from declassified secret or confidential memoranda or telegrams between the Secretary of State and various U.S. Consulate officials in Saigon in the months following their March 7, 1948 murders; details also come from French autopsy reports, the official report of the *Surete Federale*, an aerial photo of the site of the murders and where the bodies were found and communications from the *Haut Commissariat de France Pour L'Indochine*; the October 7, 1948 memorandum about the French watchtower personnel challenging, then shooting the women, per a report by an old Annamese man who witnessed the murders, was by Vice Consul Richard T. Coughlin and addressed to Charles S. Reed, Southeast Asia Division, Department of State. The documents were found in the National Archives, College Park, MD, in Record Group

59, Stack 250, State Department Central Decimal File 1945-49.

293 **it was reported:** Ibid.

293 **A week earlier:** From *The New York Times*, March 3, 1948.

293 **Danger and death in what:** Unless otherwise noted, details about Saigon 1947-53 come from: the map: *Plan de Saigon*; *Dress, heliograve et publie parle service Geographique de l'Indochine*, dated by the the New York City Public Library at 1957, three years after the French were defeated at Dienbienphu, but its *Legende* is in French. Details also come from interviews with and or letters and emails from: U.S. Air Attache Col. Edmund F. Freeman and his wife, Gillie; former Saigon vice-consul and CIA officer Tom Peck, his wife, Betty, and daughter Barbara Peck Henning; Michele Breen; the late U.S. administrative accountant Virginia Fitzpatrick; retired U.S. Vice consul and CIA officer Paul Springer and wife, Mary Jean; assistant attaché James C. Risk; manager of the British American Tobacco company Saigon cigarette factory Robert Bailey; Assistant Air Attache Col. William H. Huntley and his wife, Ruby; CIA officer John Caswell, retired U.S. consul Hendrick Van Oss; Elizabeth "Libby" Getz; Blanche Donovan; FBIS director Scott Cohen; legation clerk Roman Lotsberg; British Foreign Service Officer Ian Day Adams; Margaret Simmons; Michelle Breen, Guy Jullien; Charlotte Loris; the late CIA officer Charles Jewel Baker and his wife, Nancy; code clerk Bob Teaze; British Consulate Information Officer Dermot Swan (who provided details from his unpublished memoirs); details from six Foreign Service Officers' photo collections; copies of invitations from the Col. William and Ruby Huntley collection of some 600 for the period March 1950 to August 1953; *The Graham Greene Papers* in the Special Collections Division, Georgetown University Library; the letters to her family by Louise Heath, wife of Ambassador Donald Heath and various books and newspapers.

293 **usually necessitated an armed escort:** from interviews with and letters from the late British Consulate Information Officer Dermot J.

Swan; some details come from his unpublished memoir; used with permission.

293 **the French were spying regularly:** from May 8, 1951 declassified secret memorandum by Donald Heath, "French Surveillance of American Legation and other Official American Personnel in South Vietnam." Heath said "unwarranted surveillance by French intelligence agents of American personnel in South Vietnam" was ongoing. Heath said: "There is transmitted herewith a memorandum prepared by Second Secretary Gardner C. Carpenter, as requested by me, respecting a false account recently entered in the records of the French intelligence and counter-espionage agency known as the Brigade de Surveillance du Territoire ("BST"), such report being concerned with a purported visit to the Chinese Nationalist internment camps on PHU QUOC Island made by Mr. Carpenter…It is, moreover, a safe surmise that numerous additional reports as apocryphal as the one under discussion have been rendered to and incorporated in the permanent records of French intelligence organizations without the legation being aware of their nature and contents. Second Secretary Carpenter some weeks ago reported to me an experience which he had had while perusing, at the invitation of the Chief of the Chinese Affairs Section of the High Commissariat for South Vietnam, a daily summary of reports respecting local Chinese affairs; Mr. Carpenter, came upon a section entitled "Affaires Americaines" and was able, before he was requested, with evident embarrassment on the part of the official concerned, to return the errant summary, to observe that the section comprised some six or seven pages devoted to news of the activities of personnel of the legation as well as of other official American organizations in South Vietnam." Carpenter, in his April 23, 1951 memorandum to Heath said his source had found that the BST was using part-time informants who were paid on a per-story basis and the one responsible for fabricating the story of his visit to PHU QUOC Island was thus "understandably overzealous in the purveyal of his tales." Also, a CIA officer in Saigon at the time said a Vietnamese spy for the

French had "wormed" his way into his home, having been employed as a servant who spoke "beautiful French."

293 **U.S. Navy bearcat fighter planes:** *The New York Times*, February 11, 1951; American Air Attaché Col. Edmund "Buck" Freeman said they were painted by the French at night.

294 **U.S. Central Intelligence Agency officers were recruiting:** from the wife of a CIA officer there at the time.

294 **The French editor of Saigon's second largest daily:** *The New York Times*, January 13, 1951.

294 **The manager of:** From interview with Robert Bailey, 91 in 2003, who succeeded the murdered manager of the BAT cigarette factory in Saigon.

294 **The Indian consul was shot at:** From interviews with Gillie Freeman, wife of the U.S. Air Attaché in Saigon; this happened at their home.

294 **The blonde pregnant:** Ibid.

294 **Two French priests:** from declassified June 14, 1951 telegram from Heath to the Secretary of State.

294 **Mike was born in Ide:** From Mike Wilton's birth certificate. His early life details came from his first wife and his service record. His crash details come from his service record and the Air Historical Branch, Ministry of Defence, United Kingdom. His involvement in the battle for Imphal is documented in the "Operations Record Book" for RAF Squadrons No. 4, No. 28 and No. 60, April 4, 1944 through December 1, 1944. His decoration details are from the RAF, Innsworth, Gloucester, England.

294 **summers at his Scottish mother's house:** Interviews with his first wife, the late Joan Kinloch, formerly Joan Bainbridge Landon, February, 2004, in Kootenay Lake Hospital, Nelson, British Columbia.

294 **His father, a surgeon:** Mike's father, Dr. Stanley James Wilton, formerly Welby, took his B.A. from Trinity College, then his Bachelor of Medicine, his MA, and his Doctor of Medicine degrees from Oxford. Mike's half sister, Evelyn Mary Welby, matriculated Somerville College in 1920. From Oxford University Archives, Bodleian Library, Oxford, England.

295 **In September, 1940:** from the service record of R.A.F. Squadron Leader Michael S.J. Wilton.

295 **the granddaughter of:** from Ariel Marguin; Joan's grandfather was Sir Frederick Landon and her father was Col. James Landon.

295 **Joan said he boasted:** February 17, 2004 interview with Joan Kinloch, Kootenay Lake Hospital, Nelson, British Columbia.

295 **"I'd rather ruin her…":** from *The Quiet American.*

295 **"You pick up women…":** Ibid.

296 **In October, 1947:** from their marriage certificate.

296 **By then she was used to:** details in this paragraph come from interviews with former Saigon residents Gillie Freeman, Libby Getz, Michelle Breen and Barbara Peck Henning.

297 **Servants chased:** details in this paragraph came with permission for use from British Consulate Information Officer Dermot Swan's unpublished memoir –, retired vice-consul Thomas B. Peck, and the unpublished letters home from Saigon of Louise Heath.

297 **aircraft carrier Boxer:** *The New York Times*, March 20 and 21, 1950.

297 **Around this time she:** March 21, 2002 phone Interview with Charlotte Loris, Powhatan Nursing Home, Falls Church, VA.

298 **A high French police:** *The New York Times*, June 2, 1950.

298 **the under secretary:** *The New York Times*, July 1, 1950.

298 **The French publisher:** *The New York Times*, July 19, 1950 and Dermot Swan.

298 **The next day 84:** *The New York Times*, July 20, 1950.

298 **then eleven were wounded:** *The New York Times*, August 20, 1950.

298 **Police uncovered a:** *The New York Times*, September 3, 1950.

298 **Loris said Mike and Mom:** March 21, 2002 interview with Charlotte Loris.

298 **What's the difference:** Ibid.

299 **Phuong had been a taxi:** details in this paragraph about Phuong come from *The Quiet American*.

299 **Mom lived with Mike:** Phone interview with Margaret Simmons, Warwickshire, England, September 13, 2002.

300 **Mrs. Simmons said the Foreign Office:** Ibid.

300 **big scene at the British Consulate:** July 24, 1983 letter from Jim Flood, Algarve, Portugal.

301 **I told her I was a writer:** Phone interview with Agnes Margaret Wilton, London, England, April 5, 2002.

301 **Her divorce from Mike came through:** Decree Absolute, The Court Service, Principal Registry of the Family Division, London, England.

301 **Mike's replacement, had arrived:** Details about Greene, my parents, Margaret and RAF Winger Commander Nick Simmons and Michelle Breene came from interviews with Margaret Simmons, September 13, 2002, September 29, 2003 and March 12, 2003.

301 **"At least she won't leave...The thoughts of the coming April...":** from *The Quiet American*.

302 **a strong social scene:** U.S. Air Force Col. William H. Huntley, Jr. said his collection of cocktail party and dinner invitations (March 1950 to

August 1953) numbered 600 and was incomplete as many were turned over to parking attendants.

303 **Michelle Breen, said:** Details about Arthur Breen, Greene, the Simmonses, my mother and Mike came from phone interviews with Mrs. Breene, East Sussex, England, August 7, 2002, September 18, 2002 and October 1, 2003.

304 **As a Eurasian:** confirmed by various sources who preferred not to be named. She was also considered French by the Vietnamese.

304 **effective February 16th.** From the Ministry of Defence Air Historical Branch, (RAF), Middlesex, England.

305 **short wave radio…:** From February 17, 2008 memo from Sue Flood, Pittsburgh, PA in response to questions.

305 **At 18 he joined:** details in this paragraph come from Jim Flood's Army honorable discharge papers, the Associated Press, Georgia School of Technology, Georgetown University's School of Foreign Service where he was studying in its Institute of Languages & Linguistics.

305 **"an unmistakably young…With his gangly legs…and his wide campus…":** From *The Quiet American.*

306 **I asked him if he spoke to Mike:** In the Algarve, Portugal, 1985.

306 **"I can call you Tom,...":** From *The Quiet American.*

306 **If he followed her straight from Saigon:** From November 27, 2002 email of Air France press officer Dominique Freyssenede.

307 **she returned to Saigon six months pregnant:** July 24, 1983 letter from Jim Flood, Algarve, Portugal.

307 **I was much enamoured:** Ibid.

307 **Dad's first request for permission:** all details re: Jim Flood's repeated requests come from Tom Peck. Charlotte Loris also knew of these.

307 **signed the birth register:** September 26, 1983 and July 24, 1983 letters from Jim Flood, Algarve, Portugal.

307 **"Pyle believed…":** From *The Quiet American.*

307 **"*Je vais me jete…*":** September 17, 1987 letter from Jim Flood, Algarve, Portugal.

308 **Charlotte Loris said:** Phone interview with Charlotte Loris, March 21, 2002, Powhatan Nursing Home, Falls Church, Virginia.

308 **"I love her and I'm going to…":** Ibid.

308 **January 9, 1951:** From the Department of State's *Foreign Service List*, 1951.

308 **Greene mentions "Jim" in a room:** from Greene's Vietnam diaries, *The Graham Greene Papers*, Georgetown University Library. FBIS director Scott Cohen confirmed in a February 12, 2008 phone interview that he and Jim Flood stayed in the *Hotel Continentale* longer than others at the legation due to a legation housing shortage.

308 **he spent more time with Americans:** details in this paragraph come from Greene's Vietnam diary, Gerogetown University.

308 **Hanoi, Haiphong, Macau:** Unless otherwise noted, information not from Greene diaries in this section come from his letters to his lover, Catherine Walston, Special Collections, Lauinger Library, Georgetown University

308 **"a natural":** April 21, 2005 phone interview with the late Charles Jewel Baker, McLean, Virginia.

309 **He picnicked twice:** Details of his activities with Americans in Saigon at this time come from Greene's diaries and interviews with Charlotte Loris.

309 **Per the U.S. attorney general's edict:** see *The Life of Graham Greene Volume II*, by Norman Sherry, p. 440. Greene's actual passport

however reflects the visa was shortened to one month, not three, from February 6, 1952. The passport is in the Graham Greene Collection, John J. Burns Library, Boston College.

309 **Peck said Greene was:** From a March 17, 2010 phone interview with Thomas B. Peck, Jr.

309 **Greene was "visibly angry.":** November 28, 2007 email from Tom Peck to author *Newsweek*, in its review of *The Quiet American* may have been the first publication to suggest that Greene wrote the novel in reaction to his visa problems due to his membership in the Communist Party. See *Newsweek*, January 2, 1956.

309 **met Greene in Saigon:** Details from this paragraph come from February 12, 2008, April 15, 2008 and May 13, 2008 interviews with Scott Cohen, Arlington, VA.

309 **bombs exploded on January 9, 1952:** The investigation of these bombings fell under the jurisdiction of the French police and or *Surete*. The curator in charge of the Indochina files for the national archives of France, Olivia Pelletier, said in a June 3, 2008 email that there is no police report or any document pertaining to the 1952 Saigon car bombings in the files of the *Archives Nationales d'Outre Mer* (ANOM), the French national archives for overseas. "If such a document exists," she wrote, "you have my absolute assurance that we don't keep it here at the ANOM. Yet, [her boldface]**I can't tell you where you can find it**, or whether it has been destroyed or can still be found in Vietnam. Actually the archives called 'management archives' were not sent back to France but remained in Vietnam." She referred me to the national archives of Vietnam; a response to a 2008 request for those documents was not received as of April, 2016.

309 **most destructive bombing:** From *The New York Times*, January 25, 1952 and interviews with Tom Peck.

310 **In a subsequent nonfiction work:** from Greene's autobiographical *Ways of Escape*, 1980. Joseph Buttinger, the Austrian Vietnam

scholar, in his *Vietnam: A Dragon Embattled Volume II*, (Praeger, 1967) wrote that Greene's "accusation became the central point of…[*The*]*Quiet American*…Greene wrote his book not only to denounce an alleged American policy of interference in the Indochina War, an allegation that is a complete fabrication and contrary to established facts, but he also conceived the American as a ridiculous figure in his attempt to promote such a policy. A much more factual and truthful picture of the Vietnamese political situation and the American role at the time is given by Robert Shaplen in his novel *A Forest of Tigers* (New York, 1956)."

Furthermore, Greene was mistaken about his "evidence" that Americans fomented the bombings.

Greene proffers this manifestation that Americans were behind the bombings in answer to his question, "Who had supplied the material to a bandit [General Trinh Minh The, the chief suspect in the January 9 bombings] who was fighting French, Caodaists and Communists?

"There was certainly evidence of contacts between American services and General The. A jeep with the bodies of two American women was found by a French rubber planter on the route to the Holy Mountain – presumably they had been killed by the Viet Minh, but what were they doing on the plantation? The bodies were promptly collected by the American Embassy and nothing more was heard of the incident. Not a word appeared in the press.")(From Greene's memoir, *Ways of Escape, 1980.*)

Greene is not accurate about this. The women, Jeanne Skewes and Lydia James, were not found by a rubber planter: State Department communiqués say their bodies were collected by the French military. (From documents in the National Archives, College Park, MD, in Record Group 59, Stack 250, State Department Central Decimal File 1945-49.)

There is no rubber plantation on the aerial photograph of the site of their murder, which took place in the area – about 20 minutes away from the women's home in northeast Saigon – off an extension of the *rue Eyriaud des Vergnes*, a secondary road to Ton Son Nhut airport. Official reports stated their bodies were in a field or rice paddy.

The Holy Mountain, to which Greene refers, is seven miles northeast of Tay Ninh, home of the CaoDai military religious sect, and about 60 miles from Saigon. The self-proclaimed "General" The had defected from the CaoDai army in the summer of 1951 and, Heath said, "took to bush."

The story of the deaths of Mrs. Skewes and Miss James was published March 9, 1948 in *The New York Times*, in many U.S. newspapers including *Stars and Stripes* and its European edition, and in *Populaire*, a local Saigon newspaper; and there was a long letter to the editor about it published in *The Bangkok Post*, reportedly from the Vietminh.

Last but not least, the women died in 1948, almost four years before the car bombings in question.

310 ***L'Atelier CINE Photo*:** was at 118-20 *rue Catinat*, Saigon.

310 **He spoke French, a little Portugese:** This list comes from my sister, Patricia, who lived with Jim Flood longer than anyone: Earl Wilson, in a March 4, 1988 interview for Charles Stuart Kennedy's Foreign Affairs Oral History Program, (Lauinger Library, Georgetown University; also in the Library of Congress website) said Jim Flood "was a natural with languages. And he said to me one time, in studying a language like Spanish or something, don't fight it, you know. The language exists. Go with it." In the 2002 movie, the *Quiet American* character speaks fluent Vietnamese. In reality, several Saigon U.S. Foreign Service Officers said, there was only American Foreign Service Officer at the time in Indochina who spoke fluent Vietnamese. This was the late John Corwin Donnell; a vice consul

and designated specialist with USIS His wife Ruth confirmed this and said he learned Vietnamese in the Army Specialized Training Program in the 1940's and later worked for the RAND Corportation. She said people often thought he was with the CIA because he was a linguist, but she said he was not.

310 **(a suspected hub of Vietminh...)**: from declassified January 31, 1950 Department of State Bureau of Far Eastern Affairs Office Memorandum regarding Vietminh assassination committees in Thailand.

310 **"A scary thought...In my sporadic contacts..."**: January and February, 2008 memos from Sue Flood, Pittsburgh.

311 **The CIA refused:** From correspondence with the Central Intelligence Agency between November 13, 2001 and August 19, 2002.

311 **The British minister's daughter:** Louise Heath in her unpublished January 11, 1952 letter to her family wrote that she had just been to the dressmaker and went home to pick up a house guest before shopping but changed her mind because her trunks needed airing – the mold problem in Saigon was constant. She wrote: "The British minister's daughter had just parked her car in the square and gone in a shop. All its windows broken – 13 cars burned up – (our office only lost a jeep.)...Our military attache's [Naval Attache George W. Killen's] wife and 2-year-old had just walked past and were just between the two bombs." The wife of vice-consul William Leonhart had driven five minutes earlier from the area of the *Catinat* explosion. The wife of the vice-consul for security, also working undercover for the CIA, Charlie Baker, was in an Indian shop across from and damaged by the blast. Charlotte Loris was in a nearby office, ran downstairs and saw body parts in the trees. Scott Cohen, working in his office off the *Galerie de l'Eden*, across *Catinat* from one blast felt the building shake. The sources listing these Americans in close vicinity of the bombings include Donald Heath's declassified January 10, 1952 telegrams to the Secretary of State; the photos taken by Col.

Edmund "Buck" Freeman; a February 12, 2008 interview with Scott Cohen; and the fact that some legation offices were literally across the *rue Catinat* from one of the bombings.

Although the Vietminh initially claimed authorship of the bombings as marking the second anniversary of a student, *Tran Van On*, accidentally killed during a student riot on January 9, 1950, Heath in a declassified February 13, 1952 cable to the Secretary State said the French *Surete* had attributed the bombings to "*Trinh Minh The* forces." Heath said when The defected from the CaoDai (military and religious) army months before the bombing, he issued a manifesto stating he was against both French Colonialists and the Vietminh. Joseph Buttinger in his *Vietnam: A Dragon Embattled Volume II* cites sources who say *The* had far fewer than 2500 men and fomented terrorist acts for publicity purposes. Bernard Fall in *Vietnam Witness* said The had a few hundred men.

312 **He did so amidst persistent violence in the area:** details of the Cap St. Jacques massacre were in The New York Times, July 24, 1952 and in the unpublished letters home of Louise Heath, as were the details of the attack on the Vung-Liem school.

312 **Ambassador Heath and his wife gave:** From Louise Heath's unpublished July 27, 1952 Saigon letter to her family.

313 **His boss said Mom:** September 12, 2005 interview with Cliff Forester, onetime USIS regional director for Kyushu, Japan.

313 **Greene's records show:** From his letters to his lover, Catherine Walston, and his Vietnam diaries. Special Collections, Lauinger Library, Georgetown University.

314 **"One starts promiscuous..."** from *The Quiet American*.

314 ***He who rides a tiger is afraid to dismount*:** From an editorial in *The New York Times*, October 17, 1950.

Photo Album

Mas de la Prade, St. Paulet de Caisson, France, 2009. The Jullien family seat since circa 1700. The author's mother was one of several heirs to the property, including the surrounding vineyards, though she and her family were not permitted to stay in the main house as post-war refugees from French Indochina. From the collection of Ruth Schneider-Girards.

Hanoi, Tonkin, French Indochina, circa 1924.
Suzanne Jullien's mother, Marie-Jeanne Jullien, née Jarno, who was half-French and half-Vietnamese. She was in a convent school from the time she was three until she was 19. She became a professional tutor.

Hanoi, Tonkin, French Indochina, circa 1924.
Suzanne Jullien's father, Aymond Damien Henri Charles Jullien of Mas de la Prade, St. Paulet de Caisson, France, was made a chevalier by the Emperor Bao Dai for his contributions to Indochine *in the construction of a significant bridge and the Vietnam – Yunnan, China railroad line.*

Sontay, Tonkin, French Indochina, February 19, 1924.
The author's grandparents: Aymond Damien Jullien of St. Paulet de Caisson, France, marries Marie-Jeanne Jarno, whose father was from Brittany and mother was from Saigon. Jullien arrived in North Vietnam in 1896 and stayed half a century. From the collection of Agnes Jullien.

Thanh Hoa, Tonkin, French Indochina, circa 1932.
The Jullien children were dressed in matching outfits and posed in family portraits regularly. From left to right, Nicole, Suzy (the author's mother), Daniel, Alban and Guy Jullien. From the collection of Maria Jullien.

Thanh Hoa, Tonkin, French Indochina, circa 1936.
The Jullien daughters: Nicole, left, and Suzy, the author's mother, right. From the collection of Agnes Jullien.

Kim Lu, Tonkin, French Indochina, circa 1930.
The author's grandfather, Aymond Jullien, left, usually hunted for the family table. He shot the leopard above at the request of a nearby village where the cat was attacking its hens, the author's uncle, Guy Jullien said. The woman is a French neighbor. Photo by Marie-Jeanne Jullien. From the collection of Guy Jullien.

Thanh Hoa, French Indochina, circa 1940.
The author's mother, Suzanne Marie Eugenie Clara Jullien, at her First Holy Communion. From the collection of Maria Jullien.

Saigon, French Indochina, circa 1947.
The author's mother, a French army specialist with a rank equivalent to a sergeant chief grade, Suzy Jullien, shortly after arriving in Saigon. From the collection of Suzanne C. Flood.

Saigon, French Indochina, Sept. 12, 1950.
The author's mother, Suzy Jullien, who like her four siblings was part Vietnamese and part French, with her brother, Alban Jullien, also in the French army at the time on a Sunday drive. She was then a specialist equivalent to a sergeant chief grade and was about to leave the army to live with her lover in his official residence as he was in a diplomatic post. From the collection of Danielle Flood.

England, circa 1948-52.
Royal Air Force Squadron Leader Michael S.J. Wilton.
From the collection of Ariel Johnson.

American Legation, Saigon, French Indochina, circa 1951. Left to right: The author's stepfather and the legation public affairs assistant, then embassy information officer, Jim Flood; attaché Leslie ("Lee") Snowden Brady and a Vietnamese man, who bears a striking resemblance to Brigadier General Nguyen Ngoc Loan, made famous for the February 1, 1968 photo of him about to shoot in the head a Viet Cong prisoner. The AP photo won the Pulitzer prize in 1968. From the collection of James Flood.

Imperial Citadel, Hue, Annam, French Indochina, circa 1951. Left to right: Attaché Leslie ("Lee") Snowden Brady; Jim Flood, the author's stepfather, with Tran Van Tuyen, at the time he was secretary of state for information in Emperor Bao Dai's cabinet. They visit the Cuu Dinh, the Nine Dynastic Urns celebrating the Nguyen Dynasty; the urns survived major war destruction. Tran Van Tuyen, a lawyer, described by his daughter as a "Third Force" advocate of democracy and free speech in Vietnam, would later be ousted as deputy prime minister of South Vietnam by General Nguyen Van Thieu and die in a "re-education" camp after the 1975 fall of Saigon. Brady, who like Flood worked for the U.S.I.A., became its director for Eastern Europe and the Soviet Union at its Washington, D.C. headquarters. From the collection of James Flood.

St. Paulet de Caisson, France, circa 1947.
Jim Flood's comment on this photo was: "This was the girl I fell in love with."

Saigon, French Indochina, July 25, 1952.
Thelma Jenssen, left, American Embassy personnel officer, and Tom Peck, far right, vice-consul for consular affairs, were Embassy witnesses at the wedding of Suzy Jullien and Jim Flood. The mayor of Saigon officiated. Peck said the marriage was "a unique situation" in that Suzy, the author's mother, part Vietnamese, had been living with an older British man, whose wife was in England and who had been called back home by his employer. The Quiet American *character, Pyle, proposes marriage to the Vietnamese character, Phuong, who has been living with Tom Fowler, the older British man whose wife is in England and who has been called back home by his employer. Peck infuriated Graham Greene when he shortened the author's visa to one month, per an edict by the U.S. attorney general. From the collection of Tom Peck.*

Saigon, French Indochina, 1950-54.
Bảo Đại, left, the last emperor of Vietnam and Donald Read Heath, the first minister and ambassador to Vietnam, Cambodia and Laos. Heath initially would not allow Jim Flood to marry Suzanne Jullien. From the collection of Donald Heath, Jr.

American Embassy, Saigon, French Indochina, December, 1952. The author, left, with the daughter of a CIA officer at the American Embassy's first Christmas party.

Cocktail party, Saigon, French Indochina, circa 1953. Suzanne Clara Flood, the author's mother, with a dignitary at one of the many hundreds of dinner and cocktail parties that required attendance of Foreign Service Officers and their wives in Southeast Asia in the early 1950's. One FSO wife noted that it would not be unheard of to sit down to a table decorated not only with flowers but with thousands of tiny beads in paisley designs on the tablecloth laid down by the servants. From the collection of James Flood.

Saigon, French Indochina, January 9, 1952.
The author was not two months old and her parents were young and in love when this two-car bombing shook Saigon when they were there. It was a bombing with the biggest effect in Saigon's history at that time and there would be no other to surpass it until 1964. The 1952 bombing killed at least 12 and injured at least 25. Graham Greene condensed this double explosion into a single-car bombing in his novel, The Quiet American. *This heretofore unpublished photo is from the collection of Tom Peck. The author's stepfather, Jim Flood, brought six photos of the bombings stateside and put them in his family album. He joined two CIA officers in purchasing the prints from l'Atelier Cine Photo, 118-20 rue Catinat, Saigon, a shop located very close to where one car bombing took place.*

16. Saigon, French Indochina, January 9, 1952.
The author's stepfather, Jim Flood, wrote on the back of this photo. Graham Greene accused a freelance photographer for Life magazine of being "well placed" near where one of the car bombs went off. However, it was the car bombing in front of the Saigon opera house, just around the corner from the photo shop that was well placed; photographers were almost constantly stationed there in front of the landmark Hotel Continentale in hopes of getting business from tourists. The author has several various photos of her mother taken by such photographers at that spot. From the collection of James Flood.

Saigon, French Indochina, January 9, 1952.
The two-car bombing aftermath. From the collection of James Flood.

Saigon, French Indochina, 1952-53.
Jim Flood and his bride, Suzy. Sources said that because she was a quarter Vietnamese she was considered in those days to be all Vietnamese by Anglos and French. Here the couple is photographed a stone's throw to their left from where one of the two January 9, 1952 car bombs exploded in front of the Saigon opera house. From the collection of James Flood.

New York, N.Y., U.S.A., Circa 1962
Promotional photo for the author's mother, Suzanne Flood, who used the name, Danielle Dao Tien on stage and toured the mid-U.S. and east coast as an exotic dancer during the 1960's.
Photo from the collection of Danielle Flood.

The penthouse, New York, N. Y., U.S.A., spring, 1964.
The author, home from boarding school.

Off the coast of Wales, United Kingdom.
RAF Squadron Leader Mike Wilton.
From the collection of Danielle Flood.

Temple Island, Henley-on-Thames, England. January, 1987. Built circa 1771 and designed by the 18th century English architect James Wyatt, this "fishing lodge" for a nearby historic house marks the starting point of the Henley Royal Regatta. The significance of Temple Island to the author is made clear in this memoir. Photo by Danielle Flood.

Acknowledgements

How this book's path to publication has been diverted at various times over the years has been stunning. I once thought it had a supernatural enemy and then at other times, a guardian angel. It almost was published by a huge prestigious publishing company, but then Something Happened at the last minute; a long story. As they say, reading is subjective business, as is second-guessing what books will sell and what won't. When I look back upon this long struggle to get between covers I am sure I owe thanks to all the literary agents and publishers who rejected *The Unquiet Daughter* because they caused me to persist.

A number of people who read it have so believed in it, they did various things to try to shove it on its way to being in front of your eyes. You, who actually physically worked to help me that way, know who you are. Thank you from all of me – forever.

Some of you asked to read it and then told me you liked it, or liked it more than a lot. Most book writing is solitary. When you're done, even though you feel it's good enough to be read by others, you still feel like you're dangling-off-a-skyscraper alone when you offer it and so it means a great deal when people gather as your supportive audience. The feeling from it goes a long, long way. So, thank you so much to all of you for your time and care.

Thank you to Tom Holbrook of Piscataqua Press, a publishing house in the RiverRun Bookstore, Portsmouth, New Hampshire, and to its very smart editorial assistant, Kellsey Metzger.

Thank you to Kurt Andersen, Sara Nelson and David Lawrence Jr. for your special support.

I call the gang – of sparky, spunky, elderly retired Foreign Service Officers, wives and support staff, who risked their lives to be in Saigon when my parents were living and working there, when Graham Greene was visiting and mingling with them – my "quiet American people." I am grateful to them for providing details to me of my parents' lives, especially those from before and just after my birth and for descriptions of the lifestyle in Saigon, when we were there. There was much reportage that did not find its way into *The Unquiet Daughter*'s pages, but it gave me perspective and helped provide depth for what I did write. Perhaps because they knew my parents, some Foreign Service Officers, their wives and support staff gave extra effort when they answered questions. The late Blanche Donovan, for example, who like Dad was from Pittsburgh, stayed in Saigon from 1950 to 1957. She proffered this in a 2005 interview (that I wouldn't have thought of asking about): "Your Mom had a hard time; the French were not always kind to people of mixed blood; not many Vietnamese were either; things have changed today, but not then." The administrative accountant at the American Legation, Virginia Fitzpatrick, made sure I was to know that once a week for two hours, legation members were able to buy discounted liquor brought in from Hong Kong. Col. Edmund "Buck" Freeman, who as the American Air attaché chauffeured John F. Kennedy and other dignitaries around in his plane, said members of the legation took turns flying with him to Hong Kong on holiday, but also to Bangkok to buy piasters (Vietnamese money) at a discount. I asked, "How?" and he shrugged, saying he didn't know. And Libby Getz, wife of the ambassador, who with her husband, John, socialized with Graham Greene more than most, proffered that even though some people said *The Quiet American* was prophetic, Greene could never have known or guessed in 1951-53, when he was in Saigon and began working on the short novel, that the very long Vietnam War with America would ensue. "Impossible," she insisted, and said it again.

Thank you to them, and to: Buck's wife, Gillie Freeman; retired Foreign Service Officer Yale Richmond; former Saigon vice-consul Tom Peck and his wife, Betty; and their daughter Barbara Peck Henning; Michelle Breen; the late senior CIA officer Paul LeBaron Springer and his wife, Mary Jean; assistant attaché James C. Risk; Robert Bailey, manager of the British

American Tobacco company's Saigon cigarette factory; Assistant U.S. Air Attache Col. William H. Huntley and his wife, Ruby; overt CIA officer John Caswell; retired U.S. consul Hendrick Van Oss; Elizabeth "Libby" Getz; FBIS director Scott Cohen; British Foreign Service Officer Ian Day Adams; Margaret Simmons; Charlotte Loris; the late CIA North African branch chief Charles Jewel Baker and his wife, Nancy; code clerk Bob Teaze; Jim Anderson of USIS and his wife, Helen; British Consulate Information Officer Dermot Swan (who provided details from his unpublished memoirs and as Dad's British counterpart spent time with Greene.) From this group I was able to study six photo collections on Saigon and copies of invitations from the Col. William and Ruby Huntley collection of some 600 for the period March 1950 to August 1953. Also, thanks to Donald Heath, Jr., for lending to me and letting me copy and quote from the letters of his mother, Louise Heath, wife of Ambassador Donald Heath, to her family in the U.S. Thank you also to Mike Canning, for helping when he was head of the U.S.I.A. Alumni Association and also to the late Cliff Forster, retired U.S.I.A. director, for his letters about my parents. Thanks also to Ruth Donnell, wife of John Corwin Donnell, the only American Foreign Service Officer at the American Legation/Embassy when my parents were there who could speak Vietnamese, though the Pyle character in the second *Quiet American* movie seemed fluent in the language.

I never met my maternal grandmother, the beautiful Marie-Jeanne Jullien, who died in the South of France in 1956. But after she married my grandfather in 1924, she wrote letters to her new in-laws in the family seat at Mas de la Prade, St. Paulet de Caisson, France, for the next 30 years. I am grateful to have come to know her through these letters, and I must thank my-busy-with-babies-cousin in Paris, Agnes Jullien Lespagnol, for taking the trouble to find these historic letters that her father, my uncle, Daniel Jullien, kept all these years. This collection also included three letters by our grandfather, Aymond Jullien, announcing that the family, was in essence, joining the rest of the world's post-World War II refugees.

Thank you to Danielle Ferre-Culas of Alliance Francaise for translating the many hours my uncle, Guy Jullien, gave to me in interview about our family in French Indochina. And I am forever grateful for Uncle Guy's gift of this great effort. Much of what I saw in my uncle, Alban Jullien's subsequently published memoir/family history, *Typhon Sur Les Filaos*, repeated information I already had, mostly from Uncle Guy. However less than half a dozen facts I didn't have are attributed to that volume and for them and that information I thank my uncle, Alban Jullien.

I also thank my cousin, Isabelle Francois, of Aix-en-Provence, for obtaining copies from French archives of the birth certificate entries for my mother, our grandfather, and our great grandfather. To my cousin, Maria Jullien, of Cuers, France, thank you so much for lending to me many family photos – including those of the Jullien family in French Indochina – so that I could copy them and share them with my sisters and readers. Thank you also to the following persons who loaned me photos and gave me permission to use them: Donald Heath, Jr., Tom Peck, Agnes Jullien, Patricia Wheeler, Ariel Marguin and Ruth Schneider-Girards. I am also grateful for same from the late Col. Edmund ("Buck") Freeman and his wife, Gillie. I am indebted to Sarah Simmons, daughter of Wing Commander Nick Simmons and his wife, Margaret, for sharing photos of her parents with me and for her support over the years.

Thank you also to the aforementioned Mrs. Schneider-Girards, an architect, for sharing details about the Jullien family's ancestral home in St. Paulet de Caisson and for receiving me there on three occasions.

At the Associated Press, I was given help documenting Jim Flood's early career there, covering China before Mao. Thank you to Valerie Komor, Susan James, Jack Stokes, Celia Mercado and Jocko Wayland. Thanks also to Ana Tesfaye of the News Media Guild.

Thank you to Sue Flood, Jim Flood's sister, for answering questions about her brother and for her comments about the writing of Norman Sherry and Graham Greene. Thanks also to my sister, Patricia, for helping me with the list of languages Jim Flood spoke and to my sister, Evalyn, for her thoughts about him; thank you also for your kindness all of our lives. Thank you to my sister, Ariel Johnson (formerly Marguin), for sharing photos and for telling me about her mother's family. I am grateful for information received from Mike's wives, the late Joan Kinloch, the late Agnes Margaret Wilton and the late Dora Wilton.

In Ireland, I am grateful for the help in confirming the accuracy of boarding school memories from the late Sister Terence O'Keefe, the late Sister Fanchea Foley and the late Mother Lucille. Thank you so much to the Irish solicitor, Elizabeth Mullan, my best friend from when we were 13, for reading, confirming or correcting information in a couple of memories about St. Mary's Dominican Convent. It's a privilege still to have Liz in my life all these more than 50 years later.

In England my heartfelt thanks to Monica Dimitroff for all the research materials, photos and all the care you have given over the years. Thanks also to Christine Ractliff for painting Temple Island for me. Thanks to Richard Groocock in the Public Records office, Elaine Camroux-McLean in the Foreign and Commonwealth Office, and to Robin Leonard at the British American Tobacco Company. Thank you to United Kingdom military researcher Paul Baillie for his tireless patience and assistance in making Royal Air Force military life come clear to me through massive flying logs and other documents I studied for this book.

I was very moved by the kindness and attention to detail given to my information requests of the Royal Air Force by Peter Gold, S.B. Taylor and Clive Richards, of the Air Historical Branch. Thank you to UK family researcher Janice O'Brien for helping me learn of the existence of my older sister.

In France, thank you to researcher Barbara Sanchez of Archeion, Aix-en-Provence; and my gratitude to Olivia Pelletier, curator of the Indochina files for the national archives of France, (the *Archives Nationales d'Outre Mer* (ANOM).) My thanks to information officer Dominique Freyssenede at Air France

Thanks also to: John E. Taylor, Ed Barnes, Lewis Holland and Carolyn Miller at the National Archives, College Park, MD; also to Simon Evnine at the University of California, Riverside; to Vietnamese translator Thuy Anh Nguyen; and to the UK literary agent, Arabella Stein.

Thank you to Peter Javian, of Institutional Research at the University of Pennsylvania, Rodrigo Castro of the Richter Library, University of Miami, and to Richard Workman, Christine Amos and Jen Tisdale of the Harry

Ransom Humanities Research Center, The University of Texas at Austin. Thanks also to Dr. Quang Van Phu of Yale.

Thank you also to Simon Bailey, keeper of the archives, Bodleian Library, University of Oxford. My gratitude to historian Clare Hopkins at Trinity College, University of Oxford and many thanks to The President and Fellows of Trinity College, University of Oxford.

Thank you to Nicholas Scheetz, Heidi Rubenstein, Scott Taylor and Nate Albee in the Special Collections Division, Georgetown University Library where I was kindly allowed to look at and take notes from Graham Greene's letters and the Graham Greene diaries, part of *The Graham Greene Papers* in the Special Collections Division.

Thank you to the author, Anne Kreamer, for your intelligent just-right words when I needed them. It's such a pleasure to be sharing part of life with you.

Thank you also to Carole Gallagher, Leslie Daniels, Jo Manning and Jane Smiley for your support, and to Jane for asking Mollie Friedrich to explain via email the publishing world to me that time I was suffering in bewilderment of it. Thank you to my friend, the writer, Norma Horvitz, for everything – you know what for.

Thank you to Cindy Soukup for simply encouraging me repeatedly to finish, and to Eve Darcy Burhenne for reading so much for me.

My son, Spencer, once said to me: "Mom, all my life you have been writing a book." Thank you, Spence, and to my daughter, Elizabeth, for all the patience, goodness, love and support throughout the years. Thank you most of all to my husband, Jim Morin, who did many countless things to help me achieve this for you, and for the love.

Visit the author at
www.danielleflood.com

CPSIA information can be obtained
at www.ICGtesting.com
Printed in the USA
LVOW12s1928281016
510729LV00001B/42/P